D0903768

E. H. HARRIMAN

A Biography

IN TWO VOLUMES

VOLUME I

E. H. Harriman

E. H. HARRIMAN

A Biography

BY

GEORGE KENNAN

WITH ILLUSTRATIONS

VOLUME I

BOSTON AND NEW YORK
HOUGHTON MIFFLIN COMPANY
The Riverside Press Cambridge

SECOND IMPRESSION

The Riverside Press
CAMBRIDGE · MASSACHUSETTS
PRINTED IN THE U.S.A.

To the Memory of

E. H. HARRIMAN

"whose services to the science of railroading will hardly be reckoned, by those who know what his work was, as less than those rendered by George Stephenson himself"

PREFACE

IN writing this biography of E. H. Harriman I found it practically impossible to describe his many and varied activities in chronological sequence, year by year, as one might do in the case of a man who worked only in a single field and took up only one thing at a time. In every year after 1899 he was carrying on at least two or three, and sometimes half a dozen, important enterprises simultaneously; and to narrate events by years would render it necessary to put into every year a scrap, or fragment, of everything that he was doing that year, and thus make the biography a series of superimposed literary sandwiches, each made up of a slice of the Boys' Club, a slice of the Union Pacific, a slice of the Southern Pacific, etc. This would break up three or four continuing enterprises into eight or ten intermixed installments, and tend not only to confuse the reader, but to deprive each achievement of the interest that it might have if treated separately as a whole.

I have also found it necessary to devote what may seem to be a disproportionate amount of space to the details of certain transactions which, during Mr. Harriman's life, were widely misrepresented or misunderstood. In some cases these transactions were relatively unimportant; but inaccurate accounts of them were made the basis for unwarranted aspersions and attacks which, at the time, were allowed to go unanswered and which have never since been adequately dealt with. Mr. Harriman was temperamentally disinclined to engage in personal disputes and controversies. He did not like the newspaper notoriety that accompanies quarrels carried on publicly, and he often refrained from making replies to injurious charges, even when he had a perfect and convincing defense. Then, too, he regarded public controversy as a waste of time. The work in which he happened at the moment to be engaged seemed to him more important than anything else, and he would not allow himself to be diverted from it by harsh criticism of his methods, or even by unjustified attacks upon his character and personal integrity. He always thought, as Abraham Lincoln once said, that "a man has not time enough to spend half his life in quarrels." This unwillingness to engage in controversies, however, was often misinterpreted. Some people, who did not know him personally, thought that it indicated callous indifference to public opinion, while others regarded it as evidence that no convincing reply to damaging accusations could be made. Neither of these suppositions, however, had any foundation in fact. Mr. Harriman was not indifferent to public opinion, nor did he ignore attacks because he was unable to meet them. He simply did not care to spend in controversy time that he could employ more profitably in work. When an intimate friend once said to him that he certainly would be misjudged if he did not defend himself with the weapons that lay at his hand, he replied: "The people always find out what's what, in the end, and I can wait. I need all my time and energy to *do* things." In order that the people who misjudged Mr. Harriman, in his lifetime, may "find out what's what, in the end," it seems to me necessary that they should be in possession of all the facts, and I have therefore given with considerable fullness the details of such transactions as the Chicago & Alton reorganization, the contest for control of the Burlington, the Equitable Life Assurance Society case, the Interstate Commerce investigation, and the break with President Roosevelt.

I desire gratefully to acknowledge the help given me in the writing of this biography by a large number of railroad men, bankers, and civil engineers, who have not only read my manuscript for errors, but have furnished me with valuable information concerning affairs in which they participated, or of which they had accurate, first-hand knowledge.

The quoted matter in the Dedication is from an article by W. M. Acworth in the London *Economic Journal* for March, 1916.

George Kennan

CONTENTS

ILLUSTRATIONS

E. H. HARRIMAN

CHAPTER I

ANCESTRY, BOYHOOD, AND EARLY LIFE

WHEN a man greatly distinguishes himself, in any field of human endeavor, the world naturally asks: "Who were his ancestors? Where did his family line originate and what was its history? Did he inherit his ability from progenitors who had themselves won distinction in the same or a similar field?"

The history of E. H. Harriman's family in the United States begins with the arrival in New York of an Englishman named William Harriman in the early summer of 1795.[1] This ancestor of the American branch of the family had been, for some years, a dealer in stationery in the city of London. His business must have been fairly large, as well as prosperous, because the merchant to whom he sold it, when he himself started for America, afterward became Lord Mayor of the city. William Harriman came to the United States, therefore, not because he had been

[1] There are said to have been Harrimans in Massachusetts as early as 1720, in New Jersey in 1747, and in New York in 1750; but their relationship to E. H. Harriman's ancestor has not been determined.

unsuccessful at home, but partly because he had been a warm sympathizer with the American colonists in their struggle for independence, and partly because he thought he might find, in the newly established Republic across the sea, better opportunities for ability and enterprise than any that he could reasonably look for in the England of that time. This William Harriman, who was E. H. Harriman's great-grandfather, sailed from Bristol in the ship Portland on the 4th of April, 1795, and after a tedious voyage of sixty days arrived in New York on the 3d of the following June. He went, almost at once, to New Haven, Connecticut, which was then a growing and thriving city, almost as old as New York.

Most of the Europeans who came to America in the last decade of the eighteenth century were comparatively poor; but from the fact that William Harriman soon became known to his New Haven neighbors as "the rich Englishman," it may fairly be inferred that he was possessed of some capital. At any rate, he had money enough to go into business on a rather large scale, because soon after his arrival in this country he bought or chartered a number of sailing vessels and engaged in the West India trade — a field of maritime enterprise in which, if the hazards were sometimes great, the profits were generally large.

WILLIAM HARRIMAN
E. H. Harriman's great-grandfather

In the year 1800, after living five years in New Haven, William Harriman moved to the city of New York, where he continued to carry on the trade with the West Indies, but added to it a general commission business. Throughout the early part of the nineteenth century he resided with his family on Broome Street, just off Broadway, in a part of the city where many old New Yorkers then had their homes. Although he never acquired great wealth, he always lived in comfort and was generally prosperous up to the time of his death. His family consisted of eight sons and four daughters; but several of the sons were lost at sea, and only Orlando, the grandfather of E. H. Harriman, lived to transmit the family name. This surviving son succeeded to his father's business, carried it on successfully for many years, and became a prominent figure in the commercial life of New York; but in 1837 he lost a large part of his property in the great fire which then swept over the city. From this mishap he never fully recovered; but in later years he partly retrieved his fortunes, and passed the remainder of his life in comfort, if not in luxury.

His oldest son, also named Orlando, was E. H. Harriman's father. He entered Columbia University, distinguished himself as a student, and was graduated with honor, after having won the gold, silver, and bronze medals in his classes. Although most of his brothers followed the example of their ancestors by engaging in commercial pursuits, Orlando decided to enter the ministry, and in 1841, just four years after the fire which destroyed the greater part of his father's property, he was ordained as a deacon in the Episcopal Church. Whether he was qualified, in all respects, for the profession that he adopted, seems to be a matter of some doubt. He had been diligent and successful as a student, and he was unquestionably a man of character and culture; but he is remembered as somewhat cold and austere in manner, and it is possible that he lacked the magnetic personal charm which might have given popularity and success to a clergyman of much less ability. Certain it is that he did not secure the advancement, or achieve the material success, that might reasonably have been expected. He seems, however, to have had confidence in his own future, because in 1841, soon after his ordination as deacon, he assumed new responsibilities by marrying Miss Cornelia Neilson, a lady to whom he had been for some time betrothed. Miss Neilson belonged to an old and distinguished New Jersey family. Her father, who was related to the Stuyvesants and the Bleeckers, was one of the ablest and most successful physicians in New York, and her paternal ancestor, Colonel John Neilson, served on the staff of General George Washington during the Revolutionary War, and was a delegate from New Jersey to the Constitutional Convention of 1777. She was a woman of strong and well-balanced character, and from her, rather than from the Reverend Orlando Harriman, Mr. E. H. Harriman seems to have inherited his business ability.

Mr. and Mrs. Orlando Harriman were devotedly attached to each other, and the marriage was a happy and successful one; but the husband did not immediately succeed in securing adequate financial support, or in establishing a permanent home. He was still a deacon when he married, and it was not until 1843 that he became assistant rector of Christ Church in Tarrytown, New York. A year or two later he moved to Hempstead, Long Island, and took charge of the parish there, but in neither place did he receive a salary that was commensurate with his abilities. Country churches at that time were comparatively small and weak, and the few hundred dollars that they could afford to pay their ministers hardly sufficed for the support of a man with a growing family. When Edward Henry Harriman was born in the Episcopal rectory at Hempstead, on the 25th of February, 1848, his father began to feel that the increasing burden of his family obligations and responsibilities was greater than he could bear under the conditions then existing. He had four young children to care for and educate; the parish could not pay more than it was already paying; and there seemed to be little prospect of a change for the better without a change of location. In 1849, the "gold rush" to the Pacific Coast began, and when, through the influence of friends, the Reverend Orlando Harriman received in 1850 a call from a mountain parish in California, he decided to accept. He had labored six years in Tarrytown and Hempstead without much advancement or pecuniary success, and he doubtless thought that in such a field as that presented by the Pacific Coast there would be an opportunity to do much good, and at the same time secure adequate compensation for his work. In view of the uncertainties involved in this change of location, it seemed inexpedient to take his family with him, so leaving his wife and children in Hempstead, with the intention of sending or returning for them if all should go well, he sailed in May, 1850, for California by way of Panama.

Owing largely to circumstances that could not have been foreseen, this bold venture of E. H. Harriman's father proved to be unfortunate. The sanitary conditions on the Isthmus at that time were bad; there was no railway across it; and passengers had to make their way from the Atlantic to the

VIEW OF GOVERNMENT HOUSE, FACING THE BOWLING GREEN
Showing at left (directly over horse and cart) the house of E. H. Harriman's great-grandfather

Pacific as best they could, in carts, on mule-back, or on foot. When Mr. Harriman, after such a journey, arrived "wet, tired, and hungry" in Panama, he was taken seriously ill. After lying there, helpless and without much attendance, for a month or more, he was able to resume his journey; but on the voyage to San Francisco he read the burial service over the bodies of seven of his fellow passengers who, less fortunate than he, died of Chagres fever.

Upon reaching his proximate destination, Mr. Harriman was disappointed to find that the vestrymen of the church to which he had been called, having heard nothing from him during his illness, had given him up, and had filled the vacancy offered to him by appointing another rector. Left thus without a parish, he wandered about the State for nearly a year, preaching here and there in pioneer towns or mining camps; founding Episcopal churches in Stockton and Sacramento; going through an epidemic of cholera in the latter place; and rendering everywhere such service as he could to the living and the dead. Early the next year, broken in health and disappointed in the hope of establishing himself in a place to which he might bring his family, he decided to return to the East. Sailing from San Francisco in March, he again crossed the Isthmus of Panama — this time without mishap — and reached New York on the 18th of April, 1851. It would perhaps have afforded him some consolation, as he thus returned unsuccessful from his first great venture, if he could have foreseen that in that same month of April, just fifty-five years later, his baby son, Edward Henry, would start from New York for the Far Western State where he himself had failed, and would there put his wealth, his power, and the resources of his two great railway systems, at the service of the people of San Francisco, when they had been ruined and made homeless by earthquake and fire.

Upon his return to New York, the Reverend Orlando Harriman took up his residence in Jersey City and established his family in a modest but comfortable home on Hamilton Square. For several years his position there was that of a semi-attached curate, whose duty it was to assist in the work of one of the large city churches. Afterward he was called to Clairmont, and then to West Hoboken, and in the latter place he officiated, in the early sixties, as rector of a small wooden church known as St. John's, to which he walked every Sunday from Jersey City. When he voluntarily relinquished this charge, in October, 1866, the congregation was owing him more than a year's salary, although, as stated in resolutions of the vestry, he "had been the means of preserving the church edifice," and had enabled the parish to "make great progress" in the face of "numerous obstacles." The faithful rector would have been better satisfied, perhaps, if the official recognition of his services had been tendered in a monetary rather than a verbal form. But he was apparently fated, throughout his professional career, to earn comparatively little and to have great difficulty in collecting even the small sums that were his due. With a family of six children to feed, clothe, and educate, it was often difficult, in framing the domestic budget, to make ends meet; and it was not until he had passed middle life that a small inheritance from the Neilson side of the family lightened a little the burden of financial embarrassment.

When the Reverend Mr. Harriman returned from California and settled with his family in Jersey City, Edward Henry, the third son, was a little more than three years of age. During most of his boyhood he lived with his parents in the Hamilton Square house and attended the public schools of Jersey City; but as he grew older his father thought best to give him a better, or at least a different, educational training, and therefore sent him to the Trinity School in New York.[1] He still continued, however, to live at home, and walked to the school and back every day from

[1] This school was founded in 1709. In April, 1914, Mrs. Harriman, in memory of her husband, gave to the school about five and a half acres of ground in the Bronx, valued at $150,000, for an athletic field.

the old Jersey City ferry, starting early in the morning and returning at a late hour in the afternoon. So far as his early associates remember, there was little or nothing in his life as a boy to indicate extraordinary ability. He was quick, alert, and observing mentally, and very active physically; but, like many other normal boys, he was more interested in sports and athletic games than in books. He acquired knowledge, however, rapidly and with great facility, and when, at the beginning of his last term in Trinity, he made up his mind to win the first prize for scholarship, he accomplished his self-imposed task with ease. This, perhaps, was a foreshadowing of his future. Many years later, when the elderly pedestrian, Weston, started for a walk across the continent, a newspaper editor in New York conceived the idea of interviewing the successful business men of the city who had passed the prime of life, and asking them whether they thought they could accomplish a similar feat. When a reporter propounded the question to Mr. Harriman, the great financier looked at the young man for a moment and then said: "Yes, if I put my mind on it." As a boy, however, Edward Henry did not always put his mind on his school books. He was naturally restless and high-spirited, and his deportment card at Trinity showed that he was even more inclined to fun and

COLONEL JOHN NEILSON
A maternal ancestor of E. H. Harriman

mischief than to serious study. Although not a big boy, physically, he was strong and agile, and when, in his walks to and from Trinity School, he encountered the rough street boys of western Manhattan, he quickly showed that he had spirit, pugnacity, and "scrapping" ability enough to take care of himself. In this respect, too, the boy was perhaps the father of the man. That he early displayed qualifications for leadership seems to be indicated by the fact that when, at the beginning of the Civil War, his playmates in Jersey City organized a sort of Boy Scout company to march through the streets with regiments of soldiers on their way to the front, Edward Henry, although the youngest of them all, was chosen as captain.

The boy's education, so far as school training was concerned, came to an end when he reached the age of fourteen. After two years in Trinity, he seems to have made up his mind that it would be better for him, and perhaps better for his family, if he should begin at once the active work of life. Coming home from school one day, he marched into his father's study, threw his books down on the table, and said to his surprised parent: "Father, I have become convinced that there is something else in life for me besides school and books; I am going to work." The father, who himself had studious tastes, who knew that the boy had aptitude for the acquirement of knowledge, and who perhaps had plans of his own for the future of his son, objected to this precipitate abandonment of school, and tried to convince the boy that to go into business at so early an age would be very unwise. Edward Henry, however, was obdurate, and after listening impatiently to his father's arguments, merely repeated his first declaration: "I am going to work." The father at last yielded. By the exercise of parental authority he might perhaps force the young student to return to school; but it did not seem expedient to use coercion when the boy's heart was so evidently set on a business career.

Edward Henry was not long in finding the "work" that he coveted. He seems to have gravitated naturally to Wall Street, and there he soon secured a position as office boy, at a salary of five dollars a week, in the Stock Exchange house of D. C. Hays. His work, at first, was largely that of a messenger, whose duty it was to carry securities in a handbag from his own office to the offices of other bankers and brokers with whom his employers had business dealings. He did not long remain, however, in this position. In the Wall Street of that day there were no electric "tickers" to print quotations of stocks and bonds in the offices of the brokers, and business was largely carried on through the medium of messenger clerks, who carried from place to place pads of paper on which current prices of securities and offers to buy or sell were written with a pencil. These clerks were known in the slang of the Street as "pad-shovers." As soon as young Harriman had become familiar with his environment and had made the acquaintance of the men with whom his firm had dealings, he was promoted to the position of "pad-shover," and in that capacity he entered upon his Wall Street career. It was a modest beginning, and the financier of later years was justified in saying: "My capital when I began was a pencil and this" — tapping his head.

The vocation of messenger clerk or "pad-shover" in the early sixties was, in a certain sense, a kindergarten of finance, in which many men who afterward gained distinction acquired their first knowledge of monetary affairs. Among the associates of young Harriman in this primary financial school were Thomas Fortune Ryan, H. K. Burras, Eugene Bogart, and many other boys who subsequently became wealthy and prominent in financial or industrial fields. Edward Henry, as a "pad-shover," was alert, enterprising, and trustworthy, and had, even at the age of fourteen, great quickness of perception and an accurate and retentive memory. He could carry in his head and give offhand to inquiring brokers the current prices of stocks and bonds, while most of the other boys had to produce or consult their pads.

As he grew older and as more office work was given him, he began to take an interest in the reasons for the incessant changes in the prices of stocks and bonds, and to connect them with transactions and events in other and often far-distant parts of the world. A deep impression is said to have been made upon him by the panic in Wall Street which followed the advance of discount rates to ten per cent by the Bank of England after the failure of Overend, Gurney & Co. in 1866. This phenomenon showed him that the Wall Street market is not the outcome of local, or even of American conditions, and that the New York Stock Exchange is a part of the commercial machinery of the world. He then began to take a wider view of the financial field and to study changes in interest rates and fluctuations of stocks in connection with the causes that produced them. Before he was twenty he had become thoroughly familiar with the brokerage business, and in 1868 or 1869 he was made managing clerk in the Hays office. By that time he had made up his mind that Wall Street afforded the best field for the exercise of his powers and had begun to cherish the ambition of going into business for himself.

THE HOUSE AT HEMPSTEAD, L.I., WHERE E. H. HARRIMAN WAS BORN

In the summer of 1870, when Harriman was a little more than twenty-two years of age, he borrowed three thousand dollars from his uncle, Oliver Harriman, — a wealthy merchant of the firm of Low, Harriman & Co., — bought a seat on the New York Stock Exchange, and opened an office of his own on the corner of Broad Street and Exchange Place. It was a very modest office, situated on the third floor of the building, and customers had to climb two flights of stairs in order to reach it; but the young broker, during his term of service as "pad-shover" and managing clerk, had made many acquaintances among investors and financiers, and business began to find its way to him, even up two flights of stairs. But he soon moved to a more accessible location. "Dick" Schell, who was a noted speculator of that time and an occasional customer of Harriman, hated to climb stairs, and on one of his visits to the office of the young broker he offered to give him business enough to pay his rent if he would move to the ground floor. Harriman did this and at once received the trade of the Schell brothers, two of whom were bank presidents, and one an official of the New York Central Railroad Company and a personal friend of Commodore Vanderbilt. But Harriman soon gained other and equally important customers. C. J. Osborne, one of the prominent speculators of that time, frequently gave him orders and declared that he was "the best broker in Wall Street." August Belmont (senior) also made use of his knowledge and skill and said, a few years later, that he was "good to draw on his [Belmont's] credit up to a million dollars." Everybody recognized his loyalty and trustworthiness. He never made selfish speculative use of the knowledge that he gained of his customers' intentions or plans, and never failed to execute orders with intelligence and discretion. The Equitable Life Assurance Society employed him in the making of investments, and he acted as broker, now and then, for both Commodore Vanderbilt and Jay Gould.

Bank credit at that time — before the establishment of the Clearing House — was even more important in Wall Street than it is now. The nature of the business done there often made it necessary for a broker largely to overdraw his bank account, and if his credit was good, his checks were certified without much regard to his actual balance. Such transactions amounted, in effect, to temporary loans, and no active broker could get along without them. Harriman's ability and integrity soon became so generally recognized that he never lacked ample credit, and three or four banks, including the old Union, stood ready to certify his checks to almost any reasonable amount. His business was profitable almost from the beginning, and his commissions, even in the first year, were so large that he had no difficulty in paying back the three thousand dollars borrowed from his uncle.

For three or four years after he became a broker, Harriman confined himself strictly to a commission business; but as he gradually accumulated capital, he began to watch for opportunities to use it for his own benefit on a larger scale. The first of such opportunities came in 1874, when "Deacon" White, a leading speculator of that day, attempted to corner the so-called "anthracite stocks" — that is, the stocks of railroads whose chief freight business was the transportation of coal. Harriman noticed the rise in these stocks and felt sure that some one was trying to monopolize them for speculative purposes. He did not believe that the shares were intrinsically worth the prices that were being offered for them, and when the rise seemed to have reached its culmination, he sold them short. The result vindicated his judgment. "Deacon" White failed to get enough of the stocks to establish the corner, and in the "slump" of values that followed Harriman was able to cover his short sales at a profit of about $150,000. Encouraged by this success, he undertook a little later a bear campaign in Delaware & Hudson, which was then quoted at about 36. The invisible forces, however, which influence the Wall Street market cannot always be foreseen by the closest observation, nor estimated by the shrewdest judgment. At the time when Harriman began selling Delaware & Hudson stock short, John Jacob Astor, a much wealthier and more powerful man, happened to want as much of it as he could get, and the shares, instead of falling in price, as Harriman expected, rose steadily under the active demand for them by Astor's brokers, until the short seller was finally obliged to cover at a heavy loss. In this series of transactions a large part of the profit that Harriman had made out of the "slump" in the anthracite stocks was swept away. His commission business, however, continued to be profitable and in the long run his losses were more than counterbalanced by his gains. About this time he gave his friend, James B. Livingston, an interest in the business and the name of the firm became "E. H. Harriman & Co."

During the first five years of his experience as a broker, Harriman not only gained the confidence and support of many men who were then prominent in Wall Street, but made warm personal friends in the higher social circles of the city. Among such friends were Stuyvesant Fish, James B. Livingston, August Belmont, Jr., William Bayard Cutting, R. Fulton Cutting, Dr. E. L. Trudeau (of Saranac Lake fame), the two Van Burens, and George C. Clark. They were all young men of approximately his own age; many of them shared his tastes, and some of them were destined to play important parts in his future career.

In his leisure hours Harriman was not a solitary student or a recluse. He was a director in the old Travelers' Club, on Fifth Avenue, and seldom failed to attend its Saturday night dinners. He was also a member of the Union and Racquet Clubs and a private in the famous Seventh Regiment of the National Guard, which was then, and for many years afterward, the crack militia organization of the State. In Company K of this regiment he drilled with August Belmont, Jr., and other Wall Street associates and became so skillful in the use of the rifle that he won many medals and trophies for expert marksmanship. Convivial pleasures of the commoner sort never appealed to him; but he had a passion for athletics and out-of-door sports. Although not a big man physically, he was strong and well developed; his movements were quick and well coördinated, and he soon gained distinction as a gymnast, a boxer, and a field sportsman. He had always been a lover of horses, and almost the first purchase that he made, after he was able to afford luxuries, was a trotting horse. He bought the animal, for comparatively little money, at a country fair; but his judgment of horseflesh was good, and the beast that looked like a country scrub proved, after a little training, to be so fast that it was not always beaten on the speedway, even by the blooded horses of Vanderbilt and Robert Bonner.

Harriman, in his boyhood, had had many "scraps" with the street urchins of Manhattan on his way to and from the Trinity School, and it was perhaps the remembrance of these contests that turned his attention, in his early manhood, to boxing. He took lessons of "Larry" Edwards, brother of the "Billy" Edwards who then held the light-weight championship, and soon became one of the quickest and cleverest boxers in New York. He finally helped his teacher to establish, over Jones's candy shop on the corner of Broadway and Twenty-First Street, a sort of boxing academy, which ultimately became a fashionable resort for the aristocratic young men of the city who were interested in athletic sports. Harriman himself was its chief patron, but on its rolls appeared also the names of Francis Appleton, Louis Gross, the Livingston brothers, the Clark brothers, August Belmont, Jr., and many other well-known young men of that time. There Harriman boxed with his teacher and his associates, and occasionally put on the gloves with even the redoubtable "Billy" Edwards himself.

As a fisherman, a hunter, and a lover of outdoor sports in general, Harriman was naturally attracted to the Adirondacks, and he spent there, both in his early manhood and in later life, some of the most enjoyable of his summer vacations. Dr. E. L. Trudeau, then a practicing physician in New York, was also a lover of the Adirondacks, and in his autobiography, many years later, he described in the following words one of the earliest meetings that he had with Harriman at Paul Smith's:

> . . . Another friend of mine and of the Livingstons, E. H. Harriman, offered to come up and look after me,[1] and spent most of the month of August with me. A telegram which read, "Here I come! Head me!" preceded his arrival by a few hours. Paul Smith had purchased somewhere a gilt ball, which with great pride he had placed on the flag-pole in front of the hotel. I told Paul that I knew if Ed Harriman caught sight of that ball when he arrived, the first thing he would do would be to shoot at it. As the stage stopped, Ed Harriman jumped out, rifle in hand, caught sight of the bright ball at the top of the flag-pole, and put a bullet through it before shaking hands with us all. This was before Mr. Harriman began his wonderful career as a railroad organizer and a great financier — for I believe he was still a clerk in the office of D. C. Hays & Co. at that time — and a more light-hearted and better companion and friend I could not have had. Many were the beautiful summer days we spent floating over the lakes in our boats, hunting, fishing, and camping together wherever we fancied

[1] Dr. Trudeau had been ill and had gone to the mountains to recuperate.

to stop for the night. Mr. Harriman was an excellent shot with a rifle, and we soon became rivals — especially in the sport of loon-hunting. We were both light-hearted young men in those joyous days, and little did either of us know what responsibilities and struggles the future held in store for us, and how absolutely divergent would be the paths Fate had marked out for us to walk in. Many years afterward, when the financial and railway world was ringing with Mr. Harriman's name, he came to Paul Smith's in his private car to see me, and at Dr. Seward Webb's invitation he went down to inspect some of the lakes on Dr. Webb's wonderful forest preserve, taking me along with him. A special engine was sent up by the New York Central at his order to take the car wherever he wanted to go; and Dr. Webb's guides and saddle horses were there to meet us when we arrived. As I remarked upon the beauty and comfort of his car, some recollections of the old days must have crossed his mind, for he looked up at me with his keen smile and said: "This is not half as much fun, Ed, as the way we travelled about in the old days that summer at Paul Smith's." And he was right, for it certainly was not.

During the "joyous days" in the Adirondacks to which Dr. Trudeau refers, Mr. Harriman's buoyancy of spirit and love of fun found expression in many pranks and practical jokes which are still recalled by the guides and mountaineers when they gather about evening camp-fires in the great North Woods. One summer, for example, there happened to be at Paul Smith's an English traveler and sportsman who made himself tiresome and unpopular by boasting extravagantly of his exploits in the hunting of big game in various parts of the world. Mr. Harriman sent to New York for a bear's foot, and spent a large part of a moonlight night in making tracks with it in all the soft muddy places he could find along the streams and around the lake. The boastful Englishman soon discovered them, and his persistent but fruitless efforts to find and shoot the non-existent animal furnished Mr. Harriman and his friends with much secret amusement.

On another occasion, finding that some of the guides and natives at Paul Smith's were inclined to pride themselves on their proficiency in "the manly art of self-defense," Mr. Harriman brought up from New York, *incognito*, the light-weight champion boxer, "Billy" Edwards, whom he introduced, under an assumed name, as one of his Wall Street friends. The guides, most of whom were large and physically powerful men, regarded the smooth-faced, slightly-built New Yorker with more or less disdain, and hardly thought it worth while, at first, to put on the gloves with him. When, however, they were finally persuaded to do so, they found themselves, to their amazement, almost defenseless and helpless in the face of "Billy's" professional knowledge, experience, and skill. Mr. Harriman, who was himself in the light-weight class, derived a sort of mischievous boyish enjoyment from the discomfort and chagrin of the bigger men, but when they had all been compelled to admit that the youthful-looking New Yorker was "too much" for them, Harriman allayed their mortification and restored their good-humor by informing them that they had been "up against" the champion light-weight professional boxer of America.

In later years, when Harriman became a national figure, he was generally regarded by the public as a cold, reticent, austere man, who was so completely absorbed in business that he had little taste for, or sympathy with, the practical jokes, boyish play, and pure fun of life. But this was a misjudgment. Sobered, afterward, as he undoubtedly was, by the cares and responsibilities of a great business career, he always retained — although perhaps he did not so often show in public — the same characteristics which made him the "light-hearted companion" of Dr. Trudeau in the years of his young manhood. His was a personality that had many sides. No one would have supposed that the young Wall Street broker who attended Travelers' Club dinners, kept a trotting horse, excelled in rifle-shooting and athletics, practiced boxing in "Larry" Edwards's "academy," and played tricks on guides and hunters in the great North Woods, would be likely to take an interest in social-betterment work in a crowded tenement-house district of the East Side, and yet it was to the East Side that the young broker next turned his attention.

CHAPTER II

THE BOYS' CLUB

AMONG the intimate personal friends of Mr. Harriman in his early manhood was George C. Clark, of the Wall Street firm of Clark, Dodge & Co. They were both members of the Union Club, and between 1870 and 1875 they met frequently, not only there, but at Mr. Clark's house where Mr. Harriman was always a welcome visitor. It was through the influence of the Clark family that Mr. Harriman was led to take an interest in social-betterment work on the East Side. Mrs. Luther Clark, George Clark's mother, had been interested for some years in the Wilson Mission School, a charitable institution established for the purpose of giving an industrial training to poor young girls from the tenement-house population in the neighborhood of Tompkins Square. This school occupied part of a building (since torn down) at the corner of Eighth Street (St. Mark's Place) and Avenue A.

Mrs. Clark, on one of her visits to this school, invited Mr. Harriman to accompany her. He was much interested in all that he saw, and when the matron, Miss Huntington, complained that they were greatly annoyed by the mischievous activity of the lawless street boys, who teased the scholars and threw stones at the windows of the school, he asked suggestively: "Why would n't it be a good plan to have a school, or a club, for the boys, so as to get them off the streets and teach them better manners?" Miss Huntington replied that she thought it would be an excellent plan and that, judging from her own experience, it would probably be successful. Many of the girls of the neighborhood had been very wild and lawless when first taken into the school, but in the course of a few months they had become orderly and well-behaved and she saw no reason why boys of the same class might not be disciplined in a similar way.

Mr. Harriman at once decided to try the experiment, and a few days later he went to the police officer of the Tompkins Square precinct and asked his assistance in getting the boys of the neighborhood together for a preliminary conference. The police officer endeavored to do this, but the boys, remembering their recent misbehavior, were suspicious and apprehensive. The invitation, they thought, was part of a scheme to have them "pinched" and punished, and all of them, at first, declined to accept it. After much persuasion, three youngsters, out of the scores who were interviewed, consented to meet Mr.

Harriman and listen to what he had to say. Mr. Harriman first surprised them by giving them a lunch of sandwiches and hot coffee, and then laid before them his scheme of establishing a boys' club, where they could meet in the evening for social intercourse and amusement. He did not intend, he said, to open a night school, or a lecture hall. What he aimed to do was to provide them with a place of their own where they could meet one another, play games, and have a good time. The three youngsters, favorably impressed by the coffee and sandwiches, as well as by Mr. Harriman's breezy, colloquial talk, expressed approval of the scheme and said they believed the other boys of the East Side would like it. Mr. Harriman asked them to talk with their companions about it and to bring as many of them as possible to another meeting, to be held a few days later.

After several conferences, Mr. Harriman became satisfied that with patience and perseverance the scheme might be carried through, and in the early part of 1876 he interested a number of his friends in it, rented the basement of the building in which the Wilson School was situated, and opened the Tompkins Square Boys' Club, the first organization of the kind in the United States, if not in the world.[1] There

[1] There was no boys' club at that time in London, nor in any other European city so far as known.

was a newsboys' lodging-house at that time in the Bowery, but its aims and purposes differed in many respects from those of the Tompkins Square Club. The latter was strictly a place of recreation, where the boys of the East Side could meet one another in the evening, talk, sing, and play indoor games. There were no fees or dues, and no discriminations on racial, religious, or other grounds. Any boy of suitable age was eligible for membership, and the children of Russians, Italians, Germans, Hebrews, Hungarians, and Greeks, mingled on terms of perfect equality.[1] The Club, at first, was open only in the evening and was closed altogether from May to October. It had no superintendent or manager, but Mr. Harriman and his friends took turns in spending one evening a week in the Club basement for the purpose of keeping the boys in order, talking to them and helping them to amuse themselves in rational ways.

For several years the number of boys who visited the Club was so small that any other man than Mr. Harriman might have been discouraged; but he

[1] At the time when the Boys' Club was founded, the Germans had a numerical preponderance in the Tompkins Square neighborhood; but in later years the Italians were in the majority, and still later both of these nationalities were outnumbered by Hebrews from various parts of Europe and especially from Russia and Poland. There were practically no boys of pure American stock in the Club at any time. All the members were of foreign parentage, although most of them had been born in the United States.

never lost faith in the practicability of the enterprise and inspired his volunteer associates with his own belief in its ultimate success. Between 1880 and 1885, the number of boys who visited the Club with more or less regularity increased from forty or fifty to a hundred or more, and it became necessary to rent the next floor above the basement, in order not only to accommodate them all, but to segregate them in classes according to their ages and tastes. Boys of fifteen or sixteen were not interested in amusements that satisfied boys of seven or eight, and it was difficult to plan entertainment for them all without classifying them in separate rooms. As far as possible, the initiative in all matters was left to the Club members. They were encouraged to do whatever they most wanted to do, and were not made to feel that they were being educated or trained. The only rules or regulations enforced were those which the boys themselves recognized as necessary for the maintenance of order and fairness. There was some reason to fear that lawless boys from the East Side street gangs would be hard to manage, and that in their games and contests they might resort to violent or "rough-house" practices. This did happen occasionally at first, and there is a Club tradition that Mr. Harriman, who was himself an accomplished athlete and boxer, forcibly ejected from the building, on one occasion, a gang leader, seventeen or eighteen years of age, who attempted to introduce in the Club the bullying and intimidating methods of the streets. Such occurrences, however, were infrequent and finally ceased altogether. In 1907, when the nightly admissions to the Club averaged one thousand, or more, the trustees said in their annual report: "One may legitimately wonder whether any other institution in the world, with so large and unselected a clientèle, can boast a whole year's immunity from a single case of serious misdemeanor."

Five or six years after the establishment of the Club, its supporters formed a definite organization by electing a board of directors and an executive committee — with Mr. Harriman as chairman of both — and hired a clerk, at a small salary, to keep the accounts and assist the successive evening managers in the work of supervision. The expenses of the Club, at this time, including rent, fuel, lights, and the salary of the clerk, were about eleven hundred dollars a year, a sum which was made up by contributions from Mr. Harriman and his friends.

In the early eighties, the Club managers enlisted the sympathy and coöperation of a number of young college and university graduates, including Sherman Evarts, Walter Jennings, N. C. Fisher, William R.

Barbour, and Henry Stanford Brooks, all of Yale, and the late William Carey, of the "Century Magazine." These young men entered enthusiastically into the work of the Club, not only by acting in rotation as evening managers, but by supervising and directing groups of boys who were interested in particular kinds of amusement. Among the older members of the Club a liking for gymnastic exercises soon became apparent, and this taste was encouraged by the young university graduates, who had had recent experience in the gymnasium or the ball field, and who were well qualified, therefore, to act as instructors. The Club, at that time, had no gymnasium, and no room for one, but a few simple appliances were provided, and classes were formed for calisthenics, dumb-bell and club swinging, wrestling, and other similar exercises that did not require much space.

A leading part in the promotion of athletics was taken by Mr. H. S. Brooks (now of the American Telegraph & Telephone Company) who was first brought to the Club by Mr. Carey in 1886. Soon after he became interested in the work, Mr. Brooks proposed to Mr. Harriman that he (Brooks) give a series of talks to the boys on the care of the body. He had noticed, he said, that many of them paid little attention to cleanliness of either body or clothing, and he thought it would be a good idea to impress upon their minds the fact that the body cannot do its best in athletic sports unless it is properly cared for. Mr. Harriman approved the plan, and a few days later a notice was posted on the door of the Club that on Friday evening Mr. H. S. Brooks would begin a series of talks, illustrated with magic-lantern pictures, on "The Care of the Body — What to Eat, What to Wear, and How to Train the Body for Athletic Contests."

On the night when the first of these talks was to be given, Mr. Harriman and Mr. Brooks, on their way to the Club by the Eighth Street car, were stopped near Tompkins Square by a great crowd which completely filled the street. "What's the excitement?" said Mr. Harriman to a police officer as he stepped out of the halted car. "It's the boys, sir," replied the policeman. "They're trying to get into the Club to hear a lecture."

Nobody supposed that a talk on the care of the body would be particularly attractive to the street boys of the East Side; but magic-lantern pictures were then a novelty in that part of the city, and those who were not interested in athletics came to see the pictures. When Mr. Brooks rose to speak, he faced an audience of five hundred boys, of all ages, packed closely together in a room that could not comfortably accommodate more than two hundred. It was not a case of "standing room only," but of breathing room only.

The talks on the care of the body were so successful that the executive committee decided to make Friday night of every week a special Club night, and to provide for that evening some unusual entertainment, such as an athletic exhibition, a sleight-of-hand performance, a concert, or a display of magic-lantern pictures. These entertainments, accompanied by general singing, for which the boys had a great liking as well as some aptitude, proved to be very popular and were attended by hundreds of youngsters who did not visit the Club regularly, but who were gradually drawn by this means into the circle of its daily activities.

In 1887, eleven years after Mr. Harriman had his first conference with the three boys in the Mission School, it was thought expedient to give the Club a permanent organization, and in the fall or winter of that year it was legally incorporated under the name of "The Boys' Club of Tompkins Square." Control was vested in a board of directors, with Mr. Harriman as president, but the immediate direction of Club affairs was left in the hands of the executive committee. Among the incorporators were many well-known business or professional men, including Henry S. Brooks, William R. Barbour, Jabish Holmes, Jr., Sherman Evarts, Thomas G. Sloane, Walter Jennings, Nathaniel C. Fisher, and William G. Bates.

Between 1888 and 1898 there was no radical change in the Club's methods or activities, but the seeds were sown of a number of new enterprises which eventually proved to be useful and important. In 1888, for example, Mr. Carey organized a series of steamer excursions for the Club boys which finally developed into a permanent summer camp, and a few years later he collected or contributed books and periodicals which formed the nucleus of a library. Some additions were made to the appliances for gymnastic exercise, and the class managers continued to give the boys such instruction and training in athletics as it was possible to give in the limited room space then available. An attempt was also made in this decade to find a competent superintendent for the Club, but although a number of men were tried, one after another, none proved to be wholly satisfactory. At the end of 1897, ten years after its incorporation, the Club seemed to have reached the limit of its development in the quarters that it then occupied. The average evening attendance was two hundred or more, and in the basement and on the first floor of the Wilson Mission School building a greater number could not be properly classified or comfortably accommodated

Although Mr. Harriman, in the early part of 1898, was absorbed in the reorganization of the Union Pacific and in plans for the reconstruction of that road, he was not so preoccupied as to lose sight of the interests of the Boys' Club. A month or two before his election as chairman of the executive committee of the Union Pacific, he chanced to hear, through H. S. Brooks and Warren N. Goddard, of a young English gentleman then living in New York named Francis H. Tabor, who had had some experience in social-betterment work in London before coming to America, and who, it was thought, would make a good superintendent. Mr. Harriman made inquiries and learned that Mr. Tabor was a former Oxford House worker, as well as a Cambridge honor man, and that he had already had some experience on the East Side in connection with an institution for boys known as "The Educational Alliance of the Patriotic League." He therefore requested Mr. Goddard to have Mr. Tabor make a study of the Boys' Club and submit a report on its condition and future possibilities. At a dinner given by Mr. Harriman to the executive committee in the University Club a few weeks later, Mr. Tabor made the desired report and outlined a scheme of Club management based largely on Walter Besant's original plan for the People's Palace in London. Mr. Harriman was very favorably impressed by Mr. Tabor personally, as well as by the practical wisdom of his suggestions, and at the end of the dinner he intimated to him that if he would undertake to manage the Club and carry his ideas into effect, he (Mr. Harriman) would furnish ample financial support and would provide, in the near future, another and a more suitable building for the boys' use. Mr. Tabor thereupon agreed to become superintendent and assumed the management of the Club in the autumn of that year. As director of such an institution he proved to be almost an ideal man. He was an athlete, an accomplished cricket-player, and an amateur musician; he could plan and direct concerts and dramatic entertainments and train the boys for them; he was interested in natural history and gardening, and he knew more or less about half a dozen manual industries and trades. In addition to these acquirements he had an intuitive knowledge of boy nature, which enabled him to see things from the boys' point of view, and to exert strong influence over them through perfect comprehension of their wishes, impulses, and needs.

Under the competent management of Mr. Tabor the Club soon widened its scope and greatly intensified its activities. It had long suffered from the lack of indoor and outdoor room for athletic sports, and one of the first measures taken by the executive committee under the new administration was to rent suitable apartments around Tompkins Square where the boys could be better classified by ages and segregated in small groups for special pursuits. At the same time the Club was kept open in the afternoon, as well as during a part of the summer, and arrangements were made for the use of the St. George athletic field in Hoboken, where ball clubs could be trained, and where the boys could have practice in walking, running, and jumping. Subsequently the Club had the partial use for a time, of grounds in Maspeth, Long Island, and finally, in 1907, it acquired, at an annual rental of fifteen hundred dollars, an athletic field of its own near 165th Street in the Bronx.

In the summer of 1899, permission was obtained from the owner, Abram S. Hewitt, to use a part of Plum Island, at the entrance to Long Island Sound, for a summer camp, and under the supervision of the executive committee, this camp was soon prepared for occupancy, the expenses being paid out of a special fund raised for the purpose by Mr. Carey and Mr. Brooks. Trips to the camp were then substituted for the steamer excursions which Mr. Carey had initiated ten years before. As the boys who visited

Plum Island in successive relays during the summer had more time on their hands than they needed for play, they improved the camp in various ways, took up gardening, and finally, at somebody's suggestion, began to raise potatoes. As a proof of Mr. Harriman's interest in the Club, as well as of his ability to conduct great enterprises without losing sight of trivial affairs, it may be worth while to note the fact that in 1901, when he was chairman of the executive committee of the Union Pacific and was spending tens of millions of dollars in the reconstruction of that road, he kept watch of the potato-growing on Plum Island, and bought the whole crop of ten or fifteen bushels as soon as the boys had it ready for market. Absorbed as he was in the problems of the Union Pacific, he remembered those Boys' Club potatoes, and he probably would not have forgotten them if they had ripened and been dug during the panic that followed the famous "Northern Pacific corner" in Wall Street. He had that kind of a mind.

While a part of the Tompkins Square boys were cultivating flowers and raising potatoes in the Plum Island summer camp, Superintendent Tabor, in the Wilson School basement, was arranging week-end walks in the country, training baseball and football teams, forming singing classes, organizing a dramatic company, and interesting the boys in many plays and pursuits of which they had previously known little or nothing.

As the Club grew more and more attractive, membership and attendance steadily increased, and before the end of 1900 it became evident to Mr. Harriman that the organization had wholly outgrown the accommodations available in the Wilson School building and its annexes, and that a new home for it must be found or created. He therefore purchased several lots of land on the neighboring corner of Avenue A and Tenth Street, and early in 1901 laid the cornerstone of a five-story-and-basement building, fifty feet by eighty, which, he thought, would be large enough to meet all the needs of the Club for many years to come. This building was completed in December, 1901, and cost, with land and furniture, about $185,000, nearly all of which sum was contributed by Mr. Harriman personally. It contained a carpenter shop; a gymnasium with a running track in the gallery; shower baths; a reading-room and library; a spacious general room which could be used as an auditorium; a music-room, a natural history room, and a large number of convenient apartments for classes and groups interested in special pursuits.

The erection of this building marked the beginning of a new era in the history of the organization. When the Club moved into it, on the 21st of December,

1901, Superintendent Tabor had, for the first time, an opportunity to carry out fully his plan for the segregation of the boys in classes and groups according to their ages and interests. He began by dividing them broadly into three great classes — juniors, intermediates, and seniors. He then subdivided these classes into smaller groups, each having its own organization and each devoting itself to the amusement or occupation in which its members were most interested. Every such group had a leader — generally a young college graduate who volunteered his services — and by these leaders the activities of the groups were guided, and to some extent regulated. There was, however, no arbitrary compulsion. If fifteen or twenty boys wished to take up basket-ball, or natural history, or photography, they formed a group, society, or minor club, elected officers and were furnished by the superintendent with a leader who could show them how to do the particular thing that they most wanted to do. In the formation of these occupational units the superintendent of course, took the initiative; but there were always groups of boys who had a common interest, or who were eager to try any new game or amusement that the superintendent suggested. Six or eight of these groups were already in existence when the Club moved into the new building, and between that time

THE BOYS' CLUB
New York City

and 1906 the number increased to thirty-two, including two natural history societies, two out-of-door clubs, an art class, a journalists' and printers' club, a camera club, a debating society, a cricket club, three association football teams, four basket-ball teams, four baseball teams, a track team, and half a dozen clubs devoted to various forms of athletic exercise. Eugene Sandow, the famous "strong man," gave a talk and an exhibition one evening to the Club members; experts from the Natural History Museum lectured to the natural history societies and the out-of-door clubs, and more than thirty young college and university men gave instruction to as many different groups interested in all sorts of pursuits from wrestling and cricket-playing to water-color painting, journalism, and photography.

Among the group leaders during this period were W. Bayard Cutting; Henry Stanford Brooks (secretary of the Club for more than twenty-five years); G. Grosvenor Dawe, of the "Cosmopolitan Magazine" and the Butterick Publishing Company; Trowbridge Hall, of Rogers, Peet & Co.; General W. W. Skiddy; D. T. Pierce, editor of "Public Opinion"; William Osborn Taylor, author of "Ancient Ideals"; G. Gordon Brown, a nephew of J. Pierpont Morgan; and Eliphalet N. Potter, a nephew of Bishop Potter of New York.

As might naturally have been expected, the new building, with its ample facilities for entertainment of all sorts, greatly increased the Club's attractiveness, and in less than three years it had a registered membership of five or six thousand and a daily attendance of a thousand or more. A restaurant was provided where simple food could be bought at prices ranging from three cents upward; a savings bank was established in which an account could be opened with a one-cent deposit; dancing classes were formed; a billiard and pool room was opened for the seniors, and a newspaper — "The Boys' Club Record" — was published regularly by the young amateurs of the journalists' and printers' club. Every part of the building was occupied, and the art-room, music-room, camera-room, gymnasium, and roof all were used to their fullest capacity. Strange to say, the art-room proved to be unexpectedly popular. The drawing teacher had more pupils than he could properly look after, and at the annual exhibition in 1904, the number of fairly good pictures was so great that they could not all be displayed for lack of wall space. In later years the well-known artist, J. W. Alexander, acted as judge in the awarding of prizes, and one of the boys of the art club won a scholarship in the National Academy of Design.

Another recreation that proved to be popular,

when room for it became available in the new building, was dancing. The boys soon learned the steps and figures, and every Saturday night a dance was given in the large intermediate room to which the older boys were allowed to invite their girl friends. The music was furnished by the members of the Club; the management was wholly in their hands, and everything was conducted with the utmost propriety. Indeed, in later years, when the tango, the bunny hug, and other similar dances became popular in certain higher social circles, the East Side — or at least the part of it represented in the Boys' Club — disapproved and discountenanced them.

After Mr. Tabor became superintendent of the Club particular attention was paid to music. There had always been general mass singing, but under the new régime, and especially after the Club moved into its new building, vocal classes were trained, either by the superintendent or by competent instructors, and musical entertainments were given annually for the members of the Club and their friends. In 1902, forty boys, from seven to fourteen years of age, gave a very creditable public performance of "Pinafore," and this was followed in later years by "The Pirates of Penzance," "Iolanthe," "The Gondoliers," "The Mikado," "The Sorcerer," and other well-known Gilbert and Sullivan operas.

At first, these entertainments were given in the Club auditorium only; but later, as the boys gained proficiency and confidence, they were repeated uptown, either at Sherry's or in the Berkeley Lyceum, where they attracted large and fashionable audiences. This innovation not only drew public attention to the Club, but brought large sums of money into its treasury. In 1906, for example, when "The Mikado" was given at the Berkeley Lyceum, the receipts from admissions and programme advertising were $4213. In addition to its opera company, the Club had at this time three singing classes, two fife-and-drum corps, a mandolin-guitar-and-banjo club, a minstrel troupe, and a brass band. In later years an orchestra was organized and trained, and thereafter the Club gave operas with its own orchestra, directed by a boy conductor.

In the field of athletics, the successes of the boys were quite as noteworthy as in the field of music. In 1904, their wrestlers won championships in the 105- and 135-pound classes in the metropolitan and national tournaments of the American Athletic Union, and in 1907, they were sent to the World's Fair in St. Louis, by Mr. Harriman personally, and brought back two championships from there. In 1906, the Club's association football players defeated the Merion Club of Philadelphia and got into the semi-finals for the amateur cup; its four basket-ball teams played forty-eight matches, winning twenty-three; its four baseball teams played thirty-eight games, of which they won twenty-two (including the series for the inter-settlement baseball cup); and its three football teams won thirty-eight games out of fifty-four played in New York City and its vicinity. In contests with universities the crack football team of the Club defeated Princeton 3 to 1 and Columbia 3 to 0, and drew with the University of Pennsylvania. Many times in 1906, as the Club ball teams returned from hard-fought contests, they had reason to sing, and some of them did sing:

> "As we go home a-marching
> And the band begins to play,
> You can hear the people shouting,
> 'The Boys' Club won to-day!'"

All together, the Club's athletes secured that year, in various matches and contests, twenty-two trophies and medals.

Among the larger enterprises of the Boys' Club in the first decade of the twentieth century none was more successful, or more beneficent in its results, than the summer camp. It was located originally, through the courtesy of Abram S. Hewitt, on Plum Island, near Fort Fisher, but in 1902 the Government needed more land for military purposes and bought from Mr. Hewitt the ground which the Club had been using. Then, in 1903, after the death of Mr. Carey, his friends raised a fund and purchased twenty-five acres of unimproved land on Long Island, fronting the Sound, about eighty miles from New York and three miles north of the village of Jamestown. There a new camp was established, as a memorial to Mr. Carey, and was named "The William Carey Summer Camp." Part of the cost of maintenance was borne by the Club, and part was covered by special contributions made annually for the purpose by the friends of the Club and of Mr. Carey. The real creators of the camp, however, so far as work was concerned, were the boys who made use of it. Beginning in 1903, they gradually cleared and leveled the ground; laid out roads, walks, flower-beds, and a garden; cut terraces and built steps down the sixty-foot bluff to the beach, and erected several wooden buildings, including a dining-hall, a kitchen, and a commodious dormitory large enough to accommodate sixty or eighty sleepers at a time. Every year, during the summer months, successive relays of boys spent from one week to two weeks at this vacation resort, and the total number of campers gradually increased from four hundred to more than six hundred. Season after season the camp was enlarged and improved, until, in 1907, four years after its establishment, it had dormitories, a dining-hall and kitchen, a recreation hall furnished with chairs, tables, and a piano, a stable for the camp horse, a tool-and-implement house, a carpenter shop, a vegetable garden, two tennis courts, a baseball ground, a motor boat, and facilities for keeping chickens, rabbits, and bees. All of the work was done by the boys themselves, and perhaps they derived as much pleasure from it as from the bathing, fishing, boating, and ball-playing for which they had plenty of time in the intervals between their voluntary tasks. And when they came from the hot, dirty, malodorous streets of the East Side in July or August, they enjoyed all the more the garden, the flower-beds, and the green, neatly-trimmed lawns, because these improvements were the results of their own labor. In the first nine years of the camp's existence more than three thousand boys visited it and returned safely to their homes without a single death, accident, or serious case of illness.

As the Boys' Club gradually increased its membership and diversified its activities, the problem of financing it became one of importance, if not of difficulty. In the late nineties, its annual expenses were about $3200, but in 1901, when it moved into the new building and when more paid labor was needed, they mounted up to $12,000. With the establishment of the summer camp, the renting of the athletic field in the Bronx, and the engagement of technical instructors and salaried assistants to teach and take care of the largely increased number of boys, the annual budget of the Club grew to about $23,000. Fortunately, the rapidly developing organization had competent financial management. To say nothing of Mr. Harriman, it had in its board of trustees between 1901 and 1906 such men as Philip J. Dodge, president of the Mergenthaler Linotype Company; Alvin W. Krech, of the Mercantile Trust Company; Otto H. Kahn, of Kuhn, Loeb & Co.; William H. Baldwin, Jr., president of the Long Island Railroad Company; Loyall Farragut, son of Admiral Farragut; and Percy A. Rockefeller. These men not only managed the finances of the Club with prudence and skill, but interested in the work a large number of their associates and friends. In 1906, the contributors to the Club's treasury numbered three hundred and forty-three, including such prominent citizens and well-known business firms as James Stillman, Morris K. Jesup, Lord & Taylor, Spencer, Trask & Co., Jacob H. Schiff, J. Pierpont Morgan, Elbridge T. Gerry, George J. Gould, Gifford Pinchot, Brander Matthews, Francis Lynde Stetson, Victor Morawetz, Paul Warburg, and Winslow S. Pierce. At the same time these and other friends of the Club made liberal donations for special objects, such as the establishment of an employment bureau, the purchase of uniforms, the traveling expenses of football teams, and the training of the Club's orchestra.

It is a fact deserving of notice that the boys of the Club contributed to its support as far as their limited means enabled them to do so. When the Club moved into the new building, Mr. Harriman, Superintendent Tabor, and the executive committee decided that it was not wise to offer the boys everything for nothing, and that it would increase the latter's self-respect and give them a feeling of ownership if they gave what they could toward the Club's expenses. The youngest of the boys, therefore, were asked to pay one cent each for their membership tickets. Boys of ten to fourteen, who were presumably able to earn a little by working at odd jobs now and then, paid ten cents a month, while the seniors, most of whom had steady employment, were required to contribute annually two dollars and a half. Receipts from these sources, between 1904 and 1908, amounted annually to from $800 to $1200.

During the financial panic of 1907, when the Club fell more than $11,000 short of meeting its expenses, Mr. Harriman promptly stepped into the breach, made good the deficit, and notified the trustees that he would thereafter contribute annually to the support of the Club fifty per cent of the total sum that might be obtained from all other sources taken together. This amounted, in subsequent years, to an annual donation of from $5000 to $8000.

The decade from 1899 to 1909, which was the period during which the Boys' Club grew and developed most rapidly, was also the period in which Mr. Harriman's business life was most strenuous and exacting. Absorbed as he was, however, in great railroad enterprises in the West, he always found time to consider the interests and the welfare of the East Side boys. His personal visits to the Club were less frequent than they had been in the first thirty years of its existence, but his interest in it never waned. Writing in 1910, after Mr. Harriman's death Superintendent Tabor said:

Even when engaged in the most exacting and absorbing enterprises, Mr. Harriman never for one moment forgot to follow with pride and interest the continued growth of the Club. Every report was read to him and every newspaper account was laid before him. He gave liberally and was always willing to subscribe for any special undertaking. During the panic, for several months, he paid all the expenses of the Club out of his own pocket. He sent our champion wrestlers to the World's Fair at St. Louis, whence they returned with two championships. He subscribed liberally to the "William Carey Camp," the most important of all the Club's new undertakings. He always attended the annual opera given by the Junior Singing Club, missing only one performance in eight years, and it was his custom to walk behind the scenes and compliment the youngsters, not so much on any ability they had shown as on the hard work they must have done. He never missed a chance of giving pleasure to the boys, or helping them to succeed. Every year he provided one or more entertainments for the youngsters, and, personally, I never knew him to refuse to give work to any one of them whom I could confidently recommend. He was president of the Club during the first eleven years after I became superintendent, and during all those years he never refused anything which I considered of benefit to the boys. If I called at his office, the affairs of the Boys' Club were never once kept waiting, and thousands of the youth of the East Side would to-day bear witness to the help which his wise generosity has given them.

Such was Superintendent Tabor's experience with Mr. Harriman. What did the East Side boys think of him? In 1907, after one of the entertainments in the Club auditorium, a reporter of the "New York Herald" had the happy thought of interviewing some of the boys in the junior and intermediate classes and recording, in their own words, the impression that Mr. Harriman made upon them. All had seen him, some had talked with him, and it is interesting to note that in spite of their immaturity and the limitations of their knowledge and experience, they discerned, clearly and accurately, some of the salient features of his character. One of the youngest of them could only say that he was "the richest man in the world next to the King of Russia"; but others, who were a few years older, had more definite knowledge and clearer impressions. Julius Kreig, of 146 East Seventh Street, a boy twelve years of age, said:

Mr. Harriman's a great man. He's president of a railroad and he's worth a couple of thousand anyhow. He's a quiet man and never tells anybody down here anything about his business. He is n't what I would call a good-looking man, but I'll bet he could put up a good fight. He lives 'way up town somewhere in a house all to himself.

Being "worth a couple of thousand anyhow" and living in "a house all to himself" seemed to the tenement-house boy of the East Side the acme of wealth and luxury.

Another twelve-year-old boy said:

He's the nicest man I ever saw, and he gives us boys uniforms and pays for our plays. He looks just like a man that lives down here on our block, and you would n't think he is such a wonderful man. His clothes are just like my father's and he talks just like the rest of us. He works all day and all night, but he has to, because his railroads run all the time and he has to tend to them.

James Fioldo, fifteen years of age, who had evidently heard echoes of the investigation of Mr. Harriman's railroad management by the Interstate Commerce Commission, said:

I'd rather be President of the country than president of all the railroads, because if you're president of railroads people say you're a bad man. They say things like that about Mr. Harriman, but we know they ain't true. If they were he would n't treat us boys the way he does. Nobody makes him — he just does it himself.

The Boys' Club is now more than forty-five years old. It had its origin in a conference of Mr. Harriman with three "vagrom" street youngsters in a room of the old Wilson Mission School on Tompkins Square. For a decade or more it was numerically weak, and for nearly a quarter of a century its home was a basement on the corner of St. Mark's Place and Avenue A. When, however, it practically attained its full development, about eleven years ago, it had six thousand members and owned property valued at $300,000.

Although Mr. Harriman's relation to the Club ended with his death in the autumn of 1909, it seems desirable to complete its history partly because it is, in a certain sense, a memorial of him, and partly because it engaged his thoughts during a longer period than any other organization with which he was ever connected. His great public career as a railroad rebuilder and administrator was all comprised within a single decade; but he was a predominating figure in the Boys' Club for thirty-three years — more than half his entire lifetime. His successor, as president of the Club, was Temple

Bowdoin, one of the partners in the firm of J. Pierpont Morgan & Co. There was no other change in the management until 1911, when Superintendent Tabor resigned and was succeeded by Louis de Forest Downer, formerly manager of the St. George's Trade School.

Mr. Harriman, up to the time of his death, retained a mortgage of $113,000 on the Club building — probably in order to keep control of it in his own hands, but in 1910, in pursuance of his *ante-mortem* wishes, Mrs. Harriman canceled this mortgage and presented it to the Club as her husband's last gift. At the same time she notified the trustees that she would continue to contribute annually fifty per cent of the total sum obtained by the Club from all other sources, in fulfillment of the promise made by Mr. Harriman in 1907.

About five years after Mr. Harriman's death, the Club was a second time deprived of its president. In 1915, Mr. Temple Bowdoin died, leaving to the Club a bequest of $50,000 which he wished to have added to the permanent endowment fund of $50,000 created by Lorenzo G. Woodhouse. Charles H. Sabin, president of the Guaranty Trust Company, was elected to fill the vacancy caused by the death of Mr. Bowdoin, and at the same time W. Averell Harriman, Mr. Harriman's eldest son, who had before been a trustee and a member of the executive committee, was chosen as vice-president.

Between 1909 and 1916, there was no great change in the Club's various fields of activity. In minor ways, however, it continued to extend, in various directions, its beneficent influence. In 1910, or 1911, for example, the executive committee gathered in fifteen or twenty deaf and dumb boys from the neighborhood of Tompkins Square and organized them in a special group known as "The Alphabet Club." It also established an office boys' training school, where, at a cost of fifty cents, a boy could get a course of instruction that would prepare him for the first step in a business career. In the year of its organization this school graduated 158 boys, most of whom obtained places through the Club's employment bureau.

The pressure upon the accommodations and facilities of the Club in 1916 became so great that the trustees decided to erect an additional building, with another gymnasium, a larger auditorium, a new library and reading-room, a bowling-alley, and a swimming-pool in the sixth story. This building, which was so connected with the first one that they practically formed a single structure, was completed in November, 1917. The Club now has two gymnasiums, a much more spacious reading-room with a well-selected library of four or five thousand volumes, an auditorium which has twice the seating capacity of the old one, and a larger number of additional rooms for the separate groups, or minor clubs, of which there are now more than one hundred. A large number of young college men give their services as club leaders, and there are paid instructors for groups of boys interested in music, dramatics, basket-ball, running, wrestling, drawing, printing, and civil service training.

Since the Club was founded, in 1876, more than a quarter of a million boys have passed through it, or been graduated from it, and among its alumni, says President Sabin,

> are three judges, one congressman, four aldermen, two assemblymen, a member of the present Board of Estimate and Apportionment of the city, and thousands of successful professional and business men. These men have "kept the faith"; and the creed of clean living and fair dealing taught them at the Club seems to have stood them in good stead in their struggle with the world. It must be remembered that these alumni were Gas House District boys, and were poor, many of them being the sons of parents who could not read or write when they first came to this country. . . .
>
> The war record of the Boys' Club is something to be proud of. As more than ninety per cent of the boys were below enlistment age, only about two hundred of them were able to get into uniform. Of these several score were wounded and six were killed in action. The

stranger visiting the Club will find that the members do not forget their heroic dead. Every night, at nine o'clock sharp, the lights in the main rooms are extinguished for one minute, during which all stand, in silence, in memory of those who gave their lives for the ideals taught at the Club. This moment of silent darkness is most impressive. A second before, the great seven-story building rings with the cries and footsteps of about a thousand boys, and all this is hushed to the stillness of death! When the lights flash on again, it is wonderful to see the reverent faces of the boys, to whom this ceremony is a sacrament to patriotism.[1]

At the present time the Club has more than seven thousand members; the average attendance is one thousand or more, and in the warm months twenty-five hundred boys go to the William Carey Summer Camp, which now comprises fifty acres and contains twenty-eight buildings, erected by the boys themselves. And all this is the outcome of the small and feeble organization which began its existence, with a mere handful of boys, forty-six years ago.

Mr. Harriman, in his lifetime, accomplished work that increased the prosperity and added to the happiness of a myriad of people scattered here and there in the Great West; but his enterprise and labor were fruitful also in the most crowded center of population in the East. No man ever set his hand to a more important task in the field of social betterment than

[1] Statement of Charles H. Sabin, President of the Boys' Club; *New York Times*, March 6, 1921.

he did when he went to the East Side of New York City, founded the Boys' Club in the basement of the Wilson Mission School, and began to make useful American citizens out of the undisciplined children of foreign immigrants, who had no places of amusement except the streets, and few social interests other than those of the ward and precinct "gangs" to which so many of them belonged. In the forty-six years of the Club's existence, it has, more or less, formed the tastes and moulded the characters of about 250,000 street boys, and through them it has exerted an enlightening and ameliorating influence over the whole foreign-born population of the great East Side.

CHAPTER III

ENTRANCE INTO THE RAILROAD FIELD

REGARDED from the point of view of public interest, Mr. Harriman's life between 1876, when he founded the Boys' Club, and 1881, when he entered the railroad field, was comparatively uneventful. He carried on his business successfully, strengthened his credit, and gradually accumulated capital; but he did not publicly distinguish himself in any way, and was generally regarded by superficial observers as nothing more than a skillful and prosperous Wall Street broker. During these uneventful years, however, his character was steadily developing and he was gaining the knowledge, experience, and judgment which, in later life, made him a commanding figure in the financial world. A change was taking place, moreover, in his aims and purposes. He had been satisfied for a time with the mere buying and selling of securities as a means of making money for others and for himself; but the stocks and bonds in which he dealt were only symbols of real value, and as he grew older and became more conscious of his mental powers he felt an ambition to manage and control the material properties which the paper securities represented. In order to do this he needed large capital, and as he approached his thirtieth year he began to make and save money, not for its own sake, nor for the luxuries and pleasures that it could give him, but rather for the use that he could make of it as an instrument in the control and direction of the world's larger affairs. He wanted to act — to achieve — and the possession or control of capital was an indispensable prerequisite.

The first outward indication of this new ambition was the purchase, in 1877 or 1878, of the steamer Twilight, a small Hudson River boat plying between New York City and Newburgh. This was the first vehicle of transportation that he ever owned or managed, and although it played no important part in his subsequent career, its acquisition was an evidence of his early interest in the carrying trade. He retained possession of it only a short time, but he operated it successfully while he owned it and was able to sell it at a profit.

In the late seventies, Mr. Harriman met at the house of his friend George C. Clark, Miss Mary Williamson Averell, of Ogdensburg, New York, a cousin of Mrs. Clark. The young people were mutually attracted and the acquaintance ultimately resulted in a marriage engagement. The Averells were a wealthy and prominent family, whose ancestors

E. H. HARRIMAN
At thirty

settled in the valley of the St. Lawrence in the latter part of the eighteenth century, about the time when Mr. Harriman's great-grandfather arrived in New York from England. William J. Averell, Miss Averell's father, was the leading banker of Ogdensburg, and was also president of the Ogdensburg & Lake Champlain Railroad Company.

The marriage took place in 1879, at Miss Averell's home in Ogdensburg, and it was on this occasion that Mr. Harriman's name first appeared in connection with a railroad. A special train had been provided for the young couple by the bride's father, and when they reached the station in Ogdensburg they found that the name "E. H. Harriman" had been painted on the locomotive by the workman in the railroad shops. When Mr. and Mrs. Harriman returned from their wedding journey, they went to New York, where they established themselves in a home of their own on East Forty-Fourth Street.

Mr. Harriman's connection with the Averell family naturally turned his attention to affairs in the northern part of the State, and in 1881, two years after his marriage, he became interested in a small, badly managed, and unprofitable railroad, thirty-four miles in length, running from the little town of Stanley, near Canandaigua, to a harbor on Lake Ontario known as Great Sodus Bay, about forty miles west of Oswego. Although this piece of road had been in existence for seven or eight years, and although it connected with the Pennsylvania Railroad at Stanley and with the New York Central at Newark, it had never happened to be absorbed by either of these great transportation systems. It carried a few local passengers and small quantities of freight destined for, or coming from, the lake ports of Canada; but its physical condition was bad, its equipment, in the shape of cars and locomotives, was scanty, and it was regarded by most railroad men and investors as an unprofitable and undesirable piece of property. It was called, originally, the "Ontario & Southern"; but it became bankrupt, went into the hands of a receiver, and was reorganized in the middle seventies as the "Lake Ontario Southern." In 1881, it was owned or controlled by its president, William Alexander Smith, a stockbroker of New York; but it was again in financial difficulties and was about to go into the hands of a receiver for the second time when it attracted the attention of Mr. Harriman. To that shrewd observer and capable financier it seemed to have strategic possibilities, on account of its location and its connections with the New York Central and the Pennsylvania. If it were rebuilt and properly equipped, it would make a desirable branch for either of those great railroad systems, and to one or the other of them he believed that it might profitably be sold. In the fall of 1881, therefore, he, with S. J. Macy, of New York, and others, bought the interest of William Alexander Smith in the property, and about a year later reorganized the company as the "Sodus Bay & Southern," with Macy as president and Harriman as vice-president. This was the turning-point in the fortunes of the road. Betterments were soon undertaken, new equipment was bought, and in April, 1882, Mr. Harriman, in order to encourage the grain traffic and thus increase the road's business, incorporated the "Sodus Bay Elevator Company" and proceeded to erect a grain elevator on Sodus Point.

Before the fall of 1883, the physical condition of the road had been much improved, but its business was still unprofitable, and Mr. Harriman became satisfied that in order to do what he wished to do with the property, he would have to get complete control of it. At a meeting, therefore, of the board of directors in October, 1883, he named a price at which he would either sell his own stock, or buy the stock of the other owners. The price was a fair one, and nearly all of the principal shareholders, discouraged by President Macy's last report on traffic and earnings, decided to sell. Mr. Harriman thus became practically the sole owner of the property. He immediately reorganized the directorate, had himself elected president in place of Mr. Macy, and substituted George H. Strauss for Silas Stuart as superintendent or general manager.

Before the 1st of June in the following year, the road (already much improved) had been put in first-class condition, and Mr. Harriman, in pursuance of his original intention, offered it for sale to both the Pennsylvania and the New York Central. In making his proposition to the former, Harriman pointed out the desirability of extending the Northern Central to Sodus Bay and thus getting an outlet on Lake Ontario for the coal of the Pennsylvania fields which, he thought, might be sold largely and profitably in Canada. With the Vanderbilt interests, on the other hand, he used the argument that if the New York Central did not buy the road the Pennsylvania undoubtedly would, and that it was sound railroad policy to keep a rival from acquiring it, even if the Central itself did not particularly need it. Great Sodus Bay, he urged, was the best harbor on the southern shore of Lake Ontario, and the railroad that controlled it would have a great advantage over any other line in competition for the rapidly increasing trade of Canada.

The officials of both roads were impressed by Mr.

Harriman's arguments, and the president of the New York Central asked for an option which would give him time for investigation. The option was granted — for a substantial consideration — and when, a few days later, President Thompson, of the Pennsylvania, expressed a willingness to take over the rebuilt and reëquipped road, Harriman told him that he would have to wait for the decision of the New York Central. The option to the latter expired at noon on the 1st of July; but the Vanderbilt people were slow in taking action, and when, at the last moment, they sent an official to renew the option, Harriman happened to be absent from his office. Before he returned, the specified time had elapsed and the owner of the road was at liberty to conclude the bargain with the Pennsylvania, which he immediately did. Exactly how much money Harriman made out of this transaction — his first venture into the railroad field — is unknown; but his profits were large. The purchase was advantageous also to the Pennsylvania, and with the negotiations that preceded it began a friendship between Harriman and President Thompson which lasted until the latter's death. In speaking some years later of the sale of this road Mr. Harriman said:

"This property had great strategic value which nobody seemed to recognize. I knew that if I put it into good physical condition, so it could handle and develop traffic, the Pennsylvania Railroad would jump at a chance to buy it, in order to get an outlet to the lake; and that the New York Central would be equally anxious to buy it, in order to keep its rival out. My experience with this railroad taught me a lesson with respect to the importance of proper physical condition in a transportation property which I have never forgotten."

Long before Mr. Harriman finished rebuilding the Sodus Point & Southern Railroad and sold it to the Pennsylvania, his interests, outside of Wall Street, were centering more and more in the railroad field. In 1880, he became a director on the board of the Ogdensburg & Lake Champlain Railroad Company, of which his father-in-law, William J. Averell, was president, and a few years later, he, with Senator Yulee, bought railroad property in Florida, which he afterward sold at a profit to Morton Plant, of the Plant Steamship Line. These interests, however, were not important enough to satisfy his ambition, or furnish an adequate field for the exercise of his powers. The United States at that time was just entering upon a remarkable era of railroad construction. Immigrants were pouring into the country more rapidly than ever before, and railroad builders were striving to make places of settlement for them by opening up and rendering accessible the vast areas of arable land which still remained uncultivated and unoccupied in the West and South. In 1880, the year before Mr. Harriman began seriously to consider the transportation business as a promising field for enterprise, the railroad mileage of the country was only 93,000 and the annual immigration 177,000. Ten years later, the railroads in operation had a mileage of 163,000, while immigration had increased to 789,000, or more than fourfold. Twenty-nine thousand miles of new road were built between 1879 and 1882, and more than 11,000 in the first year after Harriman entered the railroad field. He probably had no idea, at that time, of engaging, himself, in railroad construction; but he already felt conscious of ability as a financier, and he believed that he could manage a railroad, or shape its policies, if an opportunity to do so were afforded him.

Singularly enough, the first road that attracted his attention was not a new one, nor one whose financial policy it would be easy to control. On the contrary, it was one of the oldest and most successful transportation lines in the United States, namely, the Illinois Central. This road was built in the early fifties by a group of wealthy New York merchants.[1]

[1] It was chartered in 1850 and completed in 1855. Abraham Lincoln was attorney for it in 1857 and had an annual pass over it.

They sold to capitalists in Holland and England five sixths or more of its stock, but it was a favorite investment also for the old families of New York, and large blocks of it were held by the Astors, the Cuttings, and the Goelets. The policies of the company, for the first twenty-five years of its existence, were mainly directed by William Henry Osborne, an old Manila merchant who came back from the Philippines with a fortune in the early forties, took a large amount of the company's stock, and in 1877 became virtually the manager of the road. For ten years or more the Central did a profitable business and no attempt was made to extend it beyond the limits of the State; but soon after the Civil War, the competition of various east-and-west lines forced Osborne to adopt a new and different policy. "Up to that time it had been strictly an Illinois road, with its southern terminus at Cairo, at the junction of the Mississippi and Ohio rivers. Its chief traffic had been in carrying grain to Chicago for shipment east on lake steamers. Then the extensions of the eastern roads came through Illinois at right angles to the Central. Any point along its line was about as near the seacoast as Chicago; consequently the new railroads could give almost as good rates from where they crossed as from Chicago, and the grain was moving directly eastward. William Henry Osborne decided to strike out south for the Gulf of Mexico. Before the panic of 1873, Osborne had advanced the Illinois Central's money to roads building south down the Mississippi Valley below Cairo. These roads failed after the panic and the Illinois Central took them over. In the late seventies Osborne formed the Chicago, St. Louis & New Orleans out of these roads, rebuilt them, and turned them over to the Illinois Central."[1]

About this time a new force appeared in the directorate of the road in the person of Stuyvesant Fish, a member of a wealthy New York family and a son of Grant's ex-Secretary of State. Young Fish, at his summer home in the little town of Garrison, New York, had been a neighbor of William Henry Osborne, and the latter, as a result of the acquaintance there formed, caused him to be elected a director of the company. Then, a few months later (November 8, 1877), Osborne made him secretary of the Chicago, St. Louis & New Orleans, which was the Central's through line to the Gulf.

It was probably the long-standing friendship between Fish and Harriman which first led the latter to take an interest in the Illinois road. He studied it attentively, became satisfied that it had great pos-

[1] "Masters of Capital in America," by John Moody, *McClure's Magazine*, January, 1911.

sibilities of development and extension, and in 1881, when Fish was placing an issue of Chicago, St. Louis & New Orleans bonds, Harriman took a large block of them. In that year Garfield was assassinated; there was a "slump" in the stock market, and Harriman, it is said, "had hard work in pulling through"; but he obtained assistance from wealthy friends, held on to the bonds, and eventually sold them at a substantial profit. The aid given by Harriman to Fish in the placing of these bonds probably added another to the ties that united the two men. At any rate, Harriman took more and more interest in the road that Fish was beginning to manage, and at every favorable opportunity invested in its securities. "Conservative New Yorkers," says Moody, "looked askance at the Illinois' new policy of extension. Its stock was selling very low and many wise men were selling it short. Harriman had made a thorough study of it. 'It's the best road in the country,' he told his customers. He himself bought it in such quantities that his partners were frightened. 'It won't cost us a cent to carry,' he said; 'the shorts will carry it for us.' He was right. He bought steadily, but just as steadily the 'shorts' appeared to borrow and carry it. The stock went up and he made a large profit on it." [1]

[1] "Masters of Capital in America," by John Moody.

In 1882, or the early part of 1883, Harriman seems to have made up his mind to get a foothold in the Illinois Central by becoming one of its directors. "There was at that time," says Moody, "a large Dutch stockholding in the railroad, whose votes, according to the Dutch custom — were cast by the firm that had placed the stock in Holland, viz. the Boissevain Brothers. One of the firm came on a visit to America. Harriman met him, and in a short time gained his confidence and arranged to hold his proxies in the Illinois Central meetings." Through the influence of the Boissevain Brothers, aided perhaps by that of Stuyvesant Fish, who had meanwhile become vice-president, Harriman was elected a director on the 30th of May, 1883, and became closely associated with Fish in the management of the road. His influence, from the first, was exerted in support of a bold policy of improvement and expansion. The management, under William Henry Osborne, had been judicious and prudent, but it had been conservative, rather than progressive, and Harriman believed that the time had come for more energy and enterprise. He therefore advocated and supported every measure that seemed likely to increase the road's business by extending its mileage. He approved the purchase of a part of the old Wabash, St. Louis & Pacific Railroad after the failure of that company in 1884; he personally managed the acquirement of the Mississippi & Tennessee Railroad, which ran from Memphis to Grenada and which was valuable to the Illinois Central as a feeder, and he favored the construction, in 1886, of the Chicago, Madison & Northern Railroad, which saved the company $200,000 a year by giving it a connection of its own between Chicago and its leased lines in Iowa. He also advocated the purchase of a number of other small properties in Illinois or the Mississippi Valley which could be made useful and profitable as feeders of the main stem. All together, in the first five years after Harriman became a director, the Illinois Central increased its mileage by about one thousand miles.

This new policy of expansion was not carried through without unfavorable comment. Many conservative financiers in New York regarded it with apprehension, and in 1884, a little less than a year after Harriman's accession to the directorate, one of the leading railroad commentators of that time, after criticizing the road's new policy, said:

> In all these facts is there not evidence of some lack of the conservative spirit so long dominant in the company's affairs? It will be seen that we do not base our remark on any one incident in the recent career of the property, but upon a whole series of events, all apparently having the same tendency. We might be less

inclined to lay stress upon this apparent departure if it were not for rumors connected with the late changes in management.[1]

This was a comparatively guarded and cautious criticism, but others were more outspoken.

"I don't like that man Harriman," said Sam Sloan, the old railroad man, who was a summer neighbor of Osborne and Fish at Garrison. "He and 'Stuyv' Fish are going to get Osborne in trouble with the Illinois Central if he don't look out." . . . But they did not break the Illinois Central — far from it. They expanded according to a definite system, made possible by the peculiar strength of their corporation. This railroad's credit was the best in the country. Railroad bonds in the United States carried seven and eight per cent in the '60's and '70's; they sold at prices that often made them cost the railroads ten per cent a year. The Illinois Central was the exception. It had sold the first six, five, four-and-one-half and four per cent bonds sold in America, and in the early '80's Stuyvesant Fish engineered the extraordinary feat of selling for it a three-and-one-half per cent bond at par.

If you buy a small railroad capable of earning six per cent with the proceeds of a sale of three-and-one-half per cent bonds, you make a profit of two and one half per cent a year; and when transactions run into the tens of millions of dollars, profits of this kind mount up. . . . In a short time Harriman had charge of this process of extension, and in the middle '90's he was buying railroads with three per cent bonds; that is, he was paying about one third the price for his capital that many a large railroad had been paying only twenty years before.[2]

[1] *Commercial & Financial Chronicle*, March 1, 1884.
[2] "Masters of Capital in America," by John Moody.

It was to this acquirement of capital by the sale of low-interest-bearing bonds that Harriman referred when, in later years, he sometimes said: "I think this is a good time to buy some money."

In the summer of 1885, a little more than two years after Harriman became a director of the Illinois Central, he retired from the firm of E. H. Harriman & Co.[1] and bought a large tract of farm land near Tuxedo for a permanent residence. The purchase of this property was, in a certain sense, fortuitous. The land belonged originally to James Parrott, who became well known during the Civil War as the inventor of the "Parrott gun." The Parrott family had become wealthy through the exploitation of the iron deposits in southern New York; but with the discovery of large quantities of iron ore in Pennsylvania the New York mines became less and less important until their owners were no longer able to carry on profitably the manufactures based upon them. By the middle eighties the fortune of James Parrott had been so reduced that he was compelled to sell at auction his eight-thousand-acre homestead farm. This farm, most of which was covered with dense forest, was situated in the Ramapo Highlands, about forty-five miles north of Jersey City and ten

[1] E. H. Harriman's younger brother, William M. Harriman, then became a partner, and the firm was afterward known as "Harriman & Co."

miles west of the Hudson River. Harriman, in his boyhood, had known it well. During the years that his father lived in Jersey City he had been acquainted with the Parrotts and had often enjoyed their hospitality. When, therefore, his former playmate, young Parrott, came to him one day in 1885 and asked him to attend an auction sale of the old farm at Tuxedo, he did not hesitate to go.

The bidding at the sale was spirited, but nearly all of it came from timber speculators whose evident purpose was to cut away the forests and leave the northern Ramapo hills stripped and bare. Harriman, perhaps, did not go to the sale with the fixed intention of buying; but when he saw that if he did not buy, one of the most picturesque and beautiful spots in Orange County would be devastated and ruined, he determined to save it. Toward the end of the bidding he entered the contest and with characteristic persistence raised the bids of his rivals, one after another, until competition ceased. The eight thousand acres of hill and forest cost him a large sum, but it soon became worth more than he paid for it, and was eventually enlarged by subsequent purchases until it comprised an area of thirty square miles and was perhaps the most extensive country estate in the vicinity of New York.

After Mr. Harriman retired from the firm of E. H.

Harriman & Co., he continued to live in New York; but his chief interest was then in Illinois and he went there from time to time, either to attend board meetings or to consult with the officers of the Illinois Central whose affairs were beginning to absorb more and more of his time and his thoughts. In 1887, about four years after he became a director and two years after he bought the Parrott farm, he had his first skirmish with J. Pierpont Morgan, the great banker and financier, with whom he was destined to cross swords more than once in his subsequent career. The Illinois Central, at that time, was operating, under a lease, a railroad in central Iowa known as the Dubuque & Sioux City, for the use of which it was paying the owners thirty-eight per cent of the gross earnings. For some years the control of the road was profitable to the Central; but as the railroad mileage of Iowa grew from less than twelve hundred to about seventy-five hundred, competition became increasingly active, net earnings declined, and in 1884 the Central began to lose money, both on the Dubuque & Sioux City and on its subsidiary the Iowa Falls & Sioux City. If the Central could have obtained a larger share of the Iowa traffic by extending its leased lines, it might have changed the annual deficit into a substantial surplus; but it could not do this without spending its own money —

largely for the benefit of the lessors who would get thirty-eight per cent of the increased earnings without any outlay of their own. This state of affairs led Mr. Harriman to bring the matter before the Illinois Central board with a recommendation that complete ownership of the Dubuque & Sioux City be secured by means of purchase. The lease was to expire October 1, 1887, and in 1886, Harriman was authorized to get possession of the road if possible, either by private negotiation or by purchase of its stock in the open market.

Hearing of this, some of the large stockholders of the Iowa corporation made up their minds that they would force the Illinois Central either to buy their shares at par, which was much above their market value, or to accept a new lease which should guarantee them dividends at four per cent per annum. In order to bring this about, they put their stock into the hands of Drexel, Morgan & Co. as trustees, and invited all other Dubuque & Sioux City stockholders to do the same. Before the 1st of January, 1887, the Morgan firm had received from the owners more than a majority of the stock and was apparently in command of the situation. Harriman, acting for the Illinois Central, had bought in the open market about fifteen thousand shares; but as this was not enough to give control, and as no more could be had, the prospect seemed to be that at the next annual meeting the Morgan interests would elect their own directors, and the Illinois Central would have to negotiate, for a purchase or a renewal of the lease, with a hostile board. Inasmuch as Drexel, Morgan & Co. held more than a majority of the stock (32,680 shares) a contest with them seemed to be almost hopeless; but Harriman and Fish had made a careful study of all the factors in the problem and were prepared to take advantage of any error or oversight that their adversaries might make.

When the annual meeting of the Dubuque & Sioux City stockholders took place at Dubuque on the 14th of February, 1887, the Illinois Central interests controlled a majority of those present. They therefore organized the meeting and nominated five directors (a majority of the board) friendly to themselves. The Morgan interests nominated Abram S. Hewitt, J. Pierpont Morgan, Lorenzo Blackstone, James A. Roosevelt, and William G. Hunt. The further proceedings, as described in the "Commercial & Financial Chronicle," were as follows:

During the call of the roll of stockholders, a large number of proxies, representing about 5000 shares of stock, were presented and rejected by the parties in control of the meeting, on the ground that proxy voting in Iowa is not legal. The whole block of stock held by Drexel, Morgan & Co., as trustees was rejected also, on account of the vote having been signed by Drexel, Morgan & Co. personally, and not as trustees. The only shares which could be voted were those held by Harriman & Co., who voted them personally. At the close of the meeting, the following were declared elected: Edward Harriman, Albert Wilcox, and William D. Guthrie, of New York; and Edward C. Woodruff, of New Jersey. To fill the unexpired term of George H. Warner, resigned, W. J. Knight, of Dubuque, was declared elected. During the noon recess, the persons interested with Drexel, Morgan & Co. held a meeting and elected the former directors: James A. Roosevelt, Abram S. Hewitt, J. Pierpont Morgan, and Lorenzo Blackstone for the full term, and William G. Hunt for the unexpired term. There is no doubt but the final adjudication of the matter will be made by the courts.[1]

The contest, as predicted, was carried into the courts, where litigation continued for some months. The Morgan party refused, at first, to make any compromise, but insisted on their original terms, namely, purchase of their shares at par, or a renewal of the lease upon a guarantee of four per cent dividends. The Illinois Central Company declined to be held up. Finally Harriman, by authority of the board, sent a brief note to Drexel, Morgan & Co., offering them eighty dollars a share for the stock held by them, and intimating that if this offer were rejected, it would not be renewed. Drexel, Morgan & Co. and their associates, finding themselves out-

[1] Press dispatches from Dubuque, quoted in the *Commercial & Financial Chronicle*, February 19, 1887.

generaled, accepted the offer, and the Dubuque & Sioux City became, shortly afterward, the property of the Illinois Central.

To Wall Street the result was a surprise. No one had supposed that Fish and Harriman could defeat Drexel, Morgan & Co. when the latter held a clear majority of the Dubuque & Sioux City stock. Interests hostile to the Illinois Central criticized Harriman's methods, of course, and Morgan, who had never before paid much attention to Harriman, conceived a violent dislike for him; but observant operators in the field of railroad strategy began to regard him with increasing respect.

Before the end of 1886, the intimate knowledge that Mr. Harriman had acquired of the Illinois Central and its operations, the boldness and aggressiveness of his plans, and the skill that he displayed in dealing with questions of finance, made him one of the most prominent and influential members of the board of directors; and on the 28th of September, 1887, less than a year after his successful struggle with J. Pierpont Morgan for possession of the Dubuque & Sioux City Railroad, he was elected vice-president in place of Stuyvesant Fish, who, a short time before, had succeeded James C. Clarke as president. That fall Mr. and Mrs. Harriman went to Chicago to live and remained there until the following summer. They then returned to New York; took possession of the Parrott farm to which they gave the name of "Arden," and began the transformation of it into the splendid country estate that it afterward became.

In the early part of 1887, just as Mr. Harriman was preparing to go to Dubuque to attend the meeting of the stockholders of the Dubuque & Sioux City Railroad Company, an event occurred which was destined to have an important bearing upon his subsequent career, namely, the enactment of the Interstate Commerce Law. This legislation was the outcome of instability of railroad rates due mainly to unrestricted competition among carriers. Its objects were to forbid rebates, "drawbacks," and other forms of discrimination; to prevent "pooling" and rate-fixing by agreement; and to compel railroads to compete with one another fairly and in the open. If the law had done nothing more than this, it might not perhaps have affected Mr. Harriman personally; but it not only forbade "pooling" and rate discrimination, but created a railroad commission to which it gave power "to inquire into the management of the business of all common carriers; to keep itself informed as to the manner in which the same is conducted; to compel the attendance of witnesses and the production of all books, papers, tariffs, contracts, agreements, and documents relating to any matter under investigation; to invoke the aid of any court of the United States in requiring the attendance and testimony of witnesses and the production of books, papers, and documents"; and to restrain or punish anything that "has been done, or omitted to be done in violation of the provisions of this act, or of any law cognizable by the Commission." [1]

Mr. Harriman probably did not anticipate, when he read these provisions of the new law, that it would affect particularly his future career, but on this legislation was based, twenty years later, one of the bitterest and most unjust attacks ever made upon his personal character and integrity. The attack did not succeed, but through the publicity given in the newspapers to its unfounded assertions and accusations, it caused a multitude of uninformed readers to misjudge his motives, his purposes, and his actions.

It is a curious fact that the first conflict which Harriman had with a high official of the Illinois Central Company, after he became vice-president, arose out of the very question of rates with which the Interstate Commerce Law dealt. It was customary at that time for general managers, or traffic managers, to change rates at their own discretion, putting them up or down as circumstances and the fluctua-

[1] Sections 12, 13, and 15 of the Act of February 4, 1887.

tions of competition seemed to require. In deference to public opinion, and with a view to keeping a watchful eye on its own rate-making machinery, the Illinois Central Company, in April, 1889, amended one of its by-laws so as to provide that thereafter no reduction of rates should be made without the approval of the president, who should report his decision to the board of directors. The making of rates, at that time, was in the hands of the general manager, E. T. Jeffery, a railroad man of long experience, who was regarded as one of the ablest operating officials in the Middle West. Mr. Jeffery had never approved of the change in the by-laws, and President Fish had promised him that if he would stay in the service of the Illinois Central until the end of the year, he should not be deprived of the rate-making power. In the summer of 1889, President Fish went to Europe, and Harriman, moving again to Chicago, took Fish's place as acting president. In a memorandum written by Harriman at that time his conflict with the general manager is described as follows:

September 2, 1889

E. T. Jeffery was in my office about 9.40 A.M. After some talk about the purchase of twenty new locomotives, I remarked to the General Manager that while I remained in Chicago I should expect the matter of rates, in accordance with By-Law II, to be referred to me. He sat and looked at me for about half a minute and then jumped up and said: "If that's your decision, I quit, and will turn the road over to you at 12 o'clock to-day." I said that I was very sorry and hoped he would not act hastily. He said: "Well, I quit at 5 o'clock and turn the road over to you." He then went on to tell about the arrangement with President Fish. I stated that I could not see any other way than to carry the by-law into effect. He said: "All right, then I quit," and went out.

This precipitate resignation placed the acting president in a somewhat embarrassing position. He was not regarded at that time as a practical, or at least an experienced, railroad man; he had only recently become an officer of the company, and there might be a question as to his right to disregard a promise made to Jeffery by President Fish. Harriman, however, did not shrink from responsibility, nor did he hesitate to act promptly on the merits of the case as it was presented to him. A few hours later he wrote to Mr. Jeffery the following note:

Chicago, September 2, 1889

E. T. Jeffery
General Manager
Dear Sir:

Your letter of even date containing your resignation has just been handed to me. Believing, as I do, that the wishes of the Directors, as expressed in the by-laws of the company, should be respected and an earnest attempt made to work under them, and that if then found impracticable the by-laws should be referred to the

Board for a modification, I see no other course than to accept your resignation, which I do with deep regret.

Truly yours
E. H. HARRIMAN
Acting President

On the same day Harriman appointed C. A. Beck as general manager, A. W. Sullivan as general superintendent, and E. G. Russell as superintendent of lines in Illinois; all of these officers being moved up one grade in order to fill Mr. Jeffery's place.

The resignation of the general manager of the Illinois Central was widely commented upon, both in financial circles and in the press. Jeffery, at that time, was more generally known, perhaps, as a railroad man, than Harriman, and his resignation was attributed in some quarters to an "old quarrel." But it was not the result of a quarrel; it turned on a question of principle. In a long editorial commenting on the episode, the "Commercial & Financial Chronicle" justly said:

This [the action of Acting President Harriman] is interesting as showing the position of the Illinois Central on the question of maintaining rates, than which there is at present no more important problem affecting railroad interests. The Illinois Central is evidently in accord with the prevailing determination to limit and control the rate-making power in every conceivable way, so that alterations in tariff schedules shall occur only after the most mature deliberation and with a full knowledge of the probable consequences. We all know the evils that arose under the opposite policy, by which almost every subordinate official had it within his power to upset the most carefully prepared plans for observing created compacts. We do not refer in this to the Illinois Central, which, thanks to its good management, has not been troubled in that way; but to the generally prevailing principle, up to the beginning of the present year, on most Western roads.

The evil was a crying one and had to be redressed, and there was no point on which the bankers and presidents were more strenuous than that there must be reform in this respect, and that subordinates must be shorn of the power of disturbing rates. Of course, in the Illinois Central case the circumstances were peculiar. Mr. Jeffery is not to be classed in the category of subordinate officials. His character and position, his great ability and practical services, and the fact that he had so signally justified the confidence placed in him in the past, were elements entitling him to special consideration. The rate-making power might safely have been continued in his control. But, on the other hand, the point at issue involved a principle, and the position of the Illinois Central was in some respects exceptional. It had refused to become a party to the Interstate Railway Association, and yet, public opinion would not tolerate any wide distribution of the power to make rates. It was doubtless to show that they were in full sympathy with the spirit and purposes of the Interstate Railway Association, in regard to rate matters, that the amendment to the by-laws was originally made by the Directors, and it requires no stretch of the imagination to suppose that Acting President Harriman was actuated by the same motives when he insisted that the expressed wishes of the Directors in this respect should not be disregarded. In any event, we have in the action taken an assurance that the Illinois Central management, like the Interstate Railway Association, means to make changes in rates a difficult matter, thus tending to ensure greater stability and uniformity; and if there is anything that would tend to reconcile the owners of the property, and the general public as well, to the loss of such an excellent and capable official as General Manager Jeffery, it is that very circumstance.

Harriman's action was apparently approved by the board of directors, and no exception to it seems to have been taken by President Fish when he returned from Europe.

CHAPTER IV

ILLINOIS CENTRAL AND ERIE

IN the early part of 1890, when the country was prosperous and when railroads generally were increasing their equipment and extending their mileage in eager competition for traffic, an incident occurred in the history of the Illinois Central that showed not only the strength of the influence that Mr. Harriman exerted in the directorate of that road, but also the soundness of his judgment in forecasting the future.

In the summer of 1889, the Central's board of directors appointed a special Committee on Rates, Revenues, and Expenditures, and instructed its members to make a careful study of the company's needs and resources, and to submit a full report on the financial policy that it would be best to pursue in the near future, together with a programme of expenditures for the next two or three years.

The committee considered the subject for several months and, in January, 1890, made a voluminous report in which it strongly recommended the expenditure of a large sum of money for the extension and improvement of the system. "Such expenditures," the committee said, "should be spread over a period of not less than three and one half years, so that the results will show through at least four annual reports."

Inasmuch as this recommendation was in accordance with the policy that Mr. Harriman had steadily favored throughout the period of his association with the road, no doubt seems to have been felt that he would approve it. He had never hesitated to spend money freely when prospective results seemed to justify the outlay, and for a number of years he had been more persistent than any other director in urging an aggressive policy of expansion and improvement. There was no reason, therefore, to suppose that, in a time of great prosperity, when the credit of the company was high, and when other roads were spending large sums in extending their mileage and improving their facilities, he would suddenly become conservative and advocate a policy of economy and saving.

The report of the committee was sent to Mr. Harriman in New York where he happened to be at that time lying ill.

Two days later, he wrote from his bed with his own hand the following letter to A. G. Hackstaff, the secretary for the company in Chicago:

4 West 34th Street
New York, January 24, 1890

A. G. Hackstaff, Esq.
Secretary of the Illinois Central Railroad Co.
DEAR SIR:

Your favor of the 22nd inst. enclosing printed copies of the President's report and action of Committee on Rates Revenues and Expenditures taken thereon is received. I have been too ill to go over the President's report as carefully as I would like, but I am familiar enough with the subject to be able to form a decided opinion. I do not concur with the recommendation of the Committee on Rates, Revenues, and Expenditures, and think it would be unwise at this time to pass any resolution adopting a policy for a large expenditure of money. Our organization is not prepared for it, we have n't sufficient information, and it might lead to extravagance. Our whole force should be devoted to *making* and *saving* money. We can make necessary improvements this year, during the dull season, with the equipment we already have. No large expenditure should be made at Chicago until the depot question has been decided. If I were present to-day, I would vote against the adoption of [such] a policy as [that] recommended by the Committee on Rates, Revenues, and Expenditures. Please present this to the Board of Directors.

Yours truly
E. H. HARRIMAN

When Secretary Hackstaff read this letter to the directors, they were more than surprised. Harriman had previously been the most eagerly progressive man on the board, and had often urged going forward when some of the other members were inclined to hold back. Now, when all were in favor of expenditure and expansion, he alone urged economy and restraint. It was a change of policy on his part for which no one was prepared. So greatly, however, had the directors come to rely upon the soundness of his judgment that there was little opposition to his views, and after a brief discussion the report of the Committee on Rates, Revenues, and Expenditures was laid on the table and the programme of lavish expenditure was virtually abandoned.

The subsequent course of events proved that Mr. Harriman's judgment was right, but it is hard to say upon what considerations he based it. To the ordinary observer there was nothing in the situation that warranted apprehension, or that suggested the necessity for "making and saving money." "Coming events," it is said, "cast their shadows before"; but few men, at that time, saw the approaching financial panic of 1893, and still fewer had the wisdom to prepare for it by adopting a policy of economy and retrenchment. If the recommendations of the Committee on Rates, Revenues, and Expenditures had been adopted, the financial resources of the company would have been seriously depleted at the very time when they should have been most abundant. Only a few years later, the great financial storm of 1893 broke over the country, sweeping into bankruptcy the Erie, the Baltimore & Ohio, the Southern, the Reading, the Union Pacific, the Northern Pacific, the Atchison, Topeka & Santa Fé, and one hundred and forty-nine other railroads, which had in the aggregate a capitalization of $2,500,000,000. And this great disaster came precisely at the end of the three-and-one-half-year period over which the special committee of the Illinois Central proposed to spread its lavish expenditures for betterments and extensions. What the results would have been if the committee's programme had been followed it is impossible to say; but scores of other roads in the West and Middle West which had adopted a similar programme found themselves, when the panic came, over-extended, destitute of reserve funds, and unable even to meet their fixed charges. Largely to Mr. Harriman's sagacity and foresight is attributable the fact that the Illinois Central went through the panic and the years of depression that followed it not only without embarrassment, but with a great enhancement of its credit. It paid its dividends regularly, and the only bond issue that it made ($2,500,000 in August, 1895) was floated without difficulty at three per cent.

It was about this time that close observers of the Illinois Central began to give due credit to the chairman of its finance committee. "It was then a well-known circumstance among bankers," says Mr. Kahn, "that the Illinois Central's finances were managed with remarkable skill and foresight. Somehow or other, it never had bonds for sale except when bonds were in great demand; it never borrowed money except when money was cheap and abundant; periods of storm and stress found it amply prepared and fortified; its credit was of the highest. The few acquainted with the facts conceded that Mr. Harriman was a shrewd financial manager." [1] The general public gave most of the credit for this financial policy to the company's president, Stuyvesant Fish, but he himself was generous enough to admit that the prosperity of the road was largely due to Mr. Harriman's skill and foresight. In a speech that he made at the fiftieth anniversary of the company in Chicago in 1901, Mr. Fish said: "The measure of success which has been achieved by the company in the last twenty years, with regard to its finances, is due to no man more than to the chairman of our finance committee, Mr. Harriman." (Applause.) [2]

But it was not only for the skillful management of its finances that the Illinois Central was indebted to Mr. Harriman. His influence was potent also in the

[1] *Edward Henry Harriman.* An address delivered before the Finance Forum of New York by Otto H. Kahn, January 25, 1911.

[2] Memorial Volume commemorating the fiftieth anniversary of the Illinois Central Railroad, 1851–1901. Privately printed.

policies that extended its mileage, amplified its equipment, and greatly increased the scope and diversity of its traffic. He was mainly instrumental in the purchase of the leased lines in Iowa and the construction of the link that joined them to the main stem; and to him, largely, was due the acquirement of the Louisville, New Orleans & Texas with its extensive mileage, easy grades, and important terminals in Memphis and New Orleans.[1] Between 1882 and 1892 — the first decade of Mr. Harriman's service as director — the Illinois Central added more than 1500 miles to its track; built or bought 234 new passenger cars, 274 new locomotives, and 8401 new freight cars, and increased its gross annual earnings from $8,905,312 to $20,095,190. During the same period, moreover, the carrying power of its rolling stock was more than doubled. In 1883, its freight cars, in the aggregate, had a capacity of only 113,000 tons; while in 1891, they could accommodate more than 290,000 tons. This great enlargement of transportation facilities benefited the public even more than it benefited the stockholders. The dividends of the latter were not increased, but in the service rendered to the farmers, manufacturers, and shippers along the line there was an immense improvement.

[1] This road was absorbed by the Yazoo & Mississippi Valley, a subsidiary of the Illinois Central, and the united roads were afterward known as the Yazoo & Mississippi Valley.

This may be said also of every railroad whose management Mr. Harriman influenced or controlled. He made money for the shareholders if he could, but he never failed to develop and improve the property, so as to make it more serviceable to its patrons. As Mr. Kahn has justly said: "Whenever there was a question between increased results to the shareholder and increased efficiency to the railroad, Mr. Harriman invariably took the latter course." [1]

If, however, Mr. Harriman was useful to the Illinois Central, that road, in turn, was useful to him, because it afforded him an opportunity to learn the practical, physical side of the transportation business. Many years later, when his friends began to talk of his extraordinary ability as a railway manager, people who had known him only in the earlier part of his career exclaimed: "Ned Harriman! Why, I knew him, years ago, as a little 'two-dollar' broker! What should he know about practical railroading?" That he did understand practical railroading, however, was a speedily demonstrated fact, although those who did not closely observe his methods were unable to explain the apparent rapidity with which he acquired expert knowledge. He was not trained in physical science, and he made little use of technical books; but he had what may be called "the

[1] *Edward Henry Harriman*, by Otto H. Kahn (New York, 1911), p. 12.

seeing eye" and few things escaped his attention. One of his friends has since explained his habit of close and attentive observation by saying that it was due to "insatiable curiosity"; but it was not "curiosity" in the sense of aimless inquisitiveness. It was a keen, intelligent interest in everything pertaining to his work. In his trips over the Illinois Central he noticed every detail of railroad equipment and operation, from cars and locomotives to rails, ties, grades, curves, switches, and even water-supply pipes and track-bolts. If he saw anything whose working or *raison d'être* he did not fully understand, he made inquiries about it among those who knew; and no statement or explanation satisfied him unless it went to the root of the whole matter. Then, having acquired the information and stored it away in his extraordinarily retentive memory, he thought about it often, assimilated it completely, and brought it into coördinated relation with everything else that he knew. Many of the most notable economies that he afterward made in railway operation were due to this habit of observing and considering even such apparently trivial things as the surplus length of a track-bolt projecting beyond the nut, or the unnecessary width of the so-called "shoulder of ballast" outside the rails. Taken separately, or for a single mile, these were things of comparatively little importance; but multiplied by the eight or ten thousand miles of a great railroad system they made up a tremendous aggregate. All these details of physical construction and operation, as well as hundreds of others, Mr. Harriman observed, remembered, and thought about, and the practical education that he thus acquired was perhaps more useful and fruitful than that of many other railroad executives who had been trained to the business, but who had never formed the habit of noticing details and making them a subject of reflection.

After Mr. Harriman took up his residence in Arden, he became a "commuter" on the Erie Railroad, and the affairs of that corporation soon began to attract his attention. When the Erie became bankrupt and went into the hands of a receiver in the panic of 1893, he happened to be the owner of a comparatively small amount of its second mortgage six per cent bonds. In 1894, when Drexel, Morgan & Co. undertook to reorganize the company, Harriman objected to the reorganization plan, first, because it was financially unsound, and second, because it infringed the rights of the company's creditors — especially the holders of its junior securities. By the terms of the plan as summarized by Professor Daggett,

> no mortgage senior to the second consolidated mortgage was to be disturbed save the first mortgage, which

matured in 1897. The bonds to be dealt with were thus reduced to $41,481,048, besides which provision had to be made for the floating debt and for future capital requirements. The plan proposed to authorize a blanket mortgage of $70,000,000 at five per cent, of which $33,597,000 were to be exchanged at par for the six per cent second consolidated bonds and funded coupons thereof; $4,031,400 to be exchanged for the funded coupon bonds of 1885, and $508,008 for the income bonds. Of the balance, $6,512,800 were to be reserved to settle with the old first lien and collateral trust bonds; $15,915,208 to supply capital requirements in the future, and $9,915,208 to be offered for subscription in order to pay the floating debt. The new management did not believe that these last bonds could be sold to advantage in the general market, and therefore imposed as a condition of the specified exchanges that holders of second mortgage, funded coupon, and income bonds should subscribe at ninety to the extent of twenty-five per cent of their holdings. It was hoped that the grant of the right of immediate foreclosure upon default would induce the holders of the second mortgage bonds to come in. Both these second mortgage bonds and the funded coupons of 1885, it may be remarked, were to be kept alive and deposited with the trustee for the protection of the new bonds. Stated in tabular form the distribution was to be as follows:

To acquire the existing second mortgage bonds	$33,597,400
To acquire the funded coupons of 1885	4,031,400
To acquire the income bonds	508,008
For subscription as above	9,915,208
To acquire the old reorganization first lien and collateral trust bonds	6,512,800
To be expended for construction equipment, &c.	15,435,184
	$70,000,000 [1]

[1] *Railroad Reorganization*, by Stuart Daggett (University Press, Cambridge, 1908), p. 62.

The effect of this plan would be greatly to impair the security of the second mortgage bondholders; to lower their interest rate from six to five per cent; to increase the annual fixed charges instead of lessening them; and, in general, to make an assessment on the road's creditors for the benefit of its owners.

Such a plan could not be expected to go through without opposition. Some of the leading bankers of New York, who were holders of the second mortgage bonds, including Mr. Harriman, Kuhn, Loeb & Co., August Belmont, Vermilye & Co., Hallgarten & Co., and Charles A. Peabody (representing the Astor estate), drew up and sent to the Erie managers a remonstrance in which they said:

> Your plan seems unjust, inasmuch as it demands a permanent reduction of interest on the bonded indebtedness for which no adequate equivalent is offered, and it levies a forced contribution upon the bondholders through the demand for a subscription to new bonds at a price considerably above their probable market value. It also proposes fixed charges which appear to be larger than, in the light of past earnings and experience, the company can carry with safety.[1]

To this remonstrance the directors of the company and its bankers paid scant attention, and a little later, the bondholders' protective committee, of which Mr. Harriman soon became the fighting head,

[1] *Commercial & Financial Chronicle* (1894), vol. 58, p. 264.

sent to the directors a protest which may be summarized thus:

Our objections to your plan are:

First, that by enlargement of the issue from which the bonds to be exchanged for ours are to be taken, it reduces our security by more than one half.

Second, that no proper equivalent is offered for the reduction of interest on our bonds.

Third, that the requirement to purchase new bonds at more than their value (being, in effect, an assessment on the bondholders) is an unjust and hitherto unheard-of imposition by a debtor upon a secured creditor.

Fourth, that if an assessment may be forcibly demanded by a debtor from a secured creditor for the purpose of preserving the debtor's property and keeping it in his control, this plan does not go far enough. The contribution demanded is not sufficient to put the company on a sound and interest-paying basis.

Fifth, the plan calls for no effort or sacrifice on the part of the debtor company to preserve its property and redeem it from insolvency.

Sixth, the scheme, if successful, would establish a dangerous precedent, which would be a discredit to American railroad finance, because it would violate the plain obligations of a contract and tend to increase distrust of all American railroad securities. We also regard as objectionable, considering the relations of the parties, the language of the circular of the company and its bankers, inasmuch as it contains an implied threat of punishment to those who decline their proposition, and gives scant consideration to the suggestions made by the bondholders for a modification of the scheme.

At a meeting of the Erie stockholders on the 6th of

March, 1894, the plan of reorganization was approved, and a little later in that same week, Drexel, Morgan & Co. gave notice that inasmuch as a majority of the second mortgage bondholders had turned over their bonds to them, they would proceed with the reorganization in accordance with the plan announced. Most of the holders of junior securities then yielded and deposited their bonds; but Mr. Harriman, who never submitted to injustice without a fight, began suit in the Supreme Court for an injunction to prevent the recording of the new mortgage. Justice Ingraham, before whom the case came, did not go fully into the merits of the questions involved, but denied the application for an injunction on the ground that the plaintiffs represented only a small minority of the security-holders. "While it is clear," he said, "that there are certain obligations resting upon the majority to refrain from infringing the legal right of the minority, and that a court of equity will enforce and protect the rights of the minority, still, when the holder of a very small number of bonds, or shares of stock, seeks to enjoin a very large majority from carrying out a plan such majority deem for their benefit, I think the court should not interfere unless it plainly appears that some legal right of the minority is endangered." [1]

[1] *Railroad Gazette* (1894), vol. 26, p. 472.

Although Mr. Harriman was thus virtually defeated, he soon had the satisfaction of seeing his contentions vindicated and his predictions fulfilled by the course of events. He had warned the reorganizers that their plan would not put the Erie "on a sound and interest-paying basis," and his warning was almost immediately justified. In June, 1894, the company defaulted on the very first coupons of the new bonds; in December, it defaulted again, and in a circular issued before the end of the year Drexel, Morgan & Co. were forced to admit that the plan of reorganization had thus far proved to be a failure. In 1895, it was abandoned altogether and a new and very different plan was substituted for it. In the second reorganization most of the objections raised by Mr. Harriman and his associates were recognized and in part met. The new and final plan put the burden of readjustment on bonds and stock jointly, instead of on bonds alone; it lowered fixed charges instead of increasing them, and it procured cash from stockholders instead of from second mortgage bondholders.[1]

The result of this second conflict with Morgan was to bring Harriman into greater prominence in the field of railroad finance and to give a number of leading bankers a higher opinion of his judgment and

[1] *Railroad Reorganization*, by Stuart Daggett, p. 69.

courage. On the other hand, it deepened the dislike that Morgan had for him, and excited in the minds of the Erie managers a feeling of hostility which manifested itself, on occasion, in various undignified and petty ways.

In the fall of 1895, for example, Harriman wished to see one of the races of the trotting association at Goshen. He accidentally missed the Erie train that he intended to take, and there was no other that would bring him to his destination in time except the Chicago express. Finding that this through train made no local stops, he telephoned to the executive offices of the Erie and asked if the express might not be allowed to stop in Goshen as a personal accommodation. Inasmuch as he was vice-president of the Illinois Central and it was customary for high railroad officials to extend such courtesies to one another, this was a perfectly natural and proper request; but when it was referred to the highest authority it met with a curt refusal. Mr. Harriman, however, was a hard man to beat. Learning upon inquiry that the Chicago express could be flagged at Goshen if there happened to be any passengers there who wished to go to points west of Buffalo, he telegraphed a friend in Goshen to buy a ticket for Chicago. Then, at the appointed hour, he took his seat in the express at Jersey City. When the train reached Goshen, it was stopped by a flag-signal for the accommodation of the non-existent passenger for Chicago, and the Jersey-City-to-Goshen passenger got off and went to the race. The high officials of the Erie would perhaps have treated Mr. Harriman with more deference and courtesy if they could have foreseen that in the not distant future he would save the Erie from another bankruptcy by putting up five and a half million dollars of his own money. In that case he "heaped coals of fire" upon Mr. Morgan's head, because the Erie, at the time, was a Morgan road.

Nothing in Mr. Harriman's career is more surprising than the readiness with which he turned from one big piece of constructive work to another, and the mingled boldness and sagacity that he displayed in undertaking new and unfamiliar enterprises. While he was engaged in rebuilding the Sodus Point & Southern Railroad in northern New York in 1883–84, he made the acquaintance of W. W. Webb, a prominent lawyer of Rochester,[1] and employed him to look up and clear the titles to certain parts of the road's right of way which were unsettled or in dispute. Ten or twelve years later, Mr. Webb, who had gained Harriman's confidence by skillful accomplishment of the task assigned to him, happened to be largely interested in an iron mining cor-

[1] Now Justice of the Court of Claims.

poration known as the Furnaceville Iron Company, which was situated fifteen or twenty miles east of Rochester near the shore of Lake Ontario. In 1896, the business of this corporation became unprofitable, and it turned its attention to the work which the State had then undertaken for the improvement of the Erie Canal. The way in which Mr. Harriman was brought into this work has since been described by Mr. Justice Webb in the following words: [1]

The particular business that brought me into closer relations with Mr. Harriman grew out of the contracts made by the Furnaceville Iron Co. with the State of New York for the improvement of the Erie Canal under the so-called "Nine Million Dollar Act." Prior to 1896, our company's mining operations had been for some time at a standstill. We had a large and expensive plant, consisting of cars, tracks, engines, steam shovels, conveyors, etc., and a force of men who thoroughly understood the work of excavation. When proposals were invited by the State for canal contracts, the question at once arose, should our company bid for the work? I spent a day or two with Mr. Harriman at Arden. After a long conference, in which I did not participate, Mr. Harriman asked me what I thought of the proposition. He had before him the proposals for excavating and rebuilding the Erie Canal between Lockport and Rochester, which was divided up into different contracts, each averaging about seven miles of work. I believed that, with our experience in that line of work, we could suc-

[1] "Some Recollections of Edward H. Harriman," by Hon. William W. Webb, Justice of the Court of Claims. (An unpublished manuscript.)

cessfully handle one or two contracts, if our bids should be accepted. But this was not to Mr. Harriman's liking. He would not bother with one contract — if we could make money on one we could make money on all — and if we went into it, it should be on a broad scale, with the idea of doing the entire work between Lockport and Rochester. To him the large sums required by the State as a deposit for the performance of the work, the assemblage of the machinery and tools with which to do the work, and the engagement of the army of brain- and brawn-workers, presented no obstacles. We put in our bids, made our cash deposits, and secured five contracts covering some thirty-four miles of work.

Under the regulations prescribed by the State authorities, large amounts of money had to be provided before there was any return. There was never any question or any delay when money was called for, and from the time the bids were submitted until the final settlements of the contracts, Mr. Harriman gave his fullest confidence to the men in charge of the work. Our actual operations extended from December, 1897, until May, 1898, when, without a moment's warning, the State officials ordered us to cease work, and no more work was done after the last mentioned date.

It is unnecessary to detail the legislation and subsequent litigation growing out of the State's failure to complete the canal. There was an investigation directed by the legislature, and various bills were passed, uniformly in the interest of the State, to adjust the differences between the contractors and the State officials. Two successive Canal Boards passed upon the validity of our claims, and endeavored to defeat our recovery by attacking the measurements and classification of materials, and payments made to us years before by the State on the certificate of its engineers, inspectors, and agents. Meantime the manager of our company had died and the engineering force had been widely scattered. We had to look up our witnesses — one from the coal mines of Kentucky, one from northern Canada, and one from the far West — and bring them on at our own expense and at large cost, no part of which was ever repaid by the State.

Had it not been for Mr. Harriman's entire loyalty to the interests of the Furnaceville Iron Co. and his perfect confidence in the ultimate outcome, either before the State officials themselves, or otherwise in the courts, our company, like many others, would have been bankrupt; but he never wavered a moment, or limited in any way the plans submitted to him for a complete investigation of our entire work and all of our transactions. After years of litigation the State paid us upward of $100,000.

While Mr. Harriman had but little personal acquaintance with the actual work under our contracts, I was necessarily brought into close relations with him in the proceedings to collect our dues from the State, mostly because of the death of the manager of our company and the dissolution of our working corps. His grasp of the situation was such that apparently he could take up a conversation at a point where it had ceased months before, and his knowledge of the details of the legislation, litigation, and conferences was as fresh in his recollection as if they had only that moment been brought to his attention.

In every interview I had with him on the subject I was amazed at the clearness of his intellectual vision, his wonderful memory, even on unimportant details, and at the rapidity and correctness of his conclusions.

Some time after the payment of the award which we obtained from the State, an attack was made during a political campaign upon the State officials and pretty much everybody connected with the Canal Board and the canal work, including our company. While, as it turned out, the attack did not amount to anything more than swearing at the court, nevertheless Mr. Harriman was a good deal disturbed at the time, being fearful of the effect upon the fortunes of the political party with which he was affiliated. At his request I prepared a synopsis of the experiences and trials which our company had had with the State of New York, which was greatly to his liking, and which, he felt, satisfactorily disposed of the charges made by unscrupulous newspapers and politicians.

In the autobiography of a distinguished naval officer reference is made to the necessary isolation of a ship's commander when on sea duty, except on matters immediately connected with the business in hand. I frequently drew a parallel between such a one and Mr. Harriman. From the nature of his business conditions he was, aside from his domestic life, a self-contained man, and one necessarily limited in his friendships, but his confidence, once given, was implicit; when lost, it was gone forever; and he had no patience with any one, high or low, who had evaded an obligation, or betrayed a confidence. By common consent of those who knew him best and longest he was a very extraordinary man — to me the brightest mind I ever encountered.

In this little-known episode of Mr. Harriman's earlier career may be seen some of the characteristics that were to make him famous in a wider field in later years, namely, courage, persistence, clearness of intellectual vision, retentiveness of memory, and natural taste as well as natural capacity for constructive work on a large scale.

CHAPTER V

THE REORGANIZATION OF THE UNION PACIFIC

UP to the year 1897, Mr. Harriman's great ability as a financier, and his constructive genius as a railroad executive, had not been generally recognized. His skillful management of the finances of the Illinois Central, and his victory over J. P. Morgan in the struggle for the possession of the Dubuque & Sioux City Railroad in 1887 had attracted the attention of New York bankers, but to the public generally he was known only as a shrewd and successful Wall Street broker. Even in the affairs of the Illinois Central his reputation had been overshadowed to some extent by that of the president, Stuyvesant Fish, and comparatively few people were aware that by long and intensive study of transportation problems he had already gained a thorough and accurate knowledge of the technical, as well as the financial, side of railway administration. The fact that he was well equipped for almost any great enterprise in the transportation field was known to his associates in the management of the Illinois Central, but it had not yet become known to the public at large, and no opportunity to demonstrate his great ability was afforded him until after the Union Pacific Railroad went into bankruptcy in the panic of 1893.

The causes that brought about the insolvency of this great corporation are so well known that a detailed review of them is hardly necessary. The most important of them were excessive initial cost due to rapid construction and high prices for materials; wasteful if not dishonest building contracts with the notorious Crédit Mobilier, and, at a later time, injudicious acquirement of competing but unprofitable lines, which added largely to the company's capitalization without increasing its net revenue.

The Union Pacific and the Central Pacific Railroad Companies were created by an Act of Congress in 1862 for the purpose of connecting California with the Eastern States by means of a transcontinental line. The Union Pacific was authorized to build westward from Omaha, and the Central Pacific eastward from Sacramento, until they should form a junction at or near the boundary line of Nevada. In order to encourage the enterprise, the Government not only granted to the companies twenty-five thousand square miles or more of public land, in alternate sections along the route, but issued and turned over to them a series of thirty-year six per cent bonds, which they were allowed to sell as a means of getting construction capital. As security for the money thus loaned, the United States (by the Act of 1864) took a second mortgage on the roads, allowing the companies to sell their own bonds and to secure them by a first mortgage equal in amount to the Government's second mortgage. The United States expected the companies to pay the interest and principal of the loan by setting aside for that purpose five per cent of their net earnings, and by carrying the Government mails, troops and military supplies. Under this arrangement the Union Pacific Company received $27,236,512 in Government bonds and 11,309,884 acres of public land.

Construction work began on the Central Pacific at Sacramento in 1864, and on the Union Pacific at Omaha in 1865, and was pushed with great energy by an army of laborers, which, at the time of greatest activity, numbered about twenty-five thousand men. On the 1st of January, 1867, the termini of the two roads were 1376 miles apart, but in less than two years the gap was reduced to seven hundred miles, and on the 10th of May, 1869, the construction parties of the two companies met at Promontory Point, in Utah, and the last spike in the great transcontinental line was driven. The Central Pacific had built 689 miles across the Sierra Nevada Mountains from Sacramento, and the Union Pacific 1086 miles across the plains, the Black Hills, and the Rocky Mountains from Omaha. A junction was formed at Ogden, and the whole line was put in operation on the 15th of July, 1869. The cost of the Union Pacific, as stated in the construction account contained in the balance sheet of 1870, was $97,273,549, but the actual cost to the contractors was probably not more than half that sum, as the latter were paid in stock and bonds which went into the capital account at par value while they were taken by the contractors at a much lower market value. The capitalization of the company, therefore, at the very outset, greatly exceeded the actual construction cost of the road, the difference representing the profit of the contractors and the discount on the securities that they took in payment.[1]

The earnings of the Union Pacific, in the earlier years of its existence, were comparatively small, for the reason that it ran through an almost uninhabited country. At the time when its construction was authorized, there were practically no settlements between Omaha and the Rocky Mountains except a few mining camps in Colorado; and although the tide

[1] For various estimates of the construction cost and the profits of the contractors see *Report of the U.S. Pacific Railway Commission*, Senate Exec. Doc. No. 51, 50th Congress, 1st Session, pp. 51–52 *et seq.*; also *The Union Pacific Railway*, by John P. Davis, p. 174; and *The Building and Cost of the Union Pacific*, by Henry Kirke White (in *Railway Problems*, by W. Z. Ripley, pp. 95–97).

of emigration began to flow westward as soon as the road was opened, the earnings from traffic were not large enough to justify the payment of a dividend until 1875. From that time until 1880 the company was fairly prosperous and paid its shareholders from five and one half to eight per cent per annum. Meanwhile, however, it was beginning to suffer from the competition of the Kansas Pacific — a nearly parallel line of 638 miles running westward from Kansas City to Denver. This road, poorly built and badly managed, had never been profitable, and in 1874 it had become insolvent and had gone into the hands of a receiver. In 1878, Jay Gould and a group of his associates obtained control of it (and of its subsidiary branch, the Denver Pacific), by purchasing a majority of its stock. The Union Pacific was then forced to meet the competition of a bankrupt road, which had no interest charges to pay and which was able to cut rates almost to the bare cost of operation. In 1879, Gould proposed to the Union Pacific a consolidation of the Union, Kansas, and Denver Pacific roads, in which the shares of the respective companies should be treated as if they had equal value. The terms of this proposition, as a well-known writer on the subject has said,

were absurd. . . . The Union Pacific had reported an annual surplus, the other roads an annual deficit; the

Union Pacific had not defaulted, the Kansas and Denver Pacific had done little else; the highest mark which the stock of the Kansas Pacific had touched, in January, 1879, had been 13, that of the Union Pacific 68½. But the question, as Gould well knew, was not one of productive, but of destructive capacity; and the means of coercion which he employed was a demonstration of the ease with which the Kansas Pacific could be made formidable as a competing line.

In November, 1879, Mr. Gould purchased the Missouri Pacific, from Kansas City to St. Louis, and announced his intention of extending the Kansas Pacific to Salt Lake City, there to connect with the Central Pacific and to form a third transcontinental route. . . . The result was the consent of the Union Pacific directors to the terms imposed, and the execution of an agreement dated January 14, 1880, whereby the Union and the Kansas Pacific, with all their respective assets and liabilities, were put together at par of their respective capitals . . . to which was added the capital of the Denver Pacific.[1]

By virtue of this consolidation the mileage of the Union Pacific was nearly doubled; but its financial strength was very much weakened, for the reason that the absorption of two unprofitable lines resulted in a large increase of capitalization without any commensurate increase in earning capacity. The Union Pacific had freed itself from competition, but at too high a cost, and its subsequent embarrassment and final insolvency were largely due to this taking

[1] *Railroad Reorganization: The Union Pacific*, by Stuart Daggett (Cambridge, 1898), pp. 228–29.

in of the Gould roads at far more than their actual value.[1]

Between 1880 and 1890, the mileage of the Union Pacific was further increased by the construction of the Oregon Short Line and the purchase of the Oregon Railroad & Navigation Company. These extensions, however, were profitable, for the reason that they opened up revenue-producing territory and gave the Union Pacific an outlet on the Pacific Coast at Portland.

Between 1884 and 1890, under the presidency of Charles Francis Adams, the Union Pacific acquired more than three thousand miles of branch lines, all

[1] According to the report of the U.S. Pacific Railway Commission of 1888, the average annual earnings of the three roads for a period of ten years prior to the consolidation were as follows:

	Annual net earnings per mile	*Annual interest charges per mile*
Union Pacific	$5617	$3185
Kansas Pacific	1602	2295
Denver Pacific	1333	1750

This table shows an annual surplus of $2432 per mile for the Union Pacific, and an annual deficit of $693 per mile for the Kansas Pacific, and $417 per mile for the Denver Pacific. The same report also states that as a result of the consolidation, the total indebtedness ofthe Union Pacific was increased by the sum of $57,950,925, including $14,000,000 in stock and $38,346,761 in bonds. Obviously the consolidation was detrimental to the interests of the solvent and surplus-earning road and profitable to the shareholders of the two bankrupt corporations. The merger seems to have been forced by the threat of transcontinental competition, which, if made effective, would be likely, as Mr. Gould himself admitted on the witness stand, to "destroy the Union Pacific." (*Report of the U.S. Pacific Railway Commission*, Senate Doc. No. 51, 50th Congress, 1st Session.)

under separate organizations, but with their accounts and management subject to the supervision and control of the parent company. These branch lines cost the Union Pacific nearly $42,000,000. Most of them reported annual deficits, which were covered out of earnings of the main line, or carried as floating debt; but President Adams justified the acquisition of them on the ground that, by acting as feeders, they added to the revenue of the main line at least $5,000,000 a year. Without their help, he said, the company would not have been able to meet even its fixed charges.[1]

Between 1880 and 1890, the financial condition of the road, notwithstanding the able management of President Adams, grew worse rather than better, owing partly to the inability of the company to fund the floating debt created in large part by extensions and purchases of branch lines; partly to diminished freight receipts from the transportation of an increased quantity of low-grade commodities, and partly to intensified competition for transcontinental business.[2] As a result of these unfavorable

[1] This statement was confirmed by the testimony of witnesses examined by the U.S. Pacific Railway Commission of 1888. The report of the Commission characterized the administration of President Adams as honest, intelligent, and skillful.

[2] In explaining this competition, the president said, in his annual report for 1884: "Not only has the Rio Grande been completed to Ogden, making, in connection with the Atchison, Topeka & Santa Fé

conditions, the average receipts per ton-mile decreased about forty-five per cent, and the net earnings in 1889 were $3,000,000 less than they had been eight years before. In 1892, after the resignation of President Adams, the position of the road became a very difficult one. "Its capitalization was high; its net earnings had shown hardly any increase in five years; it had to prepare to raise a large sum of money in two years for the payment of its short-time notes"; and, in addition, there was ahead of it the repayment of the Government loan, which would begin to mature in 1895, and would amount, with interest, to about $53,000,000.

Such was the condition of the Union Pacific when there came upon the country the great financial panic of 1893, in which six mortgage companies, thirteen loan and trust companies, and five hundred and fifty-four banks failed, and one hundred and fifty-six railroads, with a capitalization of $2,500,000,000, went into the hands of receivers. If this great national calamity had not occurred, the Union Pacific Company might perhaps have struggled along, in spite of its increasing difficulties; but it was in no

and the B. & M. extension of the Chicago, Burlington & Quincy, a direct competing line with the Union Pacific from Chicago and all eastern points to a common western terminus, but the Northern Pacific has been connected through, making a third transcontinental route."

condition to stand such a financial cyclone as this In the first eight months of the panic year its net revenue fell off $2,500,000, and in the next four months it would have to meet a maturing indebtedness of about $5,100,000.[1] This, in the existing state of the money market, it could not possibly do, and in October, 1893, it went into the hands of receivers. A month or six weeks later, at a conference held in New York, the company's security-holders, of various classes, appointed a reorganization committee consisting of Senator Brice, chairman; A. H. Boissevain, General Dodge, Major H. L. Higginson, and a representative of the estate of F. L. Ames. This committee, to which J. Pierpont Morgan was subsequently added, struggled for two years to reconcile conflicting interests and agree upon a plan of reorganization; but Congress would not consent to any suggested refunding of the Government debt, and in March, 1895, the committee abandoned its task and returned to the owners the securities that had been placed in its hands. The Union Pacific system, meanwhile, had been slowly disintegrating, partly through the efforts of the receivers to get rid of unprofitable branches, and partly through the action of bondholders of subsidiary roads who were impatient of

[1] Mr. John F. Dillon, counsel for the company, stated that there would be a deficit for the year 1893 of at least $3,000,000, and that the company was "without money or means" to meet its obligations.

delay and insisted on immediate foreclosure of their liens. One branch or extension after another was lopped off in this way until, in May, 1895, the mileage of the parent company had been reduced from 8167 to 4469, and was about to be still further curtailed by proceedings in bankruptcy against the Oregon Short Line and other important parts of the system.[1]

Such was the state of affairs when, in 1895, the Union Pacific — or what was left of it — fell into the hands of new and strong financial interests. In the late fall of that year, Winslow S. Pierce, personal counsel of George J. Gould, approached Mr. Jacob H. Schiff with a proposition that the reorganization of the company be undertaken by Kuhn, Loeb & Co. "But," objected Mr. Schiff, "that is J. P. Morgan's affair; I don't want to interfere with anything that he is trying to do." Mr. Pierce replied that the Brice committee, of which Mr. Morgan was a member, had abandoned the task as hopeless, and that it would greatly please large interests in the Union Pacific if Mr. Schiff would undertake the work, with his banking house as financial manager. Kuhn, Loeb

[1] Among the branch roads or extensions lost prior to May, 1895, were the Fort Worth & Denver City, the Denver, Leadville & Gunnison, the St. Joseph & Grand Island, and the Leavenworth, Topeka & Southwestern. The Oregon Short Line and the Union Pacific, Denver & Gulf were separately reorganized at a somewhat later time.

& Co. had never been particularly interested in the Union Pacific, but Mr. Schiff was much impressed by the data concerning it that Mr. Pierce laid before him and promised that he would consult his partners and take the matter into consideration. A few days later he called upon J. P. Morgan, apprised him of the Pierce proposition, and asked whether acceptance of it would interfere with any of his plans. Mr. Morgan declared emphatically that he was through with the Union Pacific and wanted nothing more to do with it. So far as he was concerned, he said, Mr. Schiff was at liberty to go ahead and do whatever he liked. He (Morgan) would give Kuhn, Loeb & Co. what help he could, but he was so disgusted with the political intriguing and wire-pulling which had defeated the Brice committee's plans in Congress, and so unfavorably impressed by the outlook for reorganization in general, that he was not willing even to take a financial participation for his firm.[1]

[1] Mr. Morgan's failure to take advantage of his opportunity to reorganize the Union Pacific is regarded as one of the chief tactical mistakes of his life. He thought that the road had no future, and that it was less valuable than the Erie. Mr. Harriman, on the contrary, with characteristic imagination and judgment, had a clear prevision of its possibilities, and when its common stock was selling below 25 he said to Mr. Otto H. Kahn: "Union Pacific is intrinsically worth as much as St. Paul, and with good management it will get there." This seemed to Mr. Kahn "the wildest kind of wild talk," and he did not at first take the prediction seriously; but in less than ten years Union Pacific was paying ten per cent dividends; the stock was selling at nearly 200, and it had left St. Paul far behind. These results, however, were

Knowing that the Union Pacific was regarded with disfavor by capitalists and investors, Mr. Schiff decided to interest in the reorganization an entirely new set of men, whose positions and abilities would be likely to inspire the public with confidence. He therefore went to Marvin Hughitt, president of the Chicago & Northwestern Railroad, and asked him to take an interest in the enterprise. Mr. Hughitt was reluctant to do this at first, but after a good deal of persuasion he finally consented to serve on the reorganization committee. Through his friend, General Louis Fitzgerald, Mr. Schiff then secured the coöperation of Chauncey M. Depew, president of the New York Central. As Hughitt and Depew were both known as "Vanderbilt men," bankers and brokers in Wall Street jumped to the conclusion that it was to be a Vanderbilt reorganization. "The New York Central," they said, "will acquire both the Northwestern and the Union Pacific and thus get a through line to the Pacific Coast." Such rumors and conjectures did not trouble Mr. Schiff, because they served a useful purpose in attracting attention and exciting public interest. Late in 1895, General Fitz-

largely if not wholly due to the "good management" of a born railroad builder and executive. Mr. Morgan, with all his great financial ability, might not have been able to make the Union Pacific what John W. Gates said it was in 1901 — "the most magnificent railroad property in the world."

gerald, Oliver Ames, a director of the Union Pacific, and T. Jefferson Coolidge, Jr., of the Old Colony Trust Company of Boston, joined Messrs. Schiff, Hughitt, and Depew, and the committee, with General Fitzgerald as chairman, took up the heavy burden of the bankrupt road's debts and liabilities.

For a time the work of reorganization proceeded satisfactorily; but in the latter part of 1896, Mr. Schiff and his associates became conscious that some secret but powerful influence was working against them. Their plans were opposed in the Pacific Roads Commission and in Congress; a large part of the press was hostile to them; objections were raised and difficulties created by many holders of the old stock, and evidences of antagonism were apparent in the financial circles of both America and Europe. The public soon noticed that the reorganization committee was encountering obstacles, and a rumor became current that they were thrown in its way by J. P. Morgan. He was jealous, it was said, of the successful progress thus far made by the committee, and wished now to get control of the reorganization himself. Thinking that there might be some basis for this rumor, Mr. Schiff called on Morgan and asked him frankly if he had changed his mind about Union Pacific and if he now wished to take an interest in the reorganization. Mr. Morgan replied in the negative. He had not changed his views, he said, and he did not care to have anything more to do with the road. Mr. Schiff then explained to him that the committee was meeting with serious opposition, and asked if he knew what influences were behind it. Mr. Morgan replied that he did not know, but that he would investigate quietly and try to find out. He did not care, he said, to be further associated with Union Pacific affairs himself, but he would gladly help Kuhn, Loeb & Co. in any way that he could.

A few weeks later, Mr. Morgan sent for Mr. Schiff and said that he believed he had ascertained the source of the opposition to the committee's plans. "It's that little fellow Harriman," said Morgan, "and you want to look out for him."

Mr. Schiff's personal acquaintance with Mr. Harriman was comparatively slight. He knew that the latter was the financial manager of the Illinois Central; and that he was generally regarded as a shrewd and resolute man; but beyond this his knowledge did not go. He could think of no good reason for opposition to the committee's plans on the part of the Illinois Central, and he determined to put the matter squarely before Harriman and find out what he, individually, was trying to do. He therefore arranged an interview with him and said to him frankly: "Mr. Harriman, my associates and I, as you doubtless know, are trying to reorganize the Union Pacific. For a long time we have been making good progress; but now we are meeting everywhere with opposition, and I understand that this opposition is being directed by you. What have you to say about it?"

"I am the man," replied Mr. Harriman.

"But why are you doing it?" asked Mr. Schiff.

"Because I intend to reorganize the Union Pacific myself."

This was somewhat surprising, but Mr. Schiff merely smiled and said: "How do you propose to do it, Mr. Harriman? Most of the securities of the company are in our possession. What means have you of reorganizing the Union Pacific?"

"The Illinois Central ought to have that road," replied Mr. Harriman, "and we are going to take charge of the reorganization. We have the best credit in the country. I am going to issue $100,000,000 in three per cent bonds of the Illinois Central Railroad Company and am going to get close to par for them. You, at the best, can't get money for less than four-and-a-half per cent. In that respect I am stronger than you are."[1]

[1] There is some reason to believe that Mr. Harriman's original intention (approved perhaps by President Fish) was to unite the Illinois Central and the Union Pacific, and that his opposition to the Fitzgerald-Schiff plan of reorganization was based on a fear that it would shut the Illinois Central out and give controlling influence to the New York Central and the Chicago & Northwestern, whose presidents

Mr. Schiff was amazed at the confident boldness of these assertions, but he merely replied: "You'll have a good time doing it, Mr. Harriman; but, meanwhile, what is your price?"

"There is no price," replied Harriman. "I am determined to get possession of the road."

Mr. Schiff then asked if there were no terms on which all parties could come together and work in harmony.

"If you'll make me chairman of the executive committee of the reorganized road," said Harriman, "I'll consider the expediency of joining forces with you."

"That is out of the question," replied the banker. "It has been decided that Mr. Pierce shall be chairman and I think he deserves the place."

"Very well, Mr. Schiff," said Harriman. "Go ahead and see what you can do. Good-day."

After this interview the opposition to the reorganization plan of the Fitzgerald-Schiff committee grew stronger rather than weaker. Stuyvesant Fish, president of the Illinois Central, attacked it vigor-

were prominent members of the reorganization committee. After he became a director of the Union Pacific, Mr. Harriman seems to have abandoned the idea of consolidating it with the Illinois Central — possibly because the stockholders of the latter had little faith in the future of the Union Pacific and were not willing to run the risk of combining with it and taking its chances of success. (See *E. H. Harriman and the Union Pacific Railroad*, by Alexander Millar, New York, 1910, p. 5.)

ously in a speech before the Pacific Roads Commission in Washington, and all the influences that he and his railroad company could control were arrayed against it. Realizing, at last, that Mr. Harriman was not a man to be ignored or pushed aside, Mr. Schiff decided to propose a compromise. It would be better, he thought, in the interest of a prompt and successful reorganization, to secure Mr. Harriman's coöperation than to work at cross-purposes with him. He therefore brought about another interview, in the course of which he explained more fully the circumstances that seemed to make necessary the election of Winslow S. Pierce as first chairman of the executive committee. The latter, Mr. Schiff said, had been instrumental in bringing the business to Kuhn, Loeb & Co. in the first place, and he was supported, moreover, by powerful Union Pacific interests which were more or less hostile to Mr. Harriman. "However," said Mr. Schiff, "if you will coöperate with us, I'll see that you are made a director of the reorganized company and a member of the executive committee. Then, if you prove to be the strongest man in that committee, you'll probably get the chairmanship in the end."

"All right," said Harriman, "I'm with you."

He then joined the syndicate and took a "participation" to the amount of $900,000.

Owing chiefly to embarrassments and difficulties growing out of the indebtedness of the Union Pacific to the Government, the progress of the reorganization committee was slow; but before the end of 1896 a plan was agreed upon which met the approval of nearly all the security-holders, and early in 1897 articles of incorporation for a new company were filed.[1]

Foreclosure proceedings had long been under way, and in January, 1897, the Government agreed to join in them provided the committee would guarantee a bid, at the forced sale, of a sum equal at least to the amount of the original Government bonds with interest at three and one-half per cent. This the committee consented to do, but when the decrees of the courts in the foreclosure proceedings were made public, the Government was dissatisfied with them and put in additional claims amounting in the aggregate to about $8,000,000. Further negotiations delayed the final sale until November 2, 1897, when the financing syndicate, headed by Kuhn, Loeb &

[1] "The plan of reorganization was a strong one. It reduced fixed charges from over $7,000,000 to under $4,000,000, with an eventual lower limit of $3,000,000, and this amount such good authorities as Messrs. Mink and Clark pronounced the road safely able to earn, in spite of the reduction of its mileage. . . . It gave to each class of securities a claim to interest strictly proportional to the earning capacity of the road, and added to this a preferred stock on which no payment was to be paid unless earned; while it provided for a liberal assessment upon stockholders and attempted no funding of the current liabilities incurred during the past troubled years." (*Railroad Reorganization: The Union Pacific*, by Stuart Daggett, pp. 252–54.)

Co., bought the road, paying the Government debt in full with interest to date of purchase, and agreeing, furthermore, to buy up all the bonds secured by the first mortgage which amounted to $27,637,436 more. Thus the syndicate, when it acquired the property, assumed liabilities amounting in the aggregate to more than $81,000,000.[1] For this sum the purchasers received only the main stem of the Union Pacific extending from Omaha to Ogden. All the rest of the old system, including the Kansas Pacific, Denver Pacific, Oregon Short Line, and Union Pacific, Denver & Gulf, had already been lost or were about to be lost, through the foreclosure of other mortgages.

[1]

U.S. 2d mortgage bonds with interest	$40,253,605
Union Pacific 1st mortgage bonds	27,637,435
Securities in sinking fund brought by committee	13,645,250
Total	$81,536,290

The sum received by the Government, in full satisfaction of its claims, was $58,448,223, as follows:

U.S. 2d mortgage bonds with interest	$40,253,605
Securities in sinking fund sold to committee	13,645,250
Cash in sinking fund, taken over	4,549,368
Total	$58,448,223

(*Commercial & Financial Chronicle*, January 15, 1898.)

This settlement was very advantageous to the United States. The Government had loaned to the company in bonds only $27,236,512, and it had not only got this sum back, with interest in full, but had saved in the thirty years almost or quite as much more through the economies secured in the transportation of mails, troops, supplies, etc., by rail instead of by wagon.

The risking of more than $81,000,000 in the purchase of the main line of the Union Pacific was one of the most daring financial undertakings of that time. The road was not in good physical condition, nor was it properly equipped. It had lost its through connection to the Pacific, as well as all of its branches in Kansas and Nebraska, and the whole of the territory through which it ran was still suffering from the business depression that followed the disastrous panic of 1893. So seriously did Mr. Schiff regard the enterprise upon which he and his associates had embarked that, on his first visit to Omaha after the purchase of the road, he spent the greater part of one night pacing the floor in his hotel room, debating anxiously with himself the question whether Kuhn, Loeb & Co., as financial managers for the reorganization committee, had not undertaken more than they could successfully carry through. Mr. Harriman, on the contrary, felt no anxiety and had no misgivings. His faith in the future growth and prosperity of the Great West was unbounded, and he intended to reconstruct and reëquip the Union Pacific so completely that when better times should come, it would be prepared to handle cheaply and profitably the immense volume of traffic that he could already foresee.

On the 6th of December, 1897, when the new

Union Pacific Company perfected its organization, Mr. Harriman was chosen a director and shortly afterward a member of the executive committee, in accordance with the promise that Mr. Schiff had made to him.[1] But he did not at first play any important part, for the reason that he was little known to his new associates and was regarded by some of them with distrust.

Almost all the members of the board had been previously connected with the Union Pacific, either through old affiliations, or through membership in the reorganization committee. Mr. Harriman was a newcomer, and by several members of the board his advent was not regarded with friendly eyes. He was looked at askance, somewhat in the light of an intruder. His ways and manners jarred upon several of his new colleagues, and he was considered by some as not quite belonging in their class, from the point of view of position, financial standing, and achievements.[2]

Mr. Harriman, however, paid little attention to this, if, in fact, he noticed it. He was intent on learn-

[1] The other members of the executive committee were Winslow S. Pierce (*ex-officio* chairman), Marvin Hughitt (president of the Chicago & Northwestern), James Stillman (president of the National City Bank), and Otto H. Kahn (of Kuhn, Loeb & Co.).

[2] *Edward Henry Harriman*, by Otto H. Kahn. Mr. Kahn was a young man of brilliant talents who, after studying banking in Germany, had six or seven years of training and experience in the London branch of the Deutsche Bank and in the firm of Speyer & Co. of New York. He became a partner in the banking house of Kuhn, Loeb & Co. in 1897, and was a member of the first board of directors of the reorganized Union Pacific Company. He soon became one of Mr. Harriman's warmest friends and staunchest supporters.

ing the exact condition of the property for which he had become in part responsible, and he devoted most of the winter of 1897–98 to an intensive study of it. This necessitated frequent requests for information from the men on the ground, and in commenting upon such requests, Mr. J. B. Berry, who was then chief engineer of the road, says:

> It was apparent to a number of us connected with the Union Pacific that, even prior to Mr. Harriman's election as chairman of the executive committee, in the spring of 1898, there was a new man at the head of affairs. He was constantly making inquiries about the staff and the condition of the road, and was evidently making up his mind as to what it would be best to do.[1]

In the early part of 1898, a number of Union Pacific directors and officials made a trip over the main line, for the purpose of ascertaining the condition and needs of the road. Mr. Harriman, who was a member of the party, had already begun to attract attention in the West, and was fast acquiring reputation in his new environment as a man of exceptional knowledge and ability. The impression that he made upon some of the employees of the road is described by Mr. W. L. Park, then division superintendent at North Platte, Nebraska, in the following words:

> The advent of the Harriman régime on the Union

[1] "Notes on Association with E. H. Harriman," by J. B. Berry, chief engineer of the Union Pacific. (An unpublished manuscript.)

Pacific, February 1st, 1898, was a matter of no small concern to the employees and officials. It was not known generally what interest had purchased the road, or who would dictate its policies. Then along came a party of financial people, who were escorted over the road by the general officers and shown the physical characteristics of the property. I heard the General Manager remark to the Superintendent of Machinery, Mr. J. H. McConnell, "Joe, did you notice that dark-complected man with glasses who seemed to know so much about scrap, and a great deal about things in general? Well, that's the man who is going to have a good deal to say about this railroad."

"Do you think so?" inquired the Superintendent of Machinery in rather a doubtful manner. "What's his name?"

"That's Ned Harriman — used to be on the Illinois Central at Chicago. He's a comer! They all defer to him, and he knows nearly as much about the property as I do, already; except the financial end, and of that he knows all and I know very little."[1]

If Mr. Harriman already knew almost as much about the Union Pacific as its general manager did, it was only because he had already spent months in the study of it, with a view to its complete reconstruction and reëquipment under his own direction.

It was about this time, or a little later, that Mr. Harriman laid the foundation of his great fortune by investing largely in Union Pacific stock. His ability

[1] "Personal Recollections of E. H. Harriman," by W. L. Park, division superintendent of the Union Pacific at North Platte, Nebraska, from 1890 to 1900. (An unpublished manuscript.)

to take a "participation" to the amount of $900,000 in the financing syndicate shows that he was already a man of means; but judged by the standards of the time, he was not yet a man of *great* wealth. It was the Union Pacific that ultimately enriched him, and when, in 1898, he began to buy its stock, he was counting on his own ability to make immensely valuable a property which was then worth comparatively little. Speaking of these early investments, Mr. Otto H. Kahn says:

> He caused his associates to wonder and doubt, by buying all of the Union Pacific common that he could accumulate up to the price of 25 or thereabouts. He must have acquired many thousands of shares, for the stock had long been selling freely between 15 and 20. It was considered to have but very little intrinsic value, and there were no dividends in sight for the preferred, much less for the common stock. I recollect an influential financial personage saying to me about these purchases, which at the time attracted a good deal of comment, "You see the man is essentially a speculator. He is putting everything he has, and more, into Union Pacific common and preferred at these prices. He will come to grief yet." [1]

Mr. Harriman, however, was not speculating, in the proper, or even the popular, sense of that word. When a capitalist buys a run-down farm, on the chance that it may appreciate in value with the in-

[1] *Edward Henry Harriman*, by Otto H. Kahn (New York, 1911), pp. 14-15.

crease of population, he is truly a speculator. He does not work the farm, and if it happens to double in value as the result of some fortuitous circumstance — the building of a railroad or a scarcity of farm products — he has not earned the profit that he takes. Such is not the case when an agricultural expert buys a worn-out farm, works it himself, puts into it his knowledge and skill, as well as his labor, and eventually doubles its value by fertilization and intensive cultivation. He does not then take a profit without earning it, as does the hypothetical capitalist; he rightfully takes possession of value that he has himself created. When Mr. Harriman invested his money in a worn-out railroad, he expected to earn, by personal labor and skill, the profit that he anticipated — and he *did* earn it. No one now questions the fact that he was virtually the creator of the reorganized Union Pacific; and if he made millions out of it, he added, at the same time, hundreds of millions to the value of the property of other men, and widened immensely the area of human happiness and prosperity.

It has sometimes been said, in disparagement of Mr. Harriman's achievement, that the ultimate success of the Union Pacific was wholly due to the growth and development of the territory that it served. "Harriman did n't create the Great West," said W. B. Thompson in an argument before the United States Industrial Commission. "God Almighty did that." This is the argument of the Russian peasant who begrudged the ten kopeks that he had to pay for a teakettleful of hot water. "God made the water," he declared, "and he gives it freely to everybody."

"Yes, my little brother," replied the dispenser of the aqueous fluid, "God made the water, but he did n't make it hot; if you want God's water, go to the river and fill your old teakettle."

The same reply may be made to Mr. Thompson. God created the Great West, but he did n't make it accessible. Railroad-builders did that and for that railroad-builders should have all the credit. It is undoubtedly true, as Mr. Kahn has said, that "the growth and prosperity of the Union Pacific was dependent upon the growth and prosperity of the territory that it served, but such growth and prosperity were universal throughout the country west of the Missouri River and their benefits were available to all other Western railroads to the same extent as to the Union Pacific. Yet there is not a single line that comes near to equaling the record made by the Union Pacific, and it is the uniqueness of the Union Pacific's attainments, considering not only the financial results to the stockholders, but also the standard of efficiency, service to the public, physical condition, and financial strength of resources, which measures the uniqueness of Mr. Harriman's genius."[1]

What his own profits were from the investments that he made in 1898 can only be conjectured; but the well-known financial expert, John Moody, has figured that the man who bought one hundred shares of Union Pacific common in 1898 for $1600 received on it, in dividends and increased value, in eight and a half years, $21,900, and was then receiving sixty-three per cent on his original investment.[2]

Most of Mr. Harriman's great fortune was made out of the increase in value of the properties that he managed, and in part owned; but the value was put into those properties by unremitting labor and by the exercise of the rare mental powers and capacities which in the business world always gain the high rewards. Mr. Harriman's attitude toward money will be considered elsewhere; but as it was at this time in his life that he began to accumulate wealth rapidly, it seems proper to say that in investing in Union Pacific stock he was not speculating on an uncertainty, but was anticipating the natural and legitimate results of work for which he knew he had a peculiar fitness.

[1] *Edward Henry Harriman*, by Otto H. Kahn (New York, 1911), p. 12.
[2] "The Growth of the Harriman Lines," by John Moody, *McClure's Magazine*, October, 1906, p. 546.

On the 1st of January, 1898, the Union Pacific was turned over by the receivers to the reorganized company, and the latter began at once to operate it, with Horace G. Burt as president; Oliver W. Mink, vice-president; Alexander Millar, secretary; Edward Dickinson, general manager; and Winslow S. Pierce, chairman of the board of directors and of the executive committee.[1]

In the course of the next three months, the new Union Pacific Company reacquired the Kansas Pacific, Denver Pacific, and the Julesburg branch of the Union Pacific, Denver & Gulf, and made plans for getting control again of the Oregon Short Line, the Oregon Railroad & Navigation Company, and other important parts of the old system. Mr. Harriman, as a director, favored all these measures and plans, and in the discussion of them showed so much accurate knowledge and shrewd judgment as greatly to impress even those of his associates who had at first doubted

[1] Mr. Burt was an engineer by profession, and prior to his election as president of the Union Pacific he had been third vice-president and traffic manager of the Chicago & Northwestern Railroad at Chicago. Messrs. Millar, Dickinson, and Mink had all been connected with the old company — Millar as secretary, Dickinson as general manager, and Mink as controller and afterward one of the receivers. Mr. Pierce was a corporation lawyer and had acted in the capacity of general counsel, or general attorney, for several Western railroads, including the Missouri Pacific, Texas & Pacific, and St. Louis Southwestern. He was the personal representative of George J. Gould, who, at that time, was interested in the Union Pacific as well as the Missouri Pacific.

his ability. Mr. Schiff, in particular, became convinced that in bringing about the election of Mr. Harriman as a director he had "builded better than he knew," and had given to the board a man of exceptional knowledge, boldness, and power. The by-laws of the reorganized company provided that the chairman of the board of directors should be, *ex officio*, chairman also of the executive committee; but when, in the spring of 1898, it became apparent that Mr. Harriman was preëminently qualified for leadership, it was decided to amend the by-laws so as to make a place for him by empowering the committee to choose a presiding officer for itself. Early in May, 1898, when this had been accomplished, Mr. Harriman was elected chairman and took his seat as chief executive officer of the board. Thus was fulfilled the half promise, half prediction made by Mr. Schiff in 1897 that if Mr. Harriman should "prove to be the strongest man in the committee," he would "probably get the chairmanship in the end."

CHAPTER VI

RECONSTRUCTION AND REËQUIPMENT OF THE UNION PACIFIC

MR. HARRIMAN'S first step, after he became chairman of the executive committee of the Union Pacific, was thoroughly characteristic of the man and his methods. He had already made a careful study of the road, and was better acquainted, perhaps, with its condition and needs than were any of his associates on the board of directors; but in order to verify his information and perfect his knowledge he determined to go personally, by daylight, over the whole line from the Missouri River to the Pacific Coast, and make a thorough examination of it from an observation car. Early in the summer of 1898, with his two older daughters, Mary and Cornelia, he went to Omaha, and there ordered a special train made up with an observation car in front and a locomotive in the rear. Then, accompanied by President Burt, Chief Engineer Berry, and a few other high officials of the road, he started for the Pacific Coast, sitting in the front of the observation car and taking note of grades, curves, rails, ballast, etc., as the locomotive in the rear pushed the train westward across the plains.

Traveling only in the daytime, and stopping at all important stations to question officials, investigate conditions, and gather information, the new chairman of the executive committee made a slower trip from Omaha to Portland, perhaps, than had ever been made before by a high railroad official; but in the weeks that the journey occupied he became thoroughly acquainted with the physical condition of the road, estimated the value of its equipment, interviewed the shippers who made use of it, judged the characters of the officials locally in charge of it, and not only devised plans for its immediate improvement, but, in many cases, put such plans into operation without waiting for the approval of the executive committee. He determined, for example, to retire as soon as possible most of the light rolling stock; and in order to prevent useless expenditure of money in repairing it, he directed that not more than ten dollars be spent in putting any single car in order. He also directed the removal of the sides and roofs of old box cars, in order that they might be used as flatcars in ballasting the track. They were too small and light for freight traffic and he intended to substitute for them cars of much greater capacity.[1] These measures he took on his own per-

[1] "Recollections of E. H. Harriman in Connection with the Union Pacific," by W. L. Park, division superintendent at North Platte, Nebraska. (An unpublished manuscript.)

sonal responsibility, merely for the purpose of saving time and money. In his examination of the road and its equipment, nothing escaped his attention. One of the division superintendents afterward declared, with pardonable exaggeration, "He saw every poor tie, blistered rail, and loose bolt on my division." He even noticed and made inquiries about such comparatively unimportant matters as the diameter of water-tank service pipes, the quality of water furnished to engines, and the effect of unsuitable water on the casing of locomotive fire-boxes. His wide knowledge, keenness of observation, and quickness of decision made a deep impression upon the minds of railway officials who had never before seen him. Mr. W. H. Bancroft, general manager of the Oregon Short Line says:

As I now recall it, I first met Mr. Harriman in 1898, when he made his first trip of inspection over the Union Pacific, the Oregon Short Line, and the other roads with which his name has been so familiarly associated. Before he became chairman of the executive committee of the Union Pacific, I had known little about him, even by reputation; but his election to that position naturally aroused interest in his personality. I had imagined a man larger in stature than I found him to be, but, although somewhat below the average size, he impressed me as a man of unusual ability, with a wonderful grasp of affairs, full of energy, and apparently of physical strength. At that time he was about fifty years of age, but he did not look it. I should have said that he was between forty and forty-five. The things that impressed me as most remarkable in his character were his general knowledge of the properties with which he had become so recently associated, and his rapid observation of all matters of detail. His view of larger and broader questions also was that which a man ought to have if he is to exercise supervisory powers and to direct the development and management of great railroad properties. He approached every question with a directness and thoroughness which enabled him to master all the phases of it in the least possible time. It was often difficult, even for an experienced employee, to answer directly and promptly his pertinent and far-reaching inquiries. A man might be acquainted in a general way with the data and information that he was called upon to furnish, but he might not have arranged the facts systematically enough in his mind to make a compendious presentation of them. Mr. Harriman's grasp of affairs, and his desire for full information in condensed form, constituted a lesson to me and to those associated with me. We learned to systematize and condense our information and to present it to him, at subsequent meetings, approximately in the brief and comprehensive form that his methods seemed to require. It was this that enabled him to deal successfully with the multitude of great questions presented to him.

His manner, at first, seemed to me brusque; but this was an erroneous impression, for I soon found that it was only his thorough way of transacting business. If the information given him with regard to any matter seemed satisfactory to his mind, he disposed of the largest questions with great rapidity and, as the results showed, with the greatest wisdom. If, on the other hand, the facts laid before him were insufficient, a pertinent suggestion from him would show his assistants what was lacking and enable them to go after the desired information understandingly. To be associated with him in business afforded an opportunity for a liberal education in business problems.[1]

Many, if not most, of the things that Mr. Harriman saw in his daylight ride over the Union Pacific would have disheartened a less far-sighted or less resolute man. In the first place, the condition of the road itself was deplorably bad. The rails were light, the track had never been properly ballasted, and the rolling stock was either old or of limited capacity. Every railroad deteriorates rapidly if adequate appropriations are not made for maintenance and repair, and in the five and a half years just prior to the reconstruction of the Union Pacific, the money spent for these purposes was less than $180,000 a year.[2]

[1] "Impressions of E. H. Harriman," by W. H. Bancroft, vice-president and general manager of the Oregon Short Line. (An unpublished manuscript.)

[2] Between January 1, 1893, and June 3, 1898, the expenditures of the Union Pacific for maintenance and repair were $983,678, as follows:

Bridges and trestles	$100,651
Fences	18,281
Real estate	1,350
Side tracks	12,193
Widening embankments	68,929
Miscellaneous betterments	147,567
Reconstruction and grade revision	129,338
New rolling stock	505,368
Total	$983,677

This sum, on a main line of a thousand miles, would make only about $179 per mile annually for maintenance, betterments, and renewal of equipment.

On the main line of the road, when Mr. Harriman went over it, there were only seven miles of ninety-pound rails, seventy miles of eighty-pound rails, and three hundred and forty-four miles of seventy-five-pound rails. Eighty per cent of the track had sixty- and seventy-pound rails, and even these were in a more or less worn and untrustworthy condition. Only two hundred miles of the main line were gravel-ballasted, and in many parts of these stretches the ballast was thin and scattered. Almost eighty per cent of the main line had no ballast at all. Not a yard of rail was tie-plated; not a mile of track had signals of any kind; and nearly half the line needed replacement of wooden sleepers. The western part of the road, moreover, abounded in heavy grades and short curves. Between Cheyenne and Sherman there was a rise of 2214 feet in a distance of only thirty miles, and maximum grades of from fifty to ninety-eight feet to the mile were not uncommon.

The rolling stock of the road was in better condition perhaps than the track, for the reason that more money had recently been spent on it, but it, too, left much to be desired. The company was carrying 10,634 freight cars on its books, but most of them were of small capacity and more than half of them were old or unserviceable.[1]

[1] A report made to Mr. Harriman in May, 1898, showed that 3597 of these cars had been built before 1880 and that 1180 were worn out.

The state of the country tributary to the road was quite as bad as that of the road itself. Nowhere, perhaps, in the United States, were the disastrous effects of the panic of 1893 and of the long period of business depression that followed it more clearly manifest than in the region west of the Missouri River. This territory, in the years previous to 1893, had enjoyed what is colloquially known as a "boom." The tide of immigration from the Eastern States had flowed into it rapidly, and thousands of newcomers, many of them with very little agricultural knowledge or experience, had bought land at inflated prices, borrowing on it all the money they could get. Loan companies in the East made easy the financing of such purchases, and even savings banks, tempted by high rates of interest, were eager to invest in Western farm mortgages. Little attention was paid, in many cases, to the intrinsic value of the land, or its productive capacity. If it was called a "farm," and if somebody stood ready to cultivate it, Eastern money-lenders were willing to finance the development of it. Speculative syndicates bought immense tracts of land, mortgaged them for more than they were worth, cut them up into farms, and sold them, or tried to sell them, to immigrants from the East. Even established farmers borrowed millions of dollars on their holdings for the purpose of building houses and barns, acquiring additional land, or purchasing live stock and machinery. Cities and towns in the agricultural area outgrew their former boundaries and expanded widely in suburban development. Money was easily made, easily borrowed, and freely spent, and there seemed to be no limit to the opportunities for speculation and profit. This apparent prosperity, however, was largely fictitious, for the reason that it was mainly based on borrowed capital; and when the panic of 1893 came, with a sudden contraction in credits and a general loss of confidence in everything and everybody, the financial structure, built up on hope and trust, collapsed and went to pieces. Interest payments on speculative loans ceased; mortgages were everywhere foreclosed; farmers were unable to meet their engagements, and a period of general embarrassment and distress followed the period of deceptive prosperity. The great tracts of land bought by speculative syndicates were no longer salable and remained uncultivated; town sites were abandoned, and municipalities which had floated loans in the East ceased to exist, leaving the holders of their bonds to foreclose on deserted town lots and empty buildings. Settlers could no longer obtain bank accommodations; solvent business men suffered great losses from the sudden shrinkage in values; and even the population decreased as ruined farmers and unemployed farm laborers drifted back into the Eastern States. Some agricultural counties lost almost their whole population, while in others there was a numerical reduction of from twenty-five to fifty per cent.

Inasmuch as Mr. Harriman had known all these conditions before he started westward from New York, he was not discouraged by them when he saw them from his observation car. He believed that the worst period of the depression had passed, and that a revival of business would come very soon. The agricultural crops for 1898 promised to be good, and he felt sure that the Great West would not only regain its prosperity, but develop more rapidly than ever before. As for the railroad, its condition was no worse than he had supposed it to be, and he had always anticipated the complete reconstruction and reëquipment of it. With capital, skill, and energy he knew that it could be made one of the best railroads in the world, as well as one of the most profitable. By reducing grades, eliminating curves, and increasing the size of cars and the tractive power of locomotives, he expected not only to lessen the road's operating expenses, but to double its carrying capacity. That the territory between the Missouri River and the Pacific would furnish, in the near future, an immense volume of traffic, he never for a moment doubted; and he did not hesitate, therefore, to take immediate and decisive action.

His first step, as described by Mr. Otto H. Kahn, was to

> telegraph the board in New York, asking for authority to purchase immediately a large quantity of cars, locomotives, rails, etc., and to start various works of improvement, the total aggregating, as I remember it, something like $25,000,000, which telegram was followed by a written communication setting forth the reasons for his request and the main details of the proposed expenditure. The reasons, in short, were that he clearly discovered signs of returning prosperity after the period of long depression; that he believed this prosperity would assume proportions corresponding to the depth and extent of the long-drawn-out and drastic reaction that preceded it; that labor and materials were then extremely cheap, but would begin to advance before very long, and that the Union Pacific should put itself in shape to take care of the largely increased traffic which he foresaw, to attract business to its lines by being better prepared for it, and thus afford shippers better facilities than its neighbors. Remember that at that time . . . $25,000,000 was a vastly greater sum than nowadays, when the stupendous development of the country has made railroad expenditures of proportionate size familiar, and that it was a pretty hazardous thing to venture upon this huge outlay simply upon a guess of coming unprecedented prosperity. There was much doubt in the board as to whether Mr. Harriman's recommendation should be followed. I remember the statement was made that, if it were followed, the Union Pacific would find itself in receivers' hands again before two years had passed. The subject was laid over until

Mr. Harriman's return to New York. . . . Incidentally I may mention, as characteristic of the man, that he felt so sure of his judgment and of his ability to carry the board with him (though he had no illusions as to the sentiment of some of its members regarding him and of the fatal consequences to his career in case his forecast should turn out to be mistaken or even premature) that, while he was still in the West, and so as to be sure not to lose time or opportunity, he took upon himself the responsibility, at his personal risk, of concluding various contracts for purchases and work included in the programme advocated by him.[1]

Soon after his arrival in Portland, Mr. Harriman went southward over the lines of the Southern Pacific to San Francisco; thence eastward over the Central Pacific to Ogden; northward to Butte, Montana, and back on a branch of the Oregon Short Line, and finally eastward on the main line of the Union Pacific to his starting-point in Omaha, thus completing a journey of more than five thousand miles, most of which he made by daylight in the observation car of a pushed train. Everywhere on the main line of the old Union Pacific between the Missouri River and Portland he saw evidences of business depression, and everywhere the road over which he passed was in an unsatisfactory if not a neglected condition; but so confident was he of coming prosperity, and so sure did he feel of his ability to

[1] *Edward Henry Harriman*, by Otto H. Kahn (New York, 1911), pp. 13–14.

reconstruct the railroad and put it into a state of high efficiency, that, as his train pulled into Omaha, he said to the officials who accompanied him: "Gentlemen, I have to-day wired New York for five thousand shares of Union Pacific preferred at sixty-six, and any one of you is welcome to take as few or as many shares as he likes at that price plus the interest until paid." [1]

Few railroad officials, or business men of any class, after going over a dilapidated and run-down railroad and through a country still suffering from an unprecedented financial débâcle, would have had courage and self-confidence enough to invest $330,000 on his personal judgment of that railroad's potential capacity and that country's future prosperity.

Upon his return to New York in the late summer of 1898, Mr. Harriman submitted to the Union Pacific directors the facts and reasonings on which his telegraphic request for $25,000,000 had been based. "After long and strenuous argument he carried the day. The appropriation for the expenditures advocated by him was made, though with considerable head-shaking and misgiving, and it was this courageous outlay, at a time when the unexampled pros-

[1] "Notes on Association with E. H. Harriman," by J. B. Berry, chief engineer of the Union Pacific. (An unpublished manuscript.)

perity to come was barely discernible, and the intelligent and efficient application of the funds, that started the Union Pacific on its amazingly successful career."[1]

This acceptance of Mr. Harriman's plan for the complete reconstruction of the Union Pacific, at an initial cost of $25,000,000, shows how deep an impression his knowledge, ability, and character had made upon the minds of the directors. When he became a member of the board, in December, 1897, he was comparatively little known, even to his associates, but in less than six months his influence had become paramount, and in less than a year (December 1, 1898) he was made chairman of the whole board, as well as chairman of the executive committee, and was practically given supreme control of Union Pacific affairs. The directors, of course, continued to manage the property, but, as a rule, they deferred to the expert knowledge and far-sighted judgment of their chairman in all questions of importance, whether technical or financial.

Few railroad officials, at that time, fully appreciated the importance of reducing the cost of transportation by using larger cars and more powerful locomotives. The average freight car then in use

[1] *Edward Henry Harriman*, by Otto H. Kahn (New York, 1911), p. 14.

weighed 20,000 to 40,000 pounds and had a carrying capacity about equal to its own weight. The average freight locomotive weighed about fifty tons and its tractive power was less than ten tons. Mr. Harriman believed that by increasing the size of the cars and the power of the locomotives he could double the carrying capacity of every train, without increasing in anything like the same ratio the operating expense. Given a suitable track, it would cost little more to run a train that would carry a thousand tons of paying freight than to run one that would carry only half that quantity, and the difference in earnings would be very great. Heavy equipment and heavy trains, however, would require an approximately straight and level track, and the western part of the Union Pacific was full of sharp curves and heavy grades. Between Rawlins and Wamsutta there was a grade of sixty-seven feet to the mile each way; between Wamsutta and Green River a grade of sixty-seven feet going west and seventy feet going east; and between Cheyenne and Laramie a grade of eighty-seven feet one way and ninety-eight the other. Long and heavy trains could not be run economically, if at all, over this part of the main line without extensive grade reductions, and Mr. Harriman's first task was to get an approximately straight and level track, on which the heavy equipment that he contemplated could be economically used. From his own observations and from the reports of his engineers, he believed that everywhere, except between Evanston and Ogden and between Cheyenne and Laramie, grades could be reduced to a maximum of forty-three feet to the mile, and this was adopted as the standard for the road. Bringing the track to this standard, however, was a work of colossal difficulty, inasmuch as it involved engineering operations of the most formidable nature and practical abandonment of the old line in a large part of the mountainous region. Fortunately Mr. Harriman had as his assistants technical experts of the first rank. Chief Engineer Berry was a man of conspicuous ability; President Burt was himself an engineer by profession; and W. L. Park, who superintended the ballasting, laying of rails, and building of bridges, was an extremely capable and energetic officer. With Kilpatrick Brothers and Collins and the MacArthurs of Chicago as contractors they made a strong directing and working force.

As soon as the appropriation of $25,000,000 had been secured, the work of reconstruction began along the whole extent of the main line. Under the active direction of President Burt, contractors enlisted an army of laborers and assembled a complete equipment of modern machinery, much of which was then used for the first time in railroad-building. In trying to get a maximum grade of forty-three feet to the mile, Harriman's engineers encountered the greatest difficulties in the mountainous region west of Cheyenne.

It is not perhaps generally understood [says a well-informed writer on the subject] that the highest barrier presented to the Union Pacific in its transcontinental run lies immediately west of the plains about Cheyenne, where the line strikes that secondary range of the Rockies known as the Black Hills. What makes the ascent of these hills of especial difficulty is a great elevation coupled with unusually short slopes. Just here, at the outset almost, the Union Pacific rises to its greatest height above the sea, and here, in the rebuilding, lay the problem before Berry, chief engineer, as to how the grade of this granite summit might possibly be reduced. New limits had been set to the gradients of the proposed improvements; but it is one thing in a directors' meeting to adopt a grade over the Rockies of forty-three feet to the mile, and quite another to go into the Rockies and run it. The chief engineer had to match his wits against those of engineers who, a generation before, had laid out the pioneer line and done it well. Thirty-five years of reflection, observation, and criticism from the best constructionists in the world had failed to develop flaws in this earliest effort of Americans to bridge the Rockies. . . .

To find the line that Berry determined he must have, he sent good men into the hills, only to be told that where he wanted a line there was none. But when they tried to maintain this, the personal equation, that subtle and incalculable factor in men which, in the overcoming of difficulties, makes the slight difference between success and failure, intervened. The chief engineer, undaunted, refused to abide by the findings. He sent the engineers again; the second time they brought the line he knew must be there. It involved staggering estimates. The Dale Creek crossing, just beyond Cheyenne, called for a single fill nine hundred feet long and one hundred and thirty feet deep. In these granite wastes the engineering figures assumed at once unheard-of proportions. Cubic yards went into the calculations in millions instead of thousands. Two creek crossings called for eight hundred thousand yards of embankment. Two miles of new line required the moving of seventeen hundred thousand cubic yards of material, and of this three hundred thousand were solid rock. Two fills, within these two miles, swallowed a million cubic yards. To eliminate three heavy reverse curves and two bridges, a summit cut was required eighty feet deep and a thousand feet long. The springing charge for a single cone of rock was a thousand pounds of giant powder, and the mountain was hurled into the cañon with twenty thousand pounds of black. For these unprecedented levelings of the continental summit new devices were constantly brought into play. Time was an essence of the undertaking, and the American contractor, following loyally the American engineer, as he has always followed him, stooped like an Atlas and took upon his shoulders the burden of the plans.

Grading machines and dump-wagons were sent into the hills in train-loads. Steam shovels, the leviathans of the railroad camp, crossed the mountains in processions. They scooped the borrow-pits, cut the shale from the tunnels, dug the Sherman ballast, and loaded even blasted granite upon cars out of the rock cuts. Track-laying machines flung out rails on one side and ties on the other like sandwiches. At one of the vital points Chicago men took the heavy work, and in order to make a three-hundred-thousand-yard fill with an embankment of one hundred and thirty-eight feet, MacArthur, to complete his contract on time, threw his own temporary suspension bridge across the thousand-foot cañon, and ran his dump-cars out upon his own rails and cables. Track-laying — ballasting even — was pushed across the Rockies in midwinter. At the summit the last hill was drilled and a tunnel eighteen hundred feet long was put through primitive granite. Here the Harriman engineers scaled two hundred and forty-seven feet off the highest elevation at which the road had formerly crossed the continent; then came the task of getting gracefully down the western slope of the hills to the Laramie plains.

There is nothing less showy in the rebuilding of the Harriman lines, and nothing that is more of a triumph, than this feat of Berry's in getting into Laramie. He has used every trick in his bag, and after moving five millions of cubic yards of earth and rock to accomplish his purpose, he comes down into Laramie with a forty-three-foot maximum grade eighteen miles long.[1] So close is the cloth cut for this entire distance that not one rail length of level track could be conceded for stations; they take their chances on the grade as best they can. Providence may, indeed, sometimes shift the axis of the granite anticlinal now so skillfully crossed at Sherman, Wyoming, and new dispositions may be called for; but until such an upheaval takes place, Berry's Laramie grade is likely to stand.

The whole road, from this eastern approach to the Black Hills far out to Medicine Bow on the Laramie plains, shows everywhere the chisel and the straight-edge of the Harriman engineers. There are but two pieces of track — both of them very short — on the entire main line where the forty-three-foot grade is ex-

[1] The grade of the old line here was ninety-eight feet.

ceeded. Curvature had to go with the heavy grades, and between the Black Hills and the Wasatch Range seven thousand degrees gradually disappeared. At one point, the new line, within a distance of four miles, crosses the old one seven times.

The Hanna cut uncovered an eight-foot seam of coal; a Green River cut revealed wide deposits of petrified fish. First and last the contractors uncovered a little of everything in the Rockies, from oil pockets to underground rivers; but in the Wasatch Range, in boring a six-thousand-foot tunnel, they struck a mountain that for startling developments broke the records in the annals of American engineering. It was here that the underground stream was encountered; but this was a mere incident among the possibilities in the mountain. The formation is carboniferous, thrown up in the Aspen Ridge at an angle of twenty-five degrees, and it includes shales, sandstone, oil, and coal. To bore a hole through the mountain at a depth of four hundred and fifty feet from the highest point was not difficult; but the curious thing was that after being bored the hole would not stay straight. The mountain, reversing every metaphor and simile of stability, refused to remain in the same position for two days together. It moved forcibly into the bore from the right side, and then stole quietly in from the left; it descended on the tunnel with crushing force from above, and rose irresistibly up into it from below. The mountain moved from every point of the compass, and from quarters hardly covered by the compass. Workmen grew superstitious and engineers stood nonplussed. Starting in huge cleavage planes, the shale became at times absolutely uncontrollable. Wall plates, well fastened into regular alignment at night, looked in the morning as if giants had twisted them. Twelve-by-twelve hard-pine timbers, laid skin to skin in the tunnel, were snapped like matches by this mysterious pressure.

Engineers are on record as stating that in the Aspen tunnel such construction timbers were broken in different directions within a distance of four feet. An engineer stood one day in the tunnel on a solid floor of these timbers, when under him and for a distance of two hundred feet ahead of him the floor rose, straining and cracking, three feet into the air. Before the tunnel could be finished it became necessary to line over seven hundred feet of it with a heavy steel and concrete construction.[1]

Speaking of the same tunnel, Superintendent Park says:

The Aspen tunnel was a Pandora box of unexpected events. The approaches were gentle and the earth parted easily before the great machines of Kilpatrick Brothers & Collins; but then it came together again and slides developed that required Herculean efforts and new devices to hold back. Farther in, at the eastern portal, docile limestone was encountered which remained where it was placed and made easy work; but beyond it shale rock appeared, and, at the western end, oily shale at a frightful angle. This slipped, squeezed, and crushed; great timbers a foot square bent and broke like toothpicks; gas appeared and ignited, ejecting men, mules, and timbers from the mouth of the tunnel like a cannon's shot. It took brave men to go back into the headings after the funerals; but they did return and conquered; and one morning Mr. Harriman appeared on the scene and went through the sink-hole of so many unexpected obstacles.[2]

[1] *The Strategy of Great Railroads*, by Frank H. Spearman (New York, 1914), pp. 59–66. Mr Spearman's account of these engineering operations has been submitted to Chief Engineer Berry and has been approved by him as substantially correct.

[2] "Recollections of E. H. Harriman in Connection with the Union

On the eastern part of the line, between Omaha and Cheyenne, the country was more nearly level and the engineering difficulties involved in the work of reconstruction were not so formidable; but even here great changes were made. Between Omaha and Lane, Nebraska, a new route was adopted which reduced the distance from twenty-four miles to fifteen miles and lowered the grade from forty-two feet to twenty-six feet. Between Lane and Grand Island, on a distance of one hundred and thirty miles, grades were reduced from thirty-nine and forty-two feet to twenty-six and thirty-one feet, and large parts of the track were abandoned and relocated in order to eliminate curves. All together, between Omaha and Ogden, the Harriman engineers abandoned more than one hundred and fifty miles of the old line (an amount equivalent to all of the New York Central Railroad between New York City and Troy), and by rebuilding it in new locations eliminated twenty-two complete circles of curvature and saved nearly forty miles of distance. At the same time the working force widened one hundred and ninety-six miles of road-bed and ballasted it with disintegrated granite; put in almost a million new cross-ties; laid forty-two thousand tons of new and heavier rails on a distance

Pacific," by W. L. Park, division superintendent at North Platte, Nebraska. (An unpublished manuscript.)

of three hundred and ninety-seven miles, and replaced nearly four thousand feet of old timber bridges with permanent earthen embankments or solid structures of steel. All this was done in the first year and a half of Mr. Harriman's administration. During the same period immense additions were made to the road's equipment. Two hundred light locomotives, which were not powerful enough to haul such trains as Mr. Harriman contemplated, were sold at about their scrap value, and were replaced with heavier engines which made it possible to more than double the tonnage of the average train. The rolling stock of the old road consisted of 10,634 freight cars, with a capacity of 400,000,000 pounds. Mr. Harriman added 4760 new cars with a capacity of 325,000,000 pounds, thus nearly doubling the road's carrying power. No such addition to equipment had ever before been made by an American railroad in the short period of sixteen months. During the first three years of Mr. Harriman's administration, he spent on the Union Pacific, for improvements, betterments and new equipment, the sum of $25,655,000, while the Atchison, Topeka & Santa Fé, with seventy per cent more mileage, spent only $11,318,000, and the Northern Pacific, with ten per cent more mileage, expended only $6,866,000. But Mr. Harriman wanted — as he said to his engineers and contractors — the best-built and best-equipped railroad that skill could devise and money pay for.

In discussing this period in the history of the Union Pacific, Superintendent Park says:

The lines east of Cheyenne did not require realignment, but they needed to be ballasted; the shoulders were thin and scant. Teams were employed along nearly every mile, widening the banks for ballast. The sidings were extended, cross-ties and heavier rails were thrown off alongside the track with such astonishing liberality that the rank and file marveled as to what it all meant. The famous Sherman disintegrated-granite gravel was dug up in train-loads and transported hundreds of miles, first in flatcars and then on a car of new design which we were told was a Rodger ballast car. Mr. Hart, the inventor, came out to show us how to operate them and I, personally, opened and unloaded near North Platte the first of thousands of such cars.

As superintendent, I was consecutively in charge of all that part of the ballasting, laying of rail, construction of bridges, etc., that fell to the operating department from Grand Island to Ogden, a distance of nearly a thousand miles. I was in this way brought intimately in contact with the construction department. Operation under heavy construction is always difficult, and construction under heavy traffic is apt to be slow and expensive. By close coöperation with the engineering department traffic was moved satisfactorily and the work of the reconstruction of the line proceeded very rapidly. There was close team work, and the most harmonious relations existed between the forces. A friendly rivalry to outdo each other stimulated to extraordinary effort and it was seldom that one department was compelled to wait on the other.

When the work was finished in Nebraska, I was moved to Cheyenne and placed in charge of the Wyoming division, where heavy reconstruction was under way. Those were strenuous days! The power was insufficient, the cars were old and decrepit. The demands upon the operating department were terrific. Only a few months could be utilized in pushing the work, as at the average height of six thousand feet winter might be expected to begin in September and to continue until March. The tunnels, at first, gave much concern. The one at the crest of the Rocky Mountains, however, developed into a matter only of persistent digging through flinty granite at so many inches an hour, the boring of which could be computed mathematically. In fact, its completion caught the engineers in other parts of the Sherman Hill line with work unfinished that should have been out of the way, and the mere filling of Dale Creek valley with eight hundred thousand cubic yards of gravel — enough to ballast three hundred miles of ordinary railroad — was not a satisfactory excuse for the chief engineer.

The work, as a whole, progressed with remarkable regularity and was free from the friction and conflict of authority quite frequently incident to such large undertakings. The pace, of course, was terrific, and men sometimes fell by the wayside — those without brains or brawn got out of the way — but the elimination was through the survival of the fittest. There was no favoritism; those who made good were remembered while those who did not were forgotten.

President Burt was on the work almost continually; his chief engineer, Mr. Berry, was everywhere, while the general manager, Mr. Dickinson, in his cool, deliberate way, steadied the organization and requisitioned for the material and equipment needed in the operating department. New locomotives and cars began to arrive. We heard that a couple of compound locomotives had been ordered; when they arrived there were sixty of them. Some freight cars were needed; five thousand were ordered. Steam shovels, wrecking derricks, and snow plows had only to be mentioned to be purchased. The road grew from a mere skeleton, a wandering contour line, into a magnificent highway, straight for miles as an arrow. Gentle curves took the place of abrupt and uncomfortable turns first one way and then the other without any apparent reason. Smooth, regular grades were substituted for sudden and alarming ascents and drops. The old depots and freight houses, with hieroglyphics of horses and wild animals cut by the Sioux Indians on doors and rough weather-boarding, were replaced by neat buildings with comfortable living-rooms. The shacks of section houses disappeared as if by magic, and in their places arose two-story buildings, grouped, properly, away from the line, so as to leave the view unobstructed for safety in operating the trains. Water-tubs, housed in with huge stoves to keep them from freezing and in close proximity to the track, were torn down, and graceful tanks with water-treating plants and frost-proof compartments were erected at proper distances. Water-pipes and cranes led to the locomotive tender, and by Mr. Harriman's personal order the discharge pipes were made twelve inches in diameter, instead of four, or six, in order to economize in the time of trains. One depot was moved three times to satisfy all concerned that it was in the right location; the last time by Mr. Harriman's personal direction, and it will remain there, because he was right.[1]

[1] "Recollections of E. H. Harriman in Connection with the Union Pacific," by W. L. Park, division superintendent at North Platte, Nebraska. (An unpublished manuscript.)

Although Mr. Harriman's work of reconstruction began on the main stem of the old system, it soon extended far beyond that. In 1899, less than a year after he became chairman of the executive committee, the Union Pacific reacquired the Oregon Short Line, one of the most important parts of the old system, and at the same time secured control of the Oregon Railroad & Navigation Company; thus increasing its mileage from 2848 to 5391 and recovering its lost outlet on the Pacific Coast at Portland.[1] Mr. Harriman had long before determined to secure possession of these roads, and when he went over them in the summer of 1898 he became deeply interested in the future development of the vast and potentially rich territory through which they ran. In riding from Butte to Salt Lake City at that time

[1] This merger, or consolidation, was effected by issuing $27,460,000 of new Union Pacific common stock and exchanging it for Short Line stock on the basis of share for share. As the Short Line owned a majority of the stock of the Railroad & Navigation Company the Union Pacific thus obtained control of both roads. Then, later in 1899, the Union Pacific increased its own preferred stock from $75,000,000 to $100,000,000 and its own common stock from $88,460,100 to $96,178,700 for the purpose of securing complete ownership of the two Oregon lines. The new shares of preferred were used in retiring the Oregon companies' bonds, and the new common shares were exchanged for all the stock of the Railroad & Navigation Company that the Short Line did not already possess. By virtue of these operations the Union Pacific became the owner of ninety-eight per cent of the Oregon Short Line and ninety-one per cent of the Oregon Railroad & Navigation Company. (*Commercial & Financial Chronicle*, July 22, September 2, and October 13, 1899.)

with the general manager of the Oregon Short Line, he asked the latter how much he thought the road would earn that year.

I told him [says Mr. Bancroft] that I believed it would earn $6,000,000. He thought that, in my enthusiasm, I had put the sum too high; but I replied that I thought not; that the road would not only earn $6,000,000 that year, but in ten years it would earn $12,000,000. He then wanted to know on what grounds I made that statement. Of course he was not familiar with the country at that time, while I was; but he was quick to grasp the possibilities of development in the territory that the road served. I explained to him that I thought Idaho, in a few years, would be the best State west of the Missouri River, if not west of the Mississippi. It had more water than any other Western State and more land to be put under cultivation. . . . There were ranges in abundance for sheep and cattle; undeveloped mines whose value had not yet been determined; undeveloped coal lands in the territory that the railroad served, and timber resources second to only one other Western State. As he became acquainted with the country, going over it from time to time, . . . he realized the possibilites of it as I fancy he had foreseen them in his first wonderful vision of the future; and he never cast aside any recommendaton made to him by me for the building of branch lines, purchase of new equipment, laying of new and heavier steel, purchase of terminals, ballasting, signaling, and making other improvements to the property.[1]

At the time when the Union Pacific acquired the

[1] "Impressions of E. H. Harriman," by W. H. Bancroft, general manager of the Oregon Short Line. (An unpublished manuscript.)

Oregon Short Line, the physical condition of the latter was no better than that of other parts of the old system. The rails were light; the track was unballasted; the grades over the mountain ranges were heavy; and the equipment, of all classes, was limited in capacity. This state of affairs, however, did not last long. The first appropriation for reconstruction work on the Oregon Short Line under the Harriman régime was $6,000,000, and thereafter, for a long term of years, large sums of money were spent, both on it and on the Oregon Railroad & Navigation Company's lines, in the relocation of tracks, reduction of grades, straightening of curves, and purchase of new and heavier equipment. Inasmuch as the reconstruction work on the main line from Omaha to Ogden has already been described, it is unnecessary, perhaps, to go fully into the details of leveling, straightening, and reëquipment on the two Oregon roads. Suffice it to say that as soon as they became a part of the new Union Pacific system, they were brought up, in every respect, to the new Union Pacific standard; and when Mr. John W. Gates, of Chicago, went over the whole road, a few years later, he said in a private letter: "I have traveled over nearly every railroad in the United States, and have just been over the Union Pacific by daylight. Its condition is the best I have ever found, East or West, and in my judgment it is the most magnificent railroad property in the world."

That the condition of its track was almost perfect is shown by the fact that when, on one occasion, Mr. Harriman found it necessary to go from San Francisco to New York quickly, he made the journey of 3255 miles, in his own special train, in less than three days (71 hours and 27 minutes). His average speed for the whole distance was 45.6 miles an hour, which included all stops for water, coal, and changing of engines, as well as unavoidable delays of every kind. Over the Union Pacific he made forty-eight miles an hour west of Cheyenne and fifty-five east of that point, with an occasional maximum of eighty-two miles an hour where the track was straight. This trip lowered the best previous record of speed across the continent by nearly eleven hours, ten of which were saved on the track of the Union Pacific.[1]

The financial results of this great work of reconstruction became apparent more quickly, perhaps, than even Mr. Harriman himself anticipated. The agricultural crops in the Western States in 1898, 1899, and 1900 were exceptionally good; there was a general revival of business, and the flow of population into the trans-Missouri region not only began again,

[1] The fastest time previously made from ocean to ocean was that of the famous Jarrett-Palmer theatrical train in 1878. This train also went over the Union Pacific, and its time was 82 hours, 24 minutes.

but increased so rapidly that between January 1, 1899, and June 30, 1900, the Union Pacific Company sold to new settlers an area of land almost equal to that of the States of Delaware and Rhode Island taken together. Increased Oriental trade and the acquisition of the Philippines also augmented the volume of transcontinental traffic and added largely to the profits of all the Pacific roads. The Union Pacific system, with its reduced grades, straightened curves, and heavy equipment, was able to handle, cheaply and expeditiously, all the business that offered, and its receipts from the transportation of both freight and passengers increased with great rapidity. In the fiscal year ending June 30, 1899, its earnings were more than $34,000,000 gross and $14,000,000 net; and six months later, the company not only had on hand an accumulated cash surplus of $11,385,793, but owned more than a thousand miles of improved track upon which there was no lien of any kind. In the fiscal year ending June 30, 1900, the road earned $39,000,000 gross and $20,000,000 net, and paid a first dividend of one and a half per cent on its common stock, as well as a semi-annual dividend of two per cent on its preferred. In October, 1900, it raised the rate on the common to four per cent per annum, and at the end of the year, after paying all dividends and putting vast sums of money back into the property, the company had a cash surplus of $4,843,961.[1]

These extraordinary financial results were due primarily to Mr. Harriman's faith in the future development and prosperity of the Great West, and to his boldness in spending tens of millions of dollars on a run-down and inefficient road, for the purpose of putting it in a condition to handle, economically and profitably, the immense volume of future traffic that he foresaw.[2] The brilliant success of this bold policy and the skill and energy shown in carrying it out have since been universally recognized. In a review of the work of reconstruction, "The Outlook," of New York, said:

[1] *Commercial & Financial Chronicle*, September 2 and December 30, 1899, February 10, August 4, and November 10, 1900.

[2] The sum spent on the Union Pacific system for betterments, new equipment, etc., in the five years from 1898 to 1902 was nearly $45,000,000, as follows:

1898	$505,368
1899	8,325,432
1900	11,560,711
1901	13,639,884
1902	10,925,686
Total	$44,957,081

In the same period — and mainly as a result of these expenditures — the density of traffic almost doubled, as shown in the following table:

Years	*Passengers carried one mile per mile of road*	*Tons of freight carried one mile per mile of road*
1898	42,854	476,000
1899	49,364	528,000
1900	59,000	626,000
1901	59,906	664,000
1902	70,126	751,000

Among all the stories in American railroading, and it has teemed with the marvelous, few chapters are so extraordinary as the building of the Union Pacific system by Edward H. Harriman. The boldness of the conception, the magnitude of the undertaking, and the constructive genius shown in the working-out of plans, are all unusual features, even in an era of undertakings that make for us, every day, new records in industrial history. . . . Mr. Harriman had faith in the mysterious, hopeless-looking, wonder-working Western empire that is wrapped in its unendng dream of sunshine beyond the Missouri River. He had the keenness of vision to map out within it a traffic confederation of unequaled strength; the determination to supply it with railways — the best of their class in the world — and the tremendous personality to persuade careful men to risk unheard-of sums of money to make good his plans.

Even Professor Ripley, who has not always been fair in his judgments of Mr. Harriman, says of the latter's work on the Union Pacific:

These early years [1898 to 1901] were devoted to an entire rebuilding of the road from end to end. Fortune favored the enterprise from the start. The unusual rainfall in the arid belt brought heavy crops and prosperity at a crucial time. For this all occurred, it should be noted, before the days of dry farming and extensive irrigation in the Far West. The annexation of the Philippine Islands also largely stimulated transcontinental and Oriental business. Gross earnings increased rapidly. Dividends began and substantial surpluses, over and above these, were turned back into the property for every form of improvement which would reduce costs of operation. . . . Double tracks were laid; solid embankments took the place of trestles, and curves were eliminated, wherever possible, all along the line. The result was a heavy decline in the operating ratio. This was sixty-two per cent in 1896. Within six years operating expenses were below fifty-three per cent of revenue from operation. Train-loads rapidly increased, so that the greatly expanding business was yielding more than proportionate net returns. Within three years, both gross and net revenues had more than doubled. By 1901, therefore, the company was in prime financial condition, with strong credit and unsurpassed banking connections.[1]

All this, it should be remembered, was the work of less than four years, and it is only a small part of what was accomplished in ten years. Throughout Mr. Harriman's connection with the Union Pacific, which lasted until his death, he never ceased to improve its physical condition. He strove to make it the best as well as the most useful railroad in the West, and when, after he became president in 1904, he had brought it almost to the point of perfection as a means of transportation, he turned his attention to beautifying it.

On one of his trips over the line says Superintendent Park he noticed the lack of vegetation in and around Rock Springs, Wyoming, which, its population considered, was the best revenue-producing station on the road. "Why don't you put in a park here?" he asked. "The station is of attractive design, and some grass and a little shrubbery would freshen things up wonderfully."

[1] *Railroads: Finance and Organization*, by W. Z. Ripley, Ropes Professor of Economics in Harvard University. (New York, 1915), p. 502.

A resident of Rock Springs interrupted my reply by saying: "Mr. Harriman, there is not a sprig of grass in Rock Springs; not because we don't want it, but because the percentage of alkali in the soil is an absolute bar to its growth."

Mr. Harriman looked at me and said: "Nothing is impossible."

Taking that for my cue, I hauled from Utah hundreds of cars of the best soil of that fertile State, distributed it around the depot, planted shrubbery and trees, and to-day one of the most attractive spots on the Union Pacific Railroad is the garden surrounding Rock Springs station. This was also a cue for further work of this character all along the line. At my own personal expense I had planted trees in many localities, and had made every effort to obtain parks without the expenditure of money, because previous managements had not been willing to "waste" money, as they termed it, in this way. Mr. Harriman was willing to spend money to make the road look attractive. The result was the beautiful park at Cheyenne, and the improvement of the landscape at all terminals, which, in a few years, transformed the Union Pacific from a road through a desert to one along which the bright green grass, trees, and flowers were in evidence at every station of importance. This movement soon spread — the section foremen began to plant trees and flowers — and now there is no other railroad so well kept, unless it be the Southern Pacific, along which Mr. Kruttschnitt had started a similar movement years before.[1]

One of Mr. Harriman's noteworthy personal char-

[1] "Recollections of E. H. Harriman in Connection with the Union Pacific," by W. L. Park, division superintendent at North Platte, Nebraska, and afterward general superintendent. (An unpublished manuscript.)

acteristics was his love of horses, and, curiously enough, it was his knowledge of the capacity of the horse for speed and endurance that enabled him to suggest a remedy for one of the evils with which, in the first decade of the twentieth century, all Western railroads had to contend, namely, train robberies.

The Wyoming division of the Union Pacific [says Superintendent Park] had long been a Mecca for outlaws. The mountainous region on each side of the road, within an average distance of a hundred miles, afforded opportunities for the "get-away" which is essential in the highwayman's profession. The trains were held up early in the evening, and before a posse could be organized the bandits were in the Hole-in-the-Wall-country to the north, or in Brown's Park, or the North Park country south, where the trail was invariably lost. Mr. Harriman, with his knowledge of the horse, suggested that we find horses that could go one hundred miles in a day and keep them in the service of our special agents, to be moved about from place to place on trains and in the country. This was done and cured the trouble. Thereafter the Union Pacific suffered no holdups, although the Northern Pacific, Great Northern, and Denver & Rio Grande were frequently victims. Our posse of train guards, which became quite celebrated, was composed of the best hunters and guides. One of them — Joe La Force — was made famous in Spearman's novel, "Whispering Smith." Sam Lawson, formerly guide and hunter for Lord and Lady Brassey, was always to be depended upon. Mr. Timothy Keliher had immediate charge of the guards and their equipment, and so maneuvered them that complete exemption was obtained from attacks. The expense was infinitesimal, compared with fruitless expenditures to capture the outlaws after robberies had occurred, to say nothing of the bad advertising such incidents gave to a railroad.

In discussing one of the holdups, which in the past had been all too numerous, Mr. Harriman asked me for a detailed description of the Wilcox train robbery. At considerable length I went over the occurrence, explaining the method adopted by the bandits; their pursuit; the killing of Sheriff Hazen of Converse County, who was in charge of one of the posses; the capture of Bob Lee at Colorado City, his trial, conviction, and sentence to the penitentiary; the killing of George Curry ("Flatnose George") near Green River, Utah, and of Lon Logan near Kansas City; and finally the capture, near Knoxville, Tennessee, of Harvey Logan, the leader of the outlaws (as merciless and bloodthirsty a villain as this country ever produced), and his escape, after conviction, from the Knoxville jail. In concluding the narrative, I stated incidentally that Harvey Logan was at that time reported to be in Wyoming, either preparing to commit another robbery, or wreak vengeance upon those who had so relentlessly pursued him and the members of his gang.

Mr. Harriman appeared to be intensely interested in the story, and after a few moments he turned to me, with one of his rare smiles, and said: "Mr. Park, there are just two men in these United States upon whom devolves the responsibility for the capture and reincarceration of Harvey Logan."

"Who are those two men, Mr. Harriman?" I asked.

Pointing his finger at me he said: "The General Superintendent of the Union Pacific Railroad, and" (indicating himself with the same finger) "the President of the Union Pacific Railroad."

Knowing full well the skill of Logan with a revolver,

and his delight in its use with a human being as its target, I replied: "The General Superintendent of the Union Pacific Railroad renigs."

Mr. Harriman laughed and said: "So does the President."[1]

Mr. Harriman, however, probably would not have "reniged" if he had been put to the test, because he was constitutionally fearless.

On one occasion [says Mr. Park] he described to me very graphically his killing of a large Yakutat bear in Alaska — an incident which, on account of his personal modesty, is not generally known. The story, if published, would illustrate a side of his character which, when occasion offered, was quite prominent — that of great personal courage. From my own observation and that of others I am convinced that he was wholly without fear. In time of war he would undoubtedly have been a splendid general. Like Napoleon and Grant, under the most trying circumstances he was at his best — cool, deliberate, and calculating — with an intensely patriotic inspiration which would have impelled him to make any sacrifice for his country.[2]

The history of the Union Pacific, in the first decade of the twentieth century, shows a progressive realization of Mr. Harriman's anticipations and a steady working-out of his far-reaching plans. No other man — with the possible exception of James J. Hill — had so clear a prevision of the development and prosperity that were coming to the Great West, and

[1] "Recollections of E. H. Harriman in Connection with the Union Pacific," by W. L. Park. (An unpublished manuscript.) [2] *Ibid.*

certainly no other railroad man made such preparations to foster that development, augment that prosperity, and provide for the increased traffic that would result therefrom. Between 1900 and 1910, the population of the trans-Missouri States increased about forty per cent, while the increase in the value of farm lands along the lines of the Union Pacific ranged from 100 to 353 per cent. In Idaho, which Mr. Bancroft predicted would be "the best State west of the Missouri River," the increase was more than threefold. This enhanced value of farm lands was partly due to better and more extensive cultivation, and partly to a greatly improved railroad service which enabled the farmers to send their crops, cheaply and promptly, to markets where there was an active demand for them. The annual value of these crops, in the States directly tributary to the Union Pacific, increased in the decade 1899–1909, by percentages that ranged from 89 to 235.[1]

[1]

	Value of crops 1899	1909	*Per cent of increase*
Kansas	$113,522,693	$214,859,597	89.3
Nebraska	92,469,326	196,125,632	112.
Oregon	21,806,687	49,040,725	124.9
Utah	8,242,985	18,484,615	124.2
Montana	10,692,515	29,714,563	177.9
Colorado	16,970,588	50,974,958	200.4
Washington	23,532,150	78,927,053	235.4
Idaho	9,267,261	34,357,851	270.7
Totals	$296,504,205	$672,484,994	
Total amount of increase		$375,980,789	

(*Thirteenth Census.*)

Agricultural crops, however, were not the only Western products that needed transportation. In the revival of business that followed the reconstruction of the Union Pacific, industrial activity increased rapidly in all the far Western States, and between 1900 and 1910 the annual value of manufactured products in Union Pacific territory rose from $257,000,000 to $530,000,000 in California; in Colorado from $89,000,000 to $130,000,000; in Idaho from $3,000,000 to $22,000,000; in Kansas from $154,000,000 to $325,000,000; in Nebraska from $13,000,000 to $199,000,000; in Utah from $18,000,000 to $62,000,000; and in Washington from $71,000,000 to $221,000,000. This group of States alone, in 1909, produced manufactured goods valued at $1,500,000,000, as well as farm crops to the value of $672,000,000 more.

It was the growth and development indicated by the above figures that Mr. Harriman anticipated when he began the reconstruction of the Union Pacific in the period of business depression that followed the panic of 1893. The expenditures made by him for railroad betterments from year to year show that he was never taken by surprise, and that the wonderful transportation system which he created was always equal to the demands made upon it by an ever-increasing volume of traffic. During the period of his administration the Union Pacific Company spent for additions, extensions, betterments, and new equipment more than $174,000,000, a large part of which came out of earnings.[1] The result of this liberal — not to say unprecedented — expenditure was a complete and radical transformation of the road. Not only were grades reduced and sharp curves eliminated, but 4029 miles of heavier rails were laid on 22,139,000 new cross-ties; 2319 miles of track were ballasted, and 137,000 lineal feet (twenty-six miles) of wooden bridges were taken away and replaced with solid earthen embankments or bridges of concrete and steel. Nearly $3,000,000 was spent, moreover, for automatic block signals, and in 1909, forty per cent of all the rail-

[1] Expenditures of the Union Pacific system (not including the Southern Pacific) for additions, betterments, and new equipment, during Mr. Harriman's administration:

Years	*Amounts*
1898	$ 505,368
1899	8,325,432
1900	11,560,711
1901	13,639,884
1902	10,894,291
1903	12,928,881
1904	11,488,467
1905	5,481,709
1906	29,175,761
1907	28,051,496
1908	23,261,746
1909	19,279,832
Total	$174,593,578

road mileage thus protected in the United States was included in the Harriman lines.

Upon a track thus improved it was safe and practicable to use much heavier equipment, and the sum spent for such equipment between 1899 and 1909 was $38,636,715. In 1898, the average weight of Union Pacific locomotives, on the drivers, was thirty-seven tons; in 1909 it was sixty-eight tons. In 1898, the total capacity of all the freight cars that the company owned was 414,858 tons. In 1909, it had grown to 984,923 tons, while the average train-load had increased from 277 tons to 548 tons. The volume of business done by means of this enlarged equipment and heavier train-loading may be measured by the traffic density — that is, by the number of tons hauled one mile per mile of road. In 1898, this tonnage was 476,009; in 1909, it was 1,054,427 (including all freight). The number of tons of all freight hauled one mile increased from 2,535,069,468 to 6,393,072,432. Only a small part of this increased volume of business was due to new branch lines and greater mileage; most of it was the direct result of greater efficiency — that is, greater carrying capacity over approximately the same length of track. Between 1898 and 1910, the average number of miles operated increased only eighteen per cent, while the volume of business done increased one hundred and seventy-six per cent. In 1898, the gross transportation revenues were only $32,631,000; in 1910, they had grown to $78,750,000.[1]

In 1905, the dividend on the common stock was raised to five per cent; a little later to six per cent, and in 1906 to ten per cent; while the market value of the stock increased in value from about $25 a share in 1898 to $195 a share in 1906.

It is evident from these figures that the reconstruction and subsequent management of the Union Pacific brought great wealth to Mr. Harriman, through his ownership of many thousand shares of its stock; but his reward was not out of proportion to the benefits that he conferred upon the Nation. Between 1898 and 1909, the service rendered by the Union Pacific to the public far more than doubled in

[1] The progressive increase in earnings due mainly to greater transportation efficiency is shown in the following table:

Years	*Miles of railway operated*	*Gross transportation revenue*	*Net surplus before dividends*
1898	5325	$32,631,769	$9,212,575
1899	5357	34,394,729	9,792,426
1900	5427	39,147,697	12,272,017
1901	5686	43,538,181	12,535,057
1902	5710	47,500,279	14,503,249
1903	5762	51,075,189	15,276,642
1904	5352	55,279,230	16,597,092
1905	5357	59,324,948	22,785,507
1906	5403	67,281,543	31,764,674
1907	5644	76,040,726	36,176,021
1908	5781	76,039,225	35,719,400
1909	6062	78,750,461	41,598,401

extent and importance. Freight transportation facilities increased in that period by one hundred and forty per cent and passenger travel facilities by nearly two hundred and fifty per cent. What this meant to the people of the trans-Missouri territory is shown by the increase in farm values in the States that the Union Pacific served. In the year 1900, the value of farm lands in Kansas, Nebraska, Oregon, Utah, Montana, Colorado, Washington, and Idaho was $2,342,000,000. In 1910, it was $6,580,000,000. Of course there could not have been anything like this increase of four billion dollars in agricultural wealth without the improved transportation service furnished by the transcontinental railroads, and largely by the Union Pacific. Such service, moreover, was rendered more and more cheaply from year to year. During the period of Mr. Harriman's administration freight rates on the Union Pacific decreased by from fifteen to seventeen per cent,[1] while the service rendered increased by one hundred and forty per cent. Freight rates in the Western territory finally became so low that for the cost of a two-cent postage stamp a farmer could have a ton of freight carried more than two miles; for the price of an ordinary lantern globe he could have it moved sixteen

[1] Testimony of Mr. Harriman before the Interstate Commerce Commission, p. 172.

miles; and for the cost of ten pounds of tenpenny nails he could send it forty-four miles. The transportation of a ton of freight for a distance of one hundred and thirty-eight miles cost him less than he had to pay for a good milk pail, and for the price of a No. 2 Ames shovel he could have a ton of freight carried one hundred and sixty-six miles.[1]

It is not surprising that with such rates, and almost unlimited railroad facilities, the States through which the Union Pacific ran doubled their crop output and trebled the value of their agricultural lands in a single decade. If, therefore, Mr. Harriman's achievement be regarded solely from the point of view of public benefit, there can be no question that by increasing cheapness and efficiency of transportation it built up American industry; enlarged the earnings of both labor and capital; and brought opportunities for greater comfort and happiness to millions of human beings.

Mr. Harriman found the Union Pacific insolvent, dismembered, decrepit, its sources of revenue curtailed, without important alliances, friendless. He left it financially powerful, its severed members restored, its roadbed and equipment renewed and of the highest type, dominating traffic conditions in a wide territory and with alliances and influence extending from the Atlantic to the farther shore of the Pacific, from the Gulf of

[1] *The Truth about the Railroads*, by Howard Elliott (New York, 1913), p. 158.

Mexico to the Great Lakes and even across the Canadian frontier. The property which had seemed to his predecessors to be fit for nothing more than to be a continuous object and means of political and financial intrigue, he transformed into a wealth-creating and disseminating machine of the highest efficiency. The transportation-buying public, those who travel and those who ship, has seen efficiency of the highest degree substituted for inefficiency of the lowest order; the Federal Government has collected millions which seemed hopelessly lost; and shareholders have received gratifying returns upon their investments. Rates have been lowered and wages raised, traffic has multiplied, and the region served has acquired prosperity without precedent. To Mr. Harriman, more than to any other single agency, is due the fact that, to an extent unknown before,

> "Through the veins
> Of that vast empire flows, in
> Strengthening tides,
> Trade, the calm health of nations!" [1]

Professor W. G. Sumner, one of the wisest and most far-sighted of American economists, said a few years ago: "The cheapening of transportation between the great centers of population and the great outlying masses of unoccupied land is the greatest fact of our time, and it is the greatest economic and

[1] "Harriman the Efficient," by H. T. Newcomb. *Railway World*, September 17, 1909. Mr. Newcomb was formerly statistician and expert of the Interstate Commerce Commission, and, with Professor Adams, acted in the same capacity for the Senate Committee on Interstate Commerce prior to the enactment of the Hepburn Law.

social revolution that has ever taken place." In this greatest of all social and economic revolutions, no single person played a more important and commanding part than E. H. Harriman.

CHAPTER VII

THE EXPEDITION TO ALASKA

IN the early spring of 1899, when the reconstruction of the Union Pacific was well under way, Mr. Harriman determined to get a little rest and recreation by making a summer cruise in a chartered steamer up the coast of Alaska to the island of Kadiak. His attention was directed to this particular part of the territory by D. G. Elliot, of the Field Columbian Museum in Chicago, who had interested him in the opportunities there offered for hunting the Kadiak bear, said to be the largest in the world. To a man who loved nature and out-of-door life as much as Mr. Harriman did, the prospect of cruising for a month or two through the wild, glacier-fringed straits and fiords of the mountainous Alaskan coast was in itself attractive, but it was made doubly so by the lure of adventurous sport in a picturesque, little known region, and the chance of getting a specimen of the great Kadiak bear. His original intention was to take with him only his own family and a few friends; but as comfort and safety required a large vessel, there was room for many more, and he therefore decided to include as his guests twenty-five or thirty scientists, artists, and photographers, who, "while adding to the interest and pleasure of the expedition, would gather useful information and distribute it for the benefit of others." In pursuance of this plan he went to Washington, in March, 1899, to confer with Dr. C. Hart Merriam, then Chief of the United States Biological Survey, with regard to the personnel of the scientific staff.

He came unannounced [says Dr. Merriam] and told me in an unassuming, matter-of-fact way that he was planning a trip along the Alaskan coast in a privately chartered steamer and desired to take along a party of scientific men. He asked my coöperation in arranging plans for the expedition and in selecting the scientific men and outfits necessary for the work. Never having heard of Mr. Harriman before, and knowing nothing of his resources, I made inquiries of a railroad official (for Mr. Harriman had incidentally remarked that he was a railroad man) and was informed that he was a man of means and a rising power in the railroad world. When therefore he called at my house later in the day, accompanied by Dr. Lewis Rutherford Morris, of New York, and told me more of his plans, I was less astonished to learn that he had already engaged the steamship George W. Elder and was having her refitted for the voyage. He remarked that he had secured a number of books and maps relating to Alaska and wished advice as to what others were needed, and added that while his plans were as yet in the formative stage, he thought there should be two men of recognized ability in each department of natural science — two zoölogists, two botanists, two geologists, and so on — and that each should have an assistant. When I raised the question of cost, remarking that few scientific men were financially able to meet the expenses incident to such a trip, he promptly put my mind at rest by replying that all the members of the expedition would be his guests.

After ascertaining his general views as to the kind of men desired for the scientific party, I suggested one of our most distinguished naturalists, Dr. William H. Dall, who had spent many years in Alaska, and the eminent geologist and physiographer, Dr. G. K. Gilbert. Mr. Harriman asked me to bring them to call at his rooms at the hotel. This I did, and the subject of the expedition was talked over at some length. In the course of the conversation we were impressed by Mr. Harriman's frankness and simplicity of manner, and by the directness and relevance of his questions. He was very much in earnest, and we realized that the expedition was bound to go, that it would afford opportunity for scientific research, and that to be a member of it would be the event of a lifetime. Before leaving Washington, Mr. Harriman invited both Dall and Gilbert to go and both accepted. Thus early was the nucleus of the scientific party established and the high character of the expedition assured.[1]

The technical staff, as finally made up, consisted of two photographers, three artists, and twenty-five men of science representing three museums of natural history, four departments or bureaus of the National Government in Washington, and six of our largest and most important universities. No more distinguished body of American scientists was ever gathered together for an expedition of this kind.

[1] "Recollections and Impressions of E. H. Harriman," by Dr. C. Hart Merriam, then Chief of the U.S. Biological Survey. (An unpublished manuscript.)

Most of its members had a national reputation, and among them were men as well known, even to the general public, as R. Swain Gifford, the New York artist; John Burroughs, author and ornithologist; John Muir, mountain-climber and expert student of glaciers; and George Bird Grinnell, author of many books on American Indians and big-game hunting, and also editor, at that time, of "Forest and Stream." Among the most eminent of the naturalists were Professor Brewer, of Yale; Dr. Dall, G. K. Gilbert, and Henry Gannett, of the U.S. Geological Survey; Dr. Merriam and Dr. Fisher, of the U.S. Biological Survey; Daniel G. Elliot, zoölogist, of the Field Columbian Museum, Chicago; Robert Ridgway, ornithologist, of the National Museum in Washington; and Professor Fernow, Dean of the School of Forestry in Cornell University. Mr. Harriman's own party numbered thirteen and consisted of Mrs. Harriman and five children; Mr. and Mrs. W. H. Averell, of Rochester, New York, and their daughter, Miss Elizabeth Averell; Miss Dorothea Draper; Dr. Lewis Rutherford Morris, of New York City; and Dr. E. L. Trudeau, Jr., of Saranac Lake. The members of the expedition from the East left New York for the Pacific Coast by special train on the 23d of May, 1899, and those from the West joined the main party at Portland or Seattle.

Mr. Harriman lost no time in organizing his scientific staff and making plans for its work.

On board the special train which carried us from New York to Seattle [says Dr. Merriam], we were given an insight into Mr. Harriman's methodical ways, and an opportunity of learning something of his power of organization and skill in dividing labor and fixing responsibility. The day after leaving New York, he called a meeting of the scientific men, said a few words about the purposes of the expedition, and announced his desire to place the specialists in control of their work, and to leave the details of the route and itinerary to those most familiar with the region and the opportunties it was likely to afford. This was followed by the suggestion that work would be facilitated and time saved by the creation of an executive committee. Before we reached Chicago such a committee was appointed, and the next day special committees on zoölogy, botany, geology, mining, and big game were added. The wisdom of this course was demonstrated over and over again by the efficiency of the organization — an organization which perfected its plans in advance and took advantage of every opportunity for work, thus accomplishing results out of all proportion to the time spent in the field.

Even the railroad journey was full of interest and profit. To take a party across the continent by special train, and thence to Alaska and Siberia by privately chartered steamer, would seem to be enough; but Mr. Harriman was not content with this; he wanted us to enjoy everything on the way. So at Omaha a special trolley took us to the Omaha Exposition; at Shoshone, Idaho, a small caravan of teams and saddle-horses (sent from Utah on telegraphic orders) carried us twenty-five miles to the lava cañon of Snake River to see the great Shoshone Falls; at Nampa the train was run up a branch to Boise, where we were shown the mint and given a plunge in the great natatorium; at Pendleton, Oregon, we were taken on a much longer detour, crossing Snake River at Riparia, traversing the famous Palouse wheat country to Colfax, and thence, by a Northern Pacific special, winding down a side cañon to Lewiston. At Lewiston we were met by a steamer which took us down the long cañon of Snake River and landed us at the bridge near the junction of the Snake with the Columbia, at which point our train was waiting to carry us through the picturesque gorge of the Columbia to Portland, where, before setting out for Seattle, a special trolley took us to the Heights.[1]

When the party arrived in Seattle, the steamship George W. Elder, which had been refitted under the supervision of President A. L. Mohler, of the Oregon Railroad & Navigation Company, was in waiting. She had a crew of sixty-five officers and men, with Peter Doran as captain, and Mr. Harriman had engaged an additional force of eleven hunters, packers, and campers to assist the landing parties. The steamer's equipment for the Northern voyage included a steam launch, two naphtha launches, extra boats, a number of folding canvas canoes, tents, sleeping-bags, camp outfits, and everything that could possibly be needed by the hunters and scientific explorers of the party.

The expedition sailed from Seattle on the 31st of

[1] Dr. Merriam's manuscript, previously cited.

ON THE CONTINENTAL DIVIDE

May, and after stopping a few hours in Victoria, proceeded northward through the channel that separates Vancouver Island from the mainland, and entered the vast labyrinth of islands, straits, passages, and mountain-enclosed fiords which extends northward along the Alaskan coast.

Before us [says John Burroughs in his narrative of the voyage] was a cruise of several thousand miles, one thousand of which was through probably the finest scenery of the kind in the world that can be seen from the deck of a ship — the scenery of fiords and mountain-locked bays and arms of the sea. Day after day a panorama unrolled before us with features that might have been gathered from the Highlands of the Hudson, from the Thousand Islands, the Saguenay, or the Rangeley Lakes in Maine, with the addition of towering snow-capped peaks thrown in for a background. The edge of this part of the continent, for a thousand miles, has been broken into fragments, great and small, as by the stroke of some earth-cracking hammer, and into the openings and channels thus formed the sea flows freely, often at a depth of from one to two thousand feet. It was along these inland ocean highways, through tortuous narrows, up smooth, placid inlets, across broad island-studded gulfs and bays, with now and then the mighty throb of the Pacific felt for an hour or two through some open door in the wall of islands, that our course lay.[1]

As the steamer proceeded northward, short stops were made at such points of interest as Lowe Inlet, the mission station of New Metlakatla, Wrangell

[1] *The Harriman Alaska Expedition*, edited by Dr. C. Hart Merriam (Doubleday, Page & Co., New York, 1901), vol. I, pp. 19–20.

and Juneau, and at Skagway the officials of the newly constructed White Pass & Yukon Railroad took the party by special train to the summit of White Pass, nearly three thousand feet above the sea, where the flags of the United States and Great Britain floated side by side over the provisional boundary between British Columbia and Alaska.

When the expedition entered Northern waters spring was already far advanced, and at all the places along the coast where the ornithologists landed they found birds in abundance. Even at the summit of the White Pass, amid snow and ice, the rosy finch, titlark, and golden-crown sparrow were singing merrily, while at lower altitudes the dwarf hermit thrush, russet-backed thrush, summer warbler, Lincoln's finch, and Townsend's sparrow were not only singing, but building their nests. Few members of the party expected to see in Northern latitudes, and in the wild environment of mountains, glaciers, and gloomy spruce forests, the diminutive hummingbird of the temperate zone; and yet, as soon as the salmon-berry begins to blossom, this mite of a bird —hardly bigger than a large moth—flies thousands of miles up the coast from southern California or Mexico, and may be found as far north as Wrangell and Juneau.

On both sides of the North American continent,

from Vancouver to Mount St. Elias and from Nova Scotia to northern Labrador, birds appear earlier in the season than flowers, but the flowers soon overtake them. In the first ten days of June, the botanists of the expedition found only violets, strawberry and salmon-berry blossoms, and the delicate white or pink bells of mountain heather; but ten days later acres of meadow-land were covered with the blue spikes of lupine, and before the first of July the whole Alaskan coast was abloom with wild geranium, columbine, Jacob's-ladder, iris, cypripedium, shooting star, rhododendron, bluebells, primroses, and forget-me-nots.

Up to the time when the members of the Alaskan expedition assembled in New York to take the train for the Pacific Coast, few of the scientific men had ever seen Mr. Harriman and many of them had never even heard his name. It is interesting, therefore, to note the impression that he made upon them when, in the close intimacy of steamer life, they had an opportunity to make his acquaintance.

I soon saw [says John Muir] that he was uncommon. He was taking a trip for rest, and at the same time managing his exploring guests as if we were a grateful, soothing, essential part of his rest cure, though scientific explorers are not easily managed, and in large mixed lots are rather inflammable and explosive, especially when compressed on a ship. Nevertheless he kept us all in smooth working order; put us ashore wherever we liked, in all sorts of places — bays, coves, the mouths of streams, etc. — to suit the convenience of the different parties into which we naturally separated, dropping each with suitable provisions, taking us aboard again at given times, looking after everything to the minutest details; work enough to bring nervous prostration to ordinary mortals instead of rest. All the Harriman family were aboard, together with Mr. and Mrs. Averell and their daughter Betty. Mrs. Harriman ably seconded her husband in making everything move harmoniously. The boys were very young, Roland only about two or three years of age. One of the telling sights that comes to mind as I write is Mr. Harriman keeping trot-step with little Roland while helping him to drag a toy canoe along the deck with a cotton string. The girls were so bright and eager to study the wonderful regions passed through that we were all proud to become their teachers.

We soon learned that Mr. Harriman was not only a wonderful manager of men, but that he was fearless. Nothing in his way could daunt him or abate one jot the vigor of his progress toward his aims, no matter what — going ashore through heavy breakers, sailing uncharted fiords, pursuing bears, etc. . . . Before I came to know him I thought, like many others, that money-making might be one of the springs of his action. One evening when the expedition was at Kadiak the scientists, assembled on the forecastle awaiting the dinner-bell, began to talk of the blessed ministry of wealth, especially in Mr. Harriman's case, now that some of it was being devoted to science. When these wealth laudations were sounding loudest, I teasingly interrupted them, saying: "I don't think Mr. Harriman is very rich. He has not as much money as I have. I have all I want and Mr. Harriman has not." This saying somehow reached

Mr. Harriman's ear, and after dinner, seating himself beside me, he said: "I never cared for money except as power for work. I was always lucky and my friends and neighbors, observing my luck, brought their money to me to invest, and in this way I have come to handle large sums. What I most enjoy is the power of creation, getting into partnership with Nature in doing good, helping to feed man and beast, and making everybody and everything a little better and happier." And this has proved true. He earned the means and inherited the courage to do and dare as his great head and heart directed.[1]

The first important objective of the Harriman expedition was the famous Muir Glacier, which is situated at the head of Glacier Bay, about one hundred and twenty-five miles north of Sitka. This great river of ice, which has a surface area of three hundred and fifty square miles or more, descends from the vast snow-fields on the high mountains west of Skagway, and abuts on the sea in a long icy palisade which rises in places to heights of from two hundred to two hundred and fifty feet. The Elder steamed into the bay on the 8th of June and anchored at 5 P.M. about two miles off the glacier front in the midst of floating bergs of all sizes and shapes. Hardly was the anchor down when the members of the party were startled by a loud explosive roar which sounded like muffled thunder. "It was," says

[1] *Edward Henry Harriman*, by John Muir (Doubleday, Page & Co., New York, 1911), pp. 35–36. (Privately printed.)

Burroughs, "the downpour of an enormous mass of ice from the glacier's front, making it, for the moment, as active as Niagara. Other and still other downpours followed, at intervals of a few minutes, with deep explosive sounds and the rising of great clouds of spray. We quickly realized that here was a new kind of Niagara, a cataract the like of which we had not before seen — a mighty congealed river that discharged into the bay intermittently in ice avalanches. The mass of ice below the water-line is vastly greater than that above, and when the upper portions fall away, enormous bergs are liberated and rise up from the bottom. They rise slowly and majestically, like huge monsters of the deep, lifting themselves to a height of fifty or a hundred feet with the water pouring off them in sheets, and then subsiding and floating away with a huge wave in front. Nothing that we had read or heard had prepared us for the color of the ice, especially of the newly exposed parts and of the bergs that rose up from beneath the water — its deep, almost indigo blue. Huge bergs were floating about that suggested masses of blue vitriol. The roar that followed the discharge of ice from the glacier constantly suggested the blasting in mines or in railroad cuts. The spray often rose nearly to the top of the glacier. Night and day, summer and winter, this intermittent and explosive discharge of ice into the inlet goes on, and has gone on for centuries. When we awoke in the night we heard its muffled thunder, sometimes so loud as to jar the windows in our staterooms, and the swells caused by the falling and rising masses rocked the ship" at a distance of two miles.[1] The quantity of ice pushed into the sea every day exceeds 200,000,000 cubic feet, and the Muir is only one of nine glaciers which discharge bergs into Glacier Bay.

In this scenically attractive and scientifically interesting environment the members of the expedition spent five or six days studying the glaciers, climbing the mountains, sketching, painting, photographing, dredging, and making large collections of animals and birds. John Muir, who had visited this part of the coast several times before, had many suggestions to offer with regard to interesting excursions and trips, and "when," says Dr. Merriam

> he excited the enthusiasm of the hunters by a fairy tale about the abundance of wolves in a little snowy valley ("Howling Valley," he called it), eighteen miles back from the front of Muir Glacier, Mr. Harriman promptly decided to go there, notwithstanding the long and fatiguing tramp over the ice and snow and the necessity of spending a night on the glacier. Nor was he deterred when Muir himself declined to go, making the clever excuse that he was no hunter. The party consisted of Mr.

[1] John Burroughs, in *The Harriman Alaska Expedition*, vol. 1, pp. 36–37.

Harriman and Doctor Morris, Grinnell, Trudeau, and myself. The grip proved much more severe than was expected. After tramping sixteen miles over the glacier, the more distant parts of which were covered with snow into which we sank at first to our ankles and later to our knees, we finally reached a point from which we could look into the valley and were disappointed to find it completely buried in snow. For some miles the increasing depth of the snow had led us to fear that this would be the case, but Mr. Harriman was unwilling to turn back until we had actually seen the goal. Both going and coming he, like the rest of us, carried a pack weighing about twenty pounds, and he was always either in the lead or near the front.[1]

This trip over glacier ice to Muir's "Howling Valley" furnished ample proof not only of Mr. Harriman's enterprise as a hunter, but of his indomitable spirit and great physical endurance. Few men, fifty-one years of age, would have undertaken a tramp of thirty-six miles over a snow-covered glacier, and still fewer would have been able, in competition with younger men, to keep "always in the lead, or near the front." Mr. Harriman was just from an office desk and was not in training for severe and long-continued physical effort; and yet, with a twenty-pound pack on his back, he waded knee-deep in snow at or near the head of his party, and refused to turn back until he had at least looked into the snow-

[1] "Recollections and Impressions of E. H. Harriman," by Dr. C. Hart Merriam. (An unpublished manuscript.)

buried "Howling Valley" and satisfied himself that it was not the habitat of howling wolves. John Burroughs afterward suggested that perhaps all the "howling" was done by Muir's imagination! In the course of the march the members of the party were sometimes roped together, to guard against the danger of falling into crevasses, and in the forty-eight hours of almost continuous tramping they had only a few hours' rest when, about midnight, they lay down in their sleeping-bags on the ice.

On the 13th of June, the expedition turned southward to Sitka, spent there "four humid days" and then proceeded northward again to Yakutat Bay and Prince William Sound. In this part of the voyage the members of the party saw and enjoyed the most beautiful scenery on the whole Alaskan coast.

In our northward journey [says Muir] dark clouds hid the mountains until we reached Yakutat. Then the heavens opened and St. Elias, gloriously arrayed, bade us welcome, while the heaving, plunging bergs roared and thundered. Here we spent immortal days, studying, gazing, sailing the blue waters, climbing the hills, glaciers, and warm flowery islands, and considering the abounding life. Everybody was naturally enthusiastic, busy, and happy to the heart. The scenery at the head of Disenchantment Bay [an extension of Yakutat] is gloriously wild and sublime — majestic mountains and glaciers, barren moraines, bloom-covered islands amid icy, swirling waters, enlivened by screaming gulls, hair seals, and roaring bergs. On the other hand, the beauty of the southern extension of the bay is tranquil and restful and perfectly enchanting. Its shores, especially on the eastern side, are flowery and finely sculptured, and the mountains, of moderate height, are charmingly combined and reflected in the quiet waters. . . . For an hour or two after we left Yakutat, we enjoyed glorious views of Malaspina's crystal prairie[1] and of St. Elias and his noble compeers; then down came clouds and fog, leaving only a dim little circle about us. But just as we entered the famous Prince William Sound, which I had so long hoped to see, the sky cleared, disclosing to the westward one of the richest, most glorious mountain landscapes I ever beheld — peak after peak dipping deep in the sky, a thousand of them, icy and shining, rising higher and higher, beyond and yet beyond one another, burning bright in the afternoon light, purple cloud bars above them, purple shadows in the hollows, and great breadths of sun-spangled, ice-dotted waters in front.

The nightless days circled away while we gazed and studied, sailing among the islands, exploring the long fiords, climbing moraines and glaciers, and hills clad in blooming heather — grandeur and beauty in a thousand forms awaiting us at every turn in this bright and spacious wonderland. But that first broad, far-reaching view in celestial light was the best of all.[2]

One of the most important geographical achieve-

[1] The Malaspina Glacier, which falls into the sea just north of Yakutat Bay, is the most extensive body of ice on the Alaskan coast. It is twenty miles long and sixty or seventy miles wide and is fed by the snow-fields of the Mount St. Elias Range. Its surface area is fifteen hundred square miles or more — almost equal to that of the State of Delaware — and the quantity of roily, sediment-charged water which runs out from under it is so great that the ocean, for a distance of thirty miles from the coast, is tinged a milky white.

[2] John Muir, in *The Harriman Alaska Expedition*, vol. I, pp. 130–32.

ments of the expedition in this "wonderland" of Prince William Sound was the finding and exploration of the Harriman Fiord, a deep but hidden arm or bay which opens off the channel known as Port Wells and which terminates, thirteen miles farther west, in the splendid Harriman Glacier. The discovery of this deep concealed fiord, which was not shown on the United States Coast Survey chart and which had never before been navigated by any vessel, was almost accidental.

On the evening of June 26th [says Dr. Merriam], as we were steaming out of Port Wells, we saw at the head of a short arm on the starboard side a very large glacier which appeared to extend entirely across the head of the fiord. It was a truly splendid glacier, presenting a high sea wall at least two miles in length, and pushed out into the water much farther than any we had previously seen. Mr. Harriman at once changed the course of the vessel and turned into the fiord. Approaching nearer, the most distant point of land on the left, which up to this time had appeared to abut against the ice, was seen to be separated from it, revealing open water beyond. Going still closer to examine the ice caves and pinnacles of the glacier front, we were amazed to discover that the open water continued, stretching away for miles and showing two fine glaciers in the distance. Every one was filled with eager excitement and anxious to continue the exploration. Mr. Harriman asked the captain to turn the ship into the new fiord, but neither he nor the pilot was willing to assume the responsibility of navigating the unknown water in the night. So Mr. Harriman himself took the wheel and pushed the ship on to the very head of the fiord, a distance of about thirteen miles. A number of new glaciers were discovered, four of which had massive fronts shedding icebergs into the sea. Others came down nearly to the water, while others hung on the towering faces of the bordering cliffs. We were completely surrounded by rugged snowy mountains, presenting an impressive and desolate spectacle of rock, ice, and snow. Then a snowstorm set in, shutting out the mountains while we were still in the new fiord, which later was named in honor of its discoverer. On our way back, as we turned the point in front of the huge glacier, the incoming tide caught the ship and swung her with great force toward the ice-wall. The rudder was put hard-a-port, but it was some time before the ship responded and for a few moments it looked as if we were going to be crushed against the ice.[1]

The fearlessness and decision of character shown by Mr. Harriman in thus taking full charge of the ship and steering her through thirteen miles of uncharted and unknown water, when the captain and the pilot declined to take the responsibility for such risky navigation, were thoroughly characteristic of the man. There seemed to be nothing that he was afraid to do, and nothing that he did not know how to do.

We were constantly surprised [says Dr. Merriam] by his physical strength and his fondness and aptitude for out-of-door pursuits. He was an expert swimmer and diver and an enduring walker and mountaineer. When on the sea he joined heartily in the daily sports on deck,

[1] "Recollections and Impressions of E. H. Harriman," by Dr. C. Hart Merriam. (An unpublished manuscript.)

HEAD OF HARRIMAN FIORD, PRINCE WILLIAM SOUND, ALASKA

and when on shore took part in the most difficult and fatiguing expeditions. Throughout the voyage he was alert, enthusiastic, and venturesome, and often took risks which many of us thought a man in his position should avoid. If a thing were worth seeing, he wanted to see it. If a difficult or dangerous trip were to be taken, by launch or on foot, he was almost certain to be in the lead. His versatility was a source of wonderment to us all. During the trip across the continent we had found out that he was not only a great railroad director and financier, but was also personally familiar with the multitude of details of railroad construction and operation. And when we came to the ocean voyage, we were still more surprised to learn that he was a trained sailor and a skillful and daring navigator of steam craft. Running the launch was one of his favorite diversions, and when so engaged he nearly always took the wheel. The greater the danger the surer he was to take this post, and we were not long in learning that we were safest when in his hands.

When exploring Yakutat Bay, two parties were landed on the north shore to hunt and collect animals and plants, and while there were blockaded by drift ice. I was a member of one of these parties. After three days the ship attempted to reach us, but was prevented by the ice. Our hopes rose as we saw the dark smoke in the distance, but as it moved about and then disappeared we knew the open water was a long way off. On the fourth day we rejoiced to again see the steamer's smoke. It was in another place, farther down the bay. It came nearer, to the edge of the drift, and stopped as before. For a long time we watched and waited, but could see nothing. Finally some one called out, and looking westerly close to the land we were thrilled by the sight of two small boats. Slowly and laboriously they came, picking their way among the loose ice in the narrow space between shore and the line of grounded bergs which kept the heavy drift from pressing in. It was a dangerous undertaking, and when they were near enough to enable us to distinguish persons, we were not surprised to see Mr. Harriman standing in the bow of the first boat, directing her course. We and our camp outfits were taken aboard, and on the return trip to the ship took the more direct but still more hazardous route through the pack-ice, which in the ocean swell constantly threatened to smash our frail craft.

This was neither the first nor the last time that Mr. Harriman took a perilous boat journey to gather in absent members of the expedition. Earlier in the season, when a party consisting of Gilbert, Muir, and Palache, who had gone in a small boat to explore the remoter glaciers in the main arm of Glacier Bay, failed to appear at the appointed place, he became anxious for their safety, took the ship up the bay as far as the drift ice permitted and sent out two launches in search. One of these he placed in my charge; the other he himself operated. We went in different directions through the floating ice, and when at six in the evening I heard four whistles from the steamer I knew that he had found them.

Some weeks later, several members of the expedition, including George Bird Grinnell, Charles Keeler, and myself, went ashore on the spit at the entrance of Port Clarence to visit the Eskimo who had come there to trade with the whaling vessels then at anchor near by. At the same time Mr. Harriman, with Dr. Morris and one or two others, took one of the launches and went on a visiting tour among the whalers, while our ship crossed the bay to take water at the mouth of a small stream on the south shore. At about half-past six in the afternoon, Mr. Harriman came for us with the launch and started to take us back to the steamer. The distance proved greater than we had supposed — fourteen miles — and the wind blew so hard that a strong sea was running. Fortunately we were going with the wind. When we had reached a point about midway between the spit and the south shore, we could see only the rigging of the whalers and only the masts and smokestack of the Elder. A little later the fireman of the launch announced that the supply of gasoline was so low that it was doubtful if we could reach the ship. Meanwhile the wind had increased to a gale, driving the water in such big waves that to lose headway meant the capsizing of the launch and, doubtless, the loss of all on board. But luck was in our favor. The gasoline held out and Mr. Harriman was at the wheel. On coming alongside, the sea was so high that we would have been dashed to pieces against the vessel had we attempted to run in close. By means of pike-poles we were kept from striking, and with the aid of a rope-ladder and the outstretched hands of the sailors most of us scrambled aboard. Mr. Harriman, however, learning that a party was ashore on the neighboring tundra, took on a new supply of gasoline, and, instead of trusting the task to another, made two trips from the ship to the shore and brought all the members back in safety. These trips were attended with no little danger, the taking on of the party and the turning of the launch in the gale requiring great skill in navigation to avoid disaster. It was nine in the evening when he returned with the last boat-load and we had supper.[1]

On the 28th of June, the Elder sailed from Prince William Sound and after a short stop in Cook Inlet proceeded to the island of Kadiak, where the party proposed to spend four or five days and where Mr.

[1] "Recollections and Impressions of E. H. Harriman," by Dr. C. Hart Merriam. (An unpublished manuscript.)

Harriman hoped to get a specimen of the largest of all known bears.

Between Prince William Sound and Kadiak there was a sudden and remarkable change in climate and scenery. The weather, under the influence of the Japan current — the Gulf Stream of the Pacific — grew noticeably warmer; the wild fiords, glaciers, spruce forests, and high, snowy mountains of the mainland disappeared, and in place of them were rounded hills tinged faintly blue with acres of wild geraniums; verdant glades threaded by cascading trout brooks, and scenery that was sometimes so beautiful and parklike as to suggest the work of an expert landscape gardener.

> We had come [says John Burroughs] from an arboreal wilderness to a grassy wilderness; from a world of spruce forests to a world of emerald heights and verdant slopes. Never had I seen such beauty of greenness, because never before had I seen it from such a vantage-ground of blue sea. To eyes sated with the wild, austere grandeur of Prince William Sound, the change was most delightful.

On the 2d of July, the Elder made fast to the wharf at the village of Kadiak, and in bright sunshine and a temperature of nearly 70°, with birds singing and flowers blooming everywhere, the members of the expedition "swarmed out of the ship like boys out of school" and began climbing the "mighty emerald billow" that rose from the rear of the village.

From the ship [says Burroughs] it looked as smooth as a meadow; but the climber soon found himself knee-deep in ferns, grasses, and a score of flowering plants, and now and then pushing through a patch of alders as high as his head. He could not go far before his hands would be full of flowers, blue predominating. The wild geranium here is light blue and it tinges the slopes as daisies and buttercups do at home. Near the summit were patches of a most exquisite forget-me-not of a pure, delicate blue with a yellow center. It grew to a height of a foot, and a handful of it looked like something just caught out of the sky above. Here, too, was a small delicate lady's-slipper, pale yellow striped with maroon, and a dwarf rhododendron, its large purple flowers sitting upon the moss and lichen. The climber also waded through patches of lupine and put his feet upon bluebells, Jacob's-ladder, iris, saxifrage, cassiope, and many other flowers.

From the village of Kadiak, Mr. Harriman, with a native Russian guide, set out on a bear-hunting expedition in the interior of the island, and after tramping two days among high, treeless mountains ten or fifteen miles back from the coast, finally shot, on a grassy hillside above a small lake, one of the great Kadiak bears and a half-grown cub. It was the only bear secured by the expedition on the Alaskan coast and was the first animal of this particular species that had ever been measured and photographed. When, therefore, Mr. Harriman, with the members of his party, celebrated on shipboard a day or two later the national holiday of July 4th, he received the hearty congratulations of his scientific associates upon having attained as a hunter one of the objects of his ambition, and upon having made at the same time an important addition to the collections of the expeditions.

But it was not only Mr. Harriman who had reason to be pleased and satisfied with this remote grassy island in the waters of the North Pacific.

> Kadiak [says John Burroughs] won a place in the hearts of all of us. Our spirits probably touched the highest point here. If we had other days that were epic, these days were lyric. To me they were certainly more exquisite and thrilling than any before or after. I feel as if I wanted to go back to Kadiak — almost as if I could return there to live — so secluded, so remote, so peaceful; such a mingling of the domestic, the pastoral, the sylvan, with the wild and the rugged; such emerald heights, such flowery vales, such blue arms and recesses of the sea, and such a vast green solitude stretching away to the west, to the north, and to the south. . . . Our stay of five days in this charming spot was a dream of rural beauty and repose; warm summer skies above us, green flower-strewn hills and slopes around us, our paths were indeed in green pastures and beside still waters.[1]

The Elder sailed from Kadiak on the 5th of July, and two days later, at daybreak, when the scientists

1 John Burroughs, in *The Harriman Alaska Expedition*, vol. 1, pp. 82, 86.

awoke, the first sounds they heard through their open windows were the musical bird voices of thrushes, song sparrows, finches, and warblers from a green slope on one of the Shumagin Islands, off which the ship was anchored. "It is a novel experience," says Burroughs, "to wake up in the morning on an ocean steamer and hear bird songs through your open window. But this was often our experience on the trip."

After landing a scientific party on Popof Island, to be picked up later, the Elder steamed westward along the Alaska peninsula; entered the Akutan Passage; touched at Dutch Harbor on the island of Unalaska; and finally, on the 8th of July, plunged into the foggy solitudes of Bering Sea. On the following afternoon the ship anchored off the island of St. Paul, one of the Pribilof group, where the scientists of the party went ashore to observe the fur seals which assemble there in thousands every summer.

"According to our original programme," says John Burroughs, "our outward journey should have ended at the Seal Islands; but Mrs. Harriman expressed a wish to see Siberia and, if all went well, the midnight sun. 'Very well,' replied Mr. Harriman, 'we will go to Siberia'; and toward that barren shore our prow was turned."

But the voyage came near ending in a fatal disaster long before Siberia was reached. At eight o'clock that same evening, in a dense fog off the island of St. Paul, the Elder struck heavily on a sunken ledge.

We were at supper [says Dr. Merriam], and the ship was going at full speed when her bottom suddenly struck the reef. A few seconds later she struck again and, rising a little, struck the third time with a fearful bumping, rasping crash. We all fully believed that the bottom was smashed and that the vessel would sink. Mr. Harriman was perfectly cool. He immediately rose, told the party to remain inside, and went at once on deck where he assisted Captain Doran in the management of the ship. Some one suggested that he be taken off in one of the boats. After an indignant reply, he turned to me with the remark: "Can you conceive of such a suggestion! What would a man want to live for if his family were drowned?"

The accident, however, was not so serious as it threatened to be. The engines were quickly reversed, a sail was hoisted, and in a few moments the steamer's prow swung to the right, and the danger was passed. The stern of the ship, which was two feet lower in the water than the bow, had raked across the rocks, but no serious damage was done.

"Some of us," says Burroughs, "hoped this incident would cause Mr. Harriman to turn back. Bering Sea is a treacherous sea; it is very shallow; it has many islands, and in summer it is nearly always draped in fog. But our host was a man not easy to turn back; in five minutes he was romping with his children again as if nothing had happened."

The Elder reached the Siberian coast safely on the 11th of July and anchored in Plover Bay, a harbor about a hundred miles southwest of Bering Strait, where there was a small encampment of Eskimos. All the members of the party went ashore and spent two or three hours in walking about on the continent of Asia, buying curios from the natives, taking photographs of the scenery, and picking handfuls of primroses, Iceland poppies, and forget-me-nots. Then, as there was not much else to see or do, they returned in the early evening to the ship and sailed across Bering Strait to Port Clarence, on the Alaskan coast, where a dozen American whaling vessels were waiting for a chance to get through the pack-ice that blocked the Strait.

Port Clarence, sixty miles from the Arctic Circle, was the northernmost point that the expedition reached, and after taking water there, the Elder sailed for home. The return voyage down the coast was uneventful; but as many stops were made — at St. Matthew's Island, Dutch Harbor, the Shumagin Islands, Kadiak, Yakutat Bay, Juneau, and other places — it was not until the 30th of July that the steamer finally arrived in Seattle. She had been gone from there just two months, and in that time had made a voyage, out and back, of about nine thousand miles.

The scientific results of the expedition were in every way satisfactory. A number of glaciers not previously known, as well as many others that had been vaguely or imperfectly known, were mapped and described, and much evidence was gathered of changes that had occurred in their length and size. The photographs taken by members of the party numbered about five thousand and constituted incomparably the best series of pictures ever taken of the Alaskan coast. The natural history collections made were very large and included thirteen genera and six hundred species that were wholly new to science. More than fifty specialists were engaged to work up this mass of new material, and twenty-two special papers, based on collections made by the expedition, were published in the "Proceedings" of the Washington Academy of Sciences. Under the auspices of the same Academy were also published, in thirteen large illustrated volumes, the narrative of the expedition by John Burroughs, and eleven special monographs by various members of the scientific party, including Muir, Grinnell, Dall, Keeler, Fernow, Gannett, Brewer, Merriam, and Washburn.[1]

[1] *The Harriman Alaska Expedition*, edited by Dr. C. Hart Merriam; 2 volumes with 369 illustrations and maps. (Doubleday, Page & Co., New York 1902.)

No single expedition to the Alaskan coast has ever made more important and valuable contributions to the world's knowledge of that region.

In the same year in which Mr. Harriman made the trip to Alaska, he formed a syndicate for the reorganization of the Chicago & Alton Railroad Company; but inasmuch as this transaction afterward became the subject of an exhaustive investigation by the Interstate Commerce Commission, and was widely misrepresented and generally condemned, both by the Commission and by the public, it seems best to defer consideration of it until the work and the criticisms can be presented together in a later chapter.[1]

[1] See vol. II, chapters XXVII. XXVIII.

CHAPTER VIII

THE KANSAS CITY SOUTHERN EPISODE

IN the early part of 1899, when Harriman's energetic work in the reconstruction of the Union Pacific had begun to attract attention, and when he was generally recognized as a rising man in the railway world, his help and coöperation were solicited by a group of men in the West who were interested in a railroad known as the Kansas City, Pittsburgh & Gulf, which had fallen into financial difficulties as the result of hasty original construction and subsequent bad management, and which was greatly in need both of assistance and of competent advice. The history of this road, prior to Mr. Harriman's connection with it, was this:

In the year 1889, a group of Western capitalists and promoters obtained a charter for a railroad to run from Kansas City to Fort Smith, Arkansas, by way of the small Missouri town known as Nevada. It was incorporated under the name of the Kansas City, Nevada & Fort Scott Railway; but, for reasons that it is not necessary here to specify, little work was ever done on it, and two or three years later its charter was acquired by another group of Western promoters and speculators headed by Arthur E. Stillwell, of Kansas City. Mr. Stillwell, who had been engaged for some years in the life insurance business in Chicago, moved to Kansas City in the early eighties, became a prominent and successful real estate operator there, organized the Missouri, Kansas & Texas Trust Company, and eventually acquired both influence and capital. He was not a railroad builder, either by training or by experience; but he seems to have been a man of pleasing and persuasive personality, and he was generally successful in raising money for the various enterprises in which he became interested. He first entered the railroad field in 1886, when he projected and built around Kansas City a circular railway known as the "Belt Line," which was intended to link together the scattered stations of a number of different roads which had there their terminals.[1]

Encouraged by the success of this enterprise, he conceived the idea of building a through trunk-line from Kansas City to the Gulf of Mexico by way of Pittsburgh (a growing town in the Kansas coal region), Joplin, Texarkana, and Shreveport. Kansas City, at that time, had become one of the most important grain and provision markets in the United

[1] This railway was subsequently reincorporated and is now called the Kansas City Terminal.

States, and there seemed every reason to believe that if a north-and-south line were built from there to tide-water, it might secure a large part of the export traffic of the Missouri River region, which was then going either eastward to Atlantic ports, or southward to the Gulf of Mexico by way of the Illinois Central.

In the early nineties, Mr. Stillwell and a small group of Western speculators and promoters bought the charter of the old Kansas City, Nevada & Fort Smith Railway, changed its name to the Kansas City, Pittsburgh & Gulf, and organized a number of construction companies to begin work on the proposed line. Owing, however, to the panic of 1893 and the long period of business depression that followed it, the promoters had difficulty in getting capital enough to push the enterprise rapidly, and it was not until the fall of 1898 that the road was nominally completed and put in operation as a whole. It then extended from Kansas City on the Missouri River to Port Arthur on the Gulf of Mexico and had a total length of about 778 miles.

If this road had been built by practical railroad men and solely with a view to traffic possibilities and economy of operation, it might perhaps have been successful; but Mr. Stillwell and his associates seem to have aimed primarily at making it a means of land speculation rather than a carrier of merchandise. They ran it, therefore, not directly into the towns that it was intended to serve, but through their outskirts, or at a considerable distance from them, with the expectation, apparently, that the towns would grow toward it, and that large profits might be made through the organization of land companies and the purchase and sale of real estate. In a number of places, moreover, the road was badly located with reference to the topography of the country; it contained a good many unnecessary curves and grades, and it was built, generally, without due regard to economy and efficiency of operation. Embankments and cuttings were only just wide enough to hold the track and permit the passage of cars; gullies and ravines that should have been crossed on substantial earthen fills were spanned by trestles or light wooden bridges; freight and passenger stations were little more than shacks thrown up hastily at the least possible expense, and shop facilities, water supply, crossings, and sidings were all more or less inadequate for a railroad that purported to be a trunk-line from one of the most important cities in the West to tide-water.

It is not surprising, perhaps, that a road so planned and built should fail to be remunerative. The separate sections of it, as they were completed and put in operation, were never profitable, and even after it had been ostensibly finished, it did not earn money enough to pay its operating expenses and meet its obligations. Early in 1899, when through trains had been running only a few months, the company became so involved in financial difficulties that it was threatened with bankruptcy, and a committee of shareholders was formed in New York for the purpose of saving it if possible by means of a reorganization. But the attempt was made too late. In April, 1899, the road went into the hands of receivers and another reorganization committee was formed in Philadelphia.

The managers of the property, as the crisis in their affairs developed, were anxious, of course, to get the support of some strong railway interest in the neighborhood, and as their line connected at Kansas City with the Union Pacific, they naturally turned for help to Mr. Harriman. In April or May, 1899, after receivers had been appointed, he was asked to become a member of the New York reorganization committee, and as he happened to own some of the company's stock he consented to do so.

Throughout the summer and fall of 1899 the two committees, one in New York and the other in Philadelphia, struggled with the problems of the company and tried, often with great differences of opinion, to straighten out its tangled affairs and put it on a sound and stable financial basis. The Philadelphia committee succeeded at last in securing the support of a majority of the security-holders, and in November, 1899, it formulated a plan of reorganization which was eventually adopted. In March, 1900, a new company, called the Kansas City Southern, was incorporated under the laws of the State of Missouri, and to it, under foreclosure proceedings, was turned over all the property of the old Kansas City, Pittsburgh & Gulf.

Meanwhile, in the summer or early fall of 1899, Mr. Stillwell and his associates, without consulting or notifying Mr. Harriman, sold all their interest in the property to a group of Western steel manufacturers headed by John W. Gates, of Chicago.[1] Mr. Harriman regarded this sale, in the circumstances of the case, as a virtual breach of trust. Stillwell and his friends had asked him to help them, and then, without his knowledge or consent, had dis-

[1] Mr. Gates and his associates had never before been actively engaged in railroading, but they were all largely interested in the American Steel & Wire Company of Illinois, and that corporation had taken a large amount of the bonds of the Kansas City, Pittsburgh & Gulf in payment for steel rails. It is quite possible, therefore, that they bought control of the road not as a speculative venture, but rather as a means of protecting their own interests as creditors and bondholders. Five of them — Gates, Lambert, Edenborn, Ellwood, and Pam — were among the incorporators of the Kansas City Southern, and four of them became directors and members of the executive committee.

posed of their interest in the road and left him in the lurch.

In an address on "Edward Henry Harriman," delivered before the Finance Forum in New York in 1915, Mr. Otto H. Kahn, referring evidently to this episode, said:

The incident which I am about to relate occurred in 1898 or 1899, at a time when Mr. Harriman was but at the threshold of his successes, and had not yet acquired the commanding prestige which came to him in later years, and which, when once attached to a man's name and personality, naturally adds very greatly to his influence over other people. At the time I speak of, he had been invited to take an interest in a certain property, and though not greatly caring for the proposition, had accepted. A few months afterwards, the people who had sought Mr. Harriman's coöperation suddenly sold out their holdings in the property to a group of men who thereupon proceeded to assume the control now rightfully theirs, and to substitute themselves and their appointees in place of Mr. Harriman and his colleagues. Having myself a somewhat indirect interest in the situation, I had occasion to discuss it with him, and referred to the cessation of his short-lived connection with the property, which I took as a matter of course. To my surprise he interrupted me, calling out: "Hold on. Not so fast! I am not through this thing yet, by any means. I can't be played fast and loose with like this. I did not care particularly to go into it, as you know; but, having been urged to do so and having done so, I am in it to stay."

I replied, "Of course you have a just grievance against the men who have quit. Having asked you, of their own initiative, to coöperate with them, it was a mean and improper act on their part to sell out without first conferring and consulting with you. But it's done, the newcomers are in rightful control, it's no use making a fuss, and it seems to me that the best, and indeed the only thing for you to do is to look pleasant and get out. As a matter of fact, why should you care? That property is of very little interest to you."

He reiterated his view and his determination not to give in. I said, "Well, what are you going to do about it? They have the right to turn you out without ceremony if you do not give way gracefully." He answered, "I don't know yet. I'll just stand pat and not budge, and watch."

After a while the newcomers found out that while all the others concerned accepted the situation, Mr. Harriman would not quit without a fight; and, though they were clearly in a position to win, as far as their immediate object was concerned, they hesitated to attack so determined an opponent. Things went on in this way for several months, Mr. Harriman retaining an attitude of quiet but uncompromising defiance. . . . One morning he called me on the telephone to ask that I accompany him to a conference at the enemy's headquarters. I went, somewhat in the capacity of a second at a duel. He gave me no indication what the proceedings were to be. The conference lasted three hours. Most of the talking was done by the other side. Mr. Harriman did not threaten, or cajole, or make promises. He simply brought to bear upon these men the stupendous force of his will and personality. When the conference broke up, not only was there no longer any question of his retiring, but the newcomers had agreed to turn over to him their votes and proxies and let him run the property.

Evidently, Mr. Gates and his associates, when

they were brought into direct personal contact with Mr. Harriman, concluded that the road would be more likely to become prosperous under his management than under theirs, and they therefore proposed not only to elect him as a director, but to make him chairman of the executive committee. In view of the fact that he was a comparatively small and uninfluential stockholder, his success in thus winning the confidence and support of his opponents must be regarded as a triumph of personal character and ability.

This particular incident [added Mr. Kahn] especially impressed itself upon my mind in all its details because it was the first time I had seen Mr. Harriman in action. I witnessed many similar cases in the further course of his career, during which it was my privilege to be closely associated with him. Over and over again did I see him bending men and events to his determination by the exercise of the truly wonderful powers of his brain and will.[1]

The property of the old Kansas City, Pittsburgh & Gulf Company was turned over to its successor, the Kansas City Southern, on the 1st of April, 1900. In cases of bankruptcy and reorganization, it was customary at that time to vest the control of the property, temporarily, in a specially appointed board of managers known as a "voting trust."

[1] *Edward Henry Harriman*, by Otto H. Kahn (New York, 1911), pp. 3-7.

"The essence of a voting trust," as described by a well-known authority on railroad reorganization, "is the deposit of stock in the hands of trustees (most frequently five in number). These trustees issue certificates in return. All dividends on the stock are paid to the holders of certificates, but all the voting power is exercised by the trustees as long as the trust endures." The object of the trust is to "avoid the dangers of fluctuating and speculative control at critical periods in a railroad's history. . . . It is of supreme importance that a reorganized company be well started on its way by men who have an interest in making the reorganizing plan permanently successful, and that conservative direction be assured until danger of bankruptcy be past."[1]

Aiming primarily at these objects, and following the example of the reorganizers of the Erie, Northern Pacific, Reading, Baltimore & Ohio, and many other railroad companies, the stockholders of the Kansas City Southern assigned all their powers, for a period of five years from April 1, 1900, to a very strong voting trust, representing about equally the friends of Mr. Harriman and the associates of Mr. Gates in the American Steel & Wire Company. Its members were E. H. Harriman, of the Union Pacific;

[1] *Railroad Reorganization*, by Stuart Daggett (Cambridge, 1908), p. 382.

Otto H. Kahn, of Kuhn, Loeb & Co., New York; James Stillman, of the National City Bank, New York; Louis Fitzgerald, president of the Mercantile Trust Company, New York; George J. Gould, president of the Missouri Pacific; John W. Gates, of the American Steel & Wire Company, and Herman Sielcken, who represented a large body of security-holders in Holland.

On the 5th of May, 1900, an executive committee composed of Harriman, Kahn, and five representatives of the Gates interests was chosen to manage the property under direction of the trustees, and about a week later it organized by electing Harriman as chairman. In July, 1900, Samuel W. Fordyce, formerly president and later one of the receivers of the Kansas City, Pittsburgh & Gulf, tendered his resignation, and upon recommendation of the executive committee Stuart R. Knott, of Savannah, Georgia, vice-president of the Plant System, was elected in his place.[1]

The task set before the trustees, the executive committee, and the new president of the Kansas City Southern was one of great if not insuperable difficulty. They had to deal not with a substantially built and properly equipped road, but with one that

[1] Mr. Knott was a trained and experienced railroad man, who, prior to his connection with the Plant System, had been for ten years or more first vice-president of the Louisville & Nashville.

had been flimsily put together in sections by half a dozen different construction companies; that had never been completely finished or adequately supplied with rolling stock; and that stood in need of capital betterments before it could even be operated with safety. In a report made to Mr. Harriman after the condition of the property had been ascertained, President Knott described it as follows:

The railway properties acquired by the Kansas City Southern Railway Company were constructed in sections during the years from 1888 to 1897. Contracts were entered into with construction companies for building the road and furnishing equipment. The greater part of the road was built by such construction companies, while other portions, consisting of logging or lumber roads built for local purposes, were purchased by the construction companies to form a part of the through line. These properties were generally hurriedly built, due regard not being paid to permanent results or efficiency of operation, and in that condition were turned over to the railway company, although the contracts with the construction companies called for a first-class, single-track, standard-gauge railroad. As a result, at the time when the properties were taken over by the present owners, the embankments were to a large extent found not to be of the proper width; the cuts were too narrow, and requisite ditching and draining were lacking. In numerous cases, long wooden trestles had been constructed where a small culvert and a permanent earthen embankment should have been placed, and many of these trestles were unsafe and required to be either rebuilt or filled. The narrow banks were also dangerous; weak or temporary bridges, unsafe for operation, had to be replaced with structures of a character to permit the movement of business; yards, sidings, and passing tracks were required; freight and passenger stations were inadequate or lacking at some of the most important points, and new section houses, new water stations, additional shop machinery and tools had to be provided.[1]

If Mr. Harriman and President Knott had had funds enough and time enough, they might perhaps have put into satisfactory condition even a half-finished, patched-up line composed largely of "logging and lumber roads built hurriedly for temporary purposes"; but, in the first place, they had very little money outside of the earnings of the road itself, and, in the second place, the period of their control lasted only until April 1, 1905. It was hardly possible, in five years, to save out of earnings a sum great enough to pay for the virtual reconstruction of 778 miles of road.

Under the plan of reorganization the new company was supposed to begin operations with an available working capital of about $3,000,000; but, as a matter of fact, the unsold treasury bonds which were expected to yield that sum hardly sufficed to meet the outstanding obligations of the old company. The trustees, upon assuming control of the property, had not only to provide for the liquidation of car-

[1] Report of President Knott to E. H. Harriman, chairman of the executive committee, February 23, 1905.

trust certificates, receivers' certificates, and other prior liens of the Kansas City, Pittsburgh & Gulf to the amount of $3,250,000, but also to complete and pay for various betterments authorized or undertaken by the receivers, including three modern steel bridges, over the Elk, Red, and Houston Rivers. After meeting these liabilities, the trustees had no available funds other than those derived from the current earnings of the road. These, however, they devoted wholly to reconstructive work.

In the last year's operation of the Kansas City, Pittsburgh & Gulf there was a deficit of $317,000; but between that time and December 31, 1904, the new managers of the property increased its gross earnings from $3,593,505 to $6,450,319 and its net earnings from $915,005 to $1,901,140. This was equivalent to a gain of $2746 per mile in gross and $1259 in net.[1]

Between April 1, 1900, when Mr. Harriman and his associates assumed the management of the road, and April 1, 1905, when they retired, they expended on capital account $9,692,967, of which amount $5,459,269 went for betterments, additions, and new equipment.[2]

On the 1st of April, 1905, when the term of the voting trust expired, the management of the road

[1] Report of President Knott to E. H. Harriman, chairman of the executive committee, February 23, 1905.

[2] Report of the board of directors to the stockholders, May 11, 1905.

reverted to the shareholders, and, as the result of changes in the ownership of the stock, the control of the property passed to other hands. In 1900, Mr. Gates and his associates owned or controlled a majority of the shares; but five years later the security-holders in Holland and certain capitalists in New York were found to hold the balance of power, and Gates and Harriman were displaced. They made no contest for supremacy, and at the annual meeting of stockholders on the 17th of May, 1905, the party then predominant elected, without opposition, a new board of directors, headed by Herman Sielcken, the American representative of the Dutch interests. The new administration made a sweeping change of officers by electing J. A. Edson as president, H. R. Duval as vice-president, and William Coughlin, formerly of the Denver & Rio Grande, as general manager.[1] Mr. Harriman then retired and soon afterward disposed of his interest in the property.

The new managers, in the first report that they made after coming into power, drew a dark picture of the physical condition of the road when it was turned over to them, and ascribed its imperfections to neglect of maintenance; but in making this charge

[1] Mr. Edson had been general manager of the Kansas City, Pittsburgh & Gulf and its successor the Kansas City Southern from January 25, 1899, to January 1, 1903. Mr. Sielcken had been a director of the Kansas City Southern and also a member of the voting trust.

they were hardly fair to their predecessors. If the latter, in April, 1900, had come into possession of a properly built and adequately equipped road, and had then allowed it to fall into decay, they might justly have been chargeable with neglect; but such was by no means the case. The line, when they became responsible for it, was — as President Knott said — "in an unfinished and disorganized state"; and although they had not been able to perfect it, they at least turned it over to Sielcken and his associates in far better condition than that in which they received it from the original builders. A road cannot increase its gross earnings by 56 per cent and its net earnings by 154 per cent, as the Kansas City Southern did under Mr. Harriman's management, without making some improvement in its physical condition. Certainly, its managers cannot fairly be accused of neglecting maintenance if they declare no dividends, "plough in" all their earnings, and spend more than a million dollars a year for physical betterments. Doubtless, the Kansas City Southern, even in 1905, stood in need of further improvement; but the need arose not from neglect of maintenance, but from faulty original construction, which Mr. Harriman and his associates had not had means enough or time enough fully to remedy.[1]

[1] As careful a writer as Edward S. Mead cites the Kansas City

There is some reason to believe that Mr. Harriman desired to have a line from Kansas City to the Gulf of Mexico as an additional outlet for the traffic of the Union Pacific, and that he would have retained control of the Kansas City Southern in 1905, if he could. One of his associates, who afterward held an important position on the road says:

"What he [Mr. Harriman] apparently wanted, as a matter of strategic development, was a connection in the neighborhood of Kansas City, which was and is the second primary grain market in the United States. The easy way of accomplishing this was by securing and improving the Kansas City Southern. I am confirmed in this impression by my knowledge of the fact that when the control passed to other

Southern as an extreme illustration of the evils of neglected maintenance; but he seems to have paid too much attention to the company's fifth annual report and not enough to President Knott's description of the condition of the road when he first became connected with it. (*Corporate Finance*, by Edward S. Mead, New York, 1914, p. 219.)

Professor Ripley, too, takes a fling at Mr. Harriman by saying that "when in 1905 the voting trust on the Kansas City Southern, set up in 1900, expired by limitation, the stockholders, coming into possession of their property, discovered that it was almost completely gutted." Inasmuch, however, as the same authority, in another place, declares that "the Kansas City, Pittsburgh & Gulf in 1900 [after the reorganization] was physically rebuilt and also structurally solidified throughout," one assertion may be set off against the other. The average reader, perhaps, will find it difficult to understand how a road can be "almost completely gutted," and, at the same time, be "physically rebuilt and structurally solidified throughout." (*Railroads: Finance and Organization*, by William Z. Ripley, New York, 1915, pp. 214 and 405.)

hands, he caused a very exhaustive survey and location to be made of a line between Kansas City and Galveston. Subsequently, just before his last trip to Europe, an opportunity was presented of securing control of the Kansas City Southern and he was giving it serious consideration. If he had lived, he would doubtless have taken over the property. No one had a clearer idea of the strategic values of railroad properties than Mr. Harriman, or more courage in seizing and developing advantageous positions."

CHAPTER IX

ACQUIREMENT AND RECONSTRUCTION OF THE SOUTHERN PACIFIC

AS the great work of rebuilding the Union Pacific progressed, Harriman saw that, in order to create a trunk-line from the Missouri River to the Pacific that would be capable of handling efficiently and economically the increasing volume of transcontinental traffic, it would be necessary greatly to improve, if not to rebuild entirely, the Central Pacific, which was the link that united the Ogden terminus with San Francisco. By straightening curves, lowering grades, and using heavier rolling stock, he might double the capacity of his own line between Ogden and Omaha; but if he could not bring up to the same high level of efficiency the line that gave him his western connection, it would be difficult, if not impossible, to increase much the carrying capacity of the transcontinental system as a whole. A chain is no stronger than its weakest link, and the weakest link in the Omaha–San Francisco line was that from Ogden to Sacramento. It was full of short curves, especially in the Sierra Nevadas and in the hilly region west of Ogden and east of Reno. Between the latter points there were many stretches of track where, without prohibitive expense, it was possible not only to eliminate sharp curvature, but to reduce short gradients — in some places running up to ninety feet to the mile — which limited the hauling capacity of locomotives over long distances. The rolling stock of the company, too, as compared with that which Mr. Harriman was introducing on the Union Pacific, was light and of limited capacity. Unless this part of the line could be improved, the betterments that were being made east of the Great Salt Lake would lose much of their value, because the Central Pacific could not accommodate half the transcontinental traffic that the Union Pacific was prepared to handle with ease. Unfortunately, Mr. Harriman had no control over the Central Pacific, and the men who did control it were unable to carry out the plans that they had made for the reconstruction of the line, because, at that time, they were facing the problem of financing the debt owed by the Central Pacific to the Government, amounting with interest to about $59,000,000. Mr. Harriman tried more than once to buy this road, with a view to doing with it what he was already doing with the Union Pacific; but the Southern Pacific, which owned it, would not sell.

On the 13th of August, 1900, Collis P. Huntington,

who had been practically the creator of the Southern Pacific,[1] and who held four hundred thousand shares of its stock, died after a brief illness in the Adirondacks. This sudden removal of the greatest railroad-builder in the Southwest gave Harriman an opportunity to acquire the long-desired link connecting his western terminus at Ogden with San Francisco. In order, however, to get it, he would have to secure control of the whole Southern Pacific system, by which it was owned; and this, at first sight, seemed to be impracticable. The capital stock of the Southern Pacific Company at that time consisted of nearly two million shares, which had a market value of almost $100,000,000. In order to secure complete control of it, the Union Pacific would have to make a cash investment of more than $50,000,000, and this, for a company that had only recently emerged from bankruptcy and that had on hand a cash surplus of less than $4,000,000, seemed an almost impossible task.

Mr. Harriman, however, was never daunted by prospective difficulties. The Union Pacific Company under his management had increased its earnings and greatly improved its credit, and while its cash assets were small, its resources, in the shape of

[1] In association with Leland Stanford, Charles Crocker, and Mark Hopkins.

unencumbered property, were very great. Relying upon his ability to raise money by selling bonds on the security of these unmortgaged assets, Mr. Harriman, almost immediately after the death of Huntington, began to lay plans for the acquirement of the whole Southern Pacific system.

In commenting shortly afterward upon his purpose in so doing, the United States Industrial Commission of 1901 said:

> In order to attain a single important end it often becomes necessary to acquire an entire system of railroads, although only a small portion of that system can add directly to the efficiency of the controlling road. Thus, the entire Burlington system is absorbed by the northern transcontinental lines for no other reason than that they may obtain a direct entrance into Chicago. The Union Pacific purchased control of the Southern Pacific System, not because it needed the additional mileage, but rather that it might indirectly acquire the Central Pacific and a direct outlet to the Pacific Coast.[1]

This comment is interesting and important for the reason that six years later the Interstate Commerce Commission cited the acquirement of the whole Southern Pacific System, not as evidence of a desire to get an outlet on the Pacific Coast, but as a proof of Mr. Harriman's alleged purpose to eliminate com-

[1] *Reports* of the U.S. Industrial Commission, vol. 19, pp. 309–10 and 313; House Documents, vol. 82; see also *Railroads: Finance and Organization*, by W. Z. Ripley, p. 217.

petition and establish a monopoly.[1] The different views of the same transaction taken by two different federal commissions seem to show that the second had a prejudice against Mr. Harriman, while the first was unbiased.

Early in 1901, Harriman recommended to the board of directors of the Union Pacific Company that the stockholders authorize an issue of $100,000,000 in convertible bonds, for the purpose of "making provision for the contemplated acquisition of the securities of other companies," and for the extension, protection, and consolidated operation of the Union Pacific lines. These bonds were to be secured by a first mortgage on 1135 miles of improved road, and by a collateral lien on certain securities of the Oregon Short Line and the Oregon Railroad and Navigation Company, which were held as free assets in the Union Pacific treasury and which had a par value of about $66,000,000.[2] The rate of interest on the proposed bonds was "not to exceed four per cent," but

[1] On "Consolidation and Combination of Carriers," *Reports* of Interstate Commerce Commission, vol. 12, p. 284.

[2] These securities consisted of:

Bonds of Oregon Short Line	$21,881,000
Stock of Oregon Short Line	27,337,650
Stock of Oregon Railroad & Navigation Company	17,505,306
Total	$66,723,956

The Union Pacific had acquired the stock of the two Oregon companies by exchanging its own stock for them.

in order to make them attractive to investors they were made convertible, at any time within five years, into the common stock of the Union Pacific Company at par.

On the 5th of February, 1901, the board of directors of the Union Pacific Company adopted a resolution authorizing the issue of these bonds and giving to Mr. Harriman, as chairman of the executive committee, discretionary power to use the money to be derived from them "as in his judgment may be practicable and desirable." This was only one of many cases in which the board showed its perfect confidence in Mr. Harriman by giving him almost unlimited discretionary power. The Interstate Commerce Commission, therefore, was perhaps justified in saying afterward that he was practically "the dominating spirit of the corporation." In all its great transactions "he acted upon his own initiative, and the policies and purposes of the company were his." [1] The advantages of this unified control under the direction of a single master mind were shown in the subsequent history and almost unexampled prosperity of the road.

When, early in May, the four per cent convertible bonds were put upon the market, they were eagerly

[1] *Report* of Interstate Commerce Commission on "Consolidation and Combination of Carriers" (1907), p. 278.

taken by the investing public. The security upon which they were based was not, perhaps, wholly adequate, but the conversion privilege gave them a speculative value which more than made up for the lack of absolute security. The increasing prosperity of the Great West, the growing volume of transcontinental traffic, and the almost complete reconstruction of the Union Pacific under Mr. Harriman's management, all indicated that, in the not-distant future, the common stock of the company would go above par. The purchasers of bonds, therefore, felt reasonably sure that for every thousand dollars invested they would eventually be able to get much more than that value in the stock for which they could exchange their holdings. Their anticipations were fully realized. Before 1906, when the conversion privilege expired, every holder of a thousand-dollar bond might have converted it into ten shares of Union Pacific stock, salable in the open market at $1565.

The Union Pacific Company began buying Southern Pacific shares soon after Mr. Huntington's death; but it was not until the following year that it went into the market for all that could be had. To secure control, however, without acquiring the four hundred thousand shares held by the Huntington estate was practically impossible, inasmuch as these shares comprised more than twenty per cent of all the stock outstanding and constituted the largest single block in existence. But it was not easy to buy the Huntington holdings, for the reason that they were desired also by many other persons, corporations, or interests. The powerful bankers, Speyer & Co., who were the fiscal agents of the Southern Pacific and who had close relations with the Huntington estate, were opposed to the sale of this stock to the Union Pacific Company, as were also many individuals in or out of the Southern Pacific who had railroad plans and ambitions of their own. Mr. Harriman, however, was a skillful and persistent negotiator, and in the end he outbid or won over all of his competitors. Early in February, 1901, Mr. Edwin Hawley, who had been closely associated with Mr. Huntington for more than twenty years, signed an agreement to transfer to the Union Pacific, on behalf of himself and the Huntington estate, 475,000 shares of Southern Pacific stock having a par value of $47,500,000. Meanwhile, Kuhn, Loeb & Co., the bankers of the Union Pacific, had bought in the open market, or at private sale, 275,000 shares more, so that on the 31st of March, 1901, the Union Pacific was virtually in possession of 750,000 shares, or thirty-eight per cent, of the outstanding capital stock of the Southern Pacific Company. This stock cost the Union Pacific a little more than $55.82 per share and therefore represented an investment of nearly $42,000,000. Although it did not constitute a majority of the shares outstanding, it was sufficient to prevent any other interest from getting control, and possession of it gave the Union Pacific Company time enough to strengthen its hold by acquiring more. This it soon afterward did by purchasing 150,000 shares of the common and 180,000 shares of the preferred, which brought its aggregate holdings up to 1,080,000 shares or 45.49 per cent of all the stock outstanding. This, for all practical purposes, united the two companies and brought them under the same management, because no opposing combination of stockholders that could probably be formed would be strong enough to outvote a corporation that owned 1,080,000 out of 2,374,000 shares.

The Southern Pacific, when Mr. Harriman and his associates thus acquired control of it, was the greatest transportation system in the world. It operated a continuous main line extending from Portland, Oregon, to New Orleans, Louisiana, by way of San Francisco, Los Angeles, Yuma, and El Paso; its equally important main line (the old Central Pacific) ran eastward across the Sierra Nevadas to the junction with the Union Pacific at Ogden; while it connected with an extension into Mexico some hundreds of miles from the Arizona border, owned by the same interests that owned the Southern Pacific. The company had also bought, leased, or absorbed more than a dozen other railroads of less importance, so that in 1901 it owned or controlled nearly nine thousand miles of continuous track in eight different States or Territories. In view of the fact that the region directly tributary to this great system comprised nearly one third of the total area of the United States, Mr. Harriman was perhaps justified in saying, when the wisdom of the purchase was afterward questioned, "We have bought not only a railroad, but an empire." The company, moreover, which furnished transportation to this "empire," had two or three steamship lines of its own, which connected its land lines on the east with Havana and New York, and on the west with Yokohama, Shanghai, and the principal ports of the Orient.

The traffic of the Southern Pacific, at that time, was large and diversified. As a transcontinental system it carried from ocean to ocean a great amount of through freight, while, at the same time, it gathered up along its own lines quantities of merchandise, locally produced, which it turned over to other roads for distribution. In 1901, for example, it moved 2,825,000 tons of forest products; 1,263,000 tons of grain; 560,000 tons of cotton; nearly 1,000,000 tons of fruit and vegetables; 3,000,000 tons of manufactured articles; and 6,000,000 tons of miscellaneous products, all of which originated in, or was carried to, the region traversed by its lines. No other railroad in the West had a better balanced traffic, or was better able to make money out of local business alone. Its principal connection, the Union Pacific, was essentially a through trunk-line and had to get its profits mainly from transcontinental traffic; but the Southern Pacific, while getting its due share of through freight, transacted also a large and profitable local business, originating in the territory directly tributary to its many lines and branches. Its gross earnings, in the year when the Union Pacific acquired control of it, were $77,729,000; but its operating expenses were large, it had a funded debt of nearly $350,000,000, and it had never paid a dividend.

Although the physical condition of the road compared favorably with that of other Western lines, it fell far short of the standard established by Mr. Harriman in the reconstruction of the Union Pacific. Six thousand miles of the system had rails weighing only sixty pounds to the yard; less than eight hundred miles had rails that exceeded seventy-five pounds to the yard, and on the main lines alone there were more than two hundred miles of timber trestles and bridges, many of which would have to be replaced with more substantial and durable structures.

The part of the system whose reconstruction presented most serious engineering difficulties was that between Ogden and Reno, where grades of forty-five to ninety feet to the mile were common, and where the curves were so sharp and so frequent that in a distance of three hundred and seventy-three miles the road made more than thirty-six complete circles. It was this part of the system, in particular, that Mr. Harriman was most desirous of improving, because upon it depended largely the prosperity of his own line. The Central Pacific must be made capable of carrying from San Francisco to Ogden as much freight as the reconstructed Union Pacific could carry from Ogden to Omaha. To this part of the line, therefore, Mr. Harriman gave particular and immediate attention. He had been over it several times, and had a good general idea of its defects and needs; but in order to plan the reconstruction of it with all the knowledge that could be obtained, he summoned to New York for a conference Mr. Julius Kruttschnitt, general manager of the system, who was a railroad engineer by education and training, who had been connected with the road, as manager or assistant manager, for sixteen years, and who presumably was better acquainted with its physical condition than was any other official. Mr. Kruttschnitt, who then knew Mr. Harriman only slightly, gave afterward the following account of the conference:

We tried to discuss our business at the office, but Mr. Harriman was too frequently interrupted by callers. He asked me to his house that night to dine. After dinner he called for blue-prints, maps, and statistics covering the contemplated reconstruction work in Nevada and Utah. He asked innumerable questions with great rapidity, always touching the crucial points. Frequently he would not wait for me to finish a sentence, but would dash off on another question. He wanted to know the advantages of one method over another; the economies to be effected, the increase in capacity to be derived, etc., etc., etc. The swiftness with which he covered the plans was astonishing. We finished the discussion in less than two hours, and thereupon he told me to be at the board room next morning when there was to be a meeting of the executive committee.

The plans called for an expenditure of $18,000,000 and I supposed that there would be no end of arguing and talking, which would result in the approval of only a part of the work. However, Mr. Harriman, in a few words, clearly explained to the committee the general scheme, what it would cost and the advantages that would follow, and recommended the approval of the entire work. It was approved without dissent. Evidently he had absorbed enough in that two hours' talk with me to satisfy himself what ought to be done and to approve the whole thing. As I left for the West, I wondered what manner of man it was who in a few hours' talk could digest the details of an $18,000,000 reconstruction work along a thousand miles of railroad through a mountainous country, expound the general principles of the plan to his executive associates in the course of a few minutes, and obtain the seal of financial approval. I asked him what speed we should make — over what period of time we should spread the expenditure. He replied, "Spend it all in a week if you can."

The virtual reconstruction of the Central Pacific, under the direction of Mr. Kruttschnitt and the immediate supervision of Chief Engineer Hood, began at once and was finished in less than three years. Some conception of the magnitude of the task may be gained from the fact that it involved the complete abandonment of three hundred and seventy-three miles of the old line and the substitution for it of three hundred and twenty-two miles of new track built in new and better locations. This was about equivalent to the construction of an entirely new railroad from Boston, Massachusetts, to Washington, D.C. The engineering difficulties, however, in the mountainous regions of Utah and Nevada, were far more serious than they would be in the comparatively level country lying between eastern Massachusetts and the District of Columbia.

As the result of these changes of location, the new line was about fifty miles shorter than the old; it had thirteen thousand degrees less of curvature, and its maximum grades were reduced from an average of forty-nine to ninety feet per mile to an average of twenty-one feet per mile. On the old line there were many curves of eight and ten degrees, while on the new the sharpest curve did not exceed four degrees. The saving in grade rise, going either east or west, was about three thousand vertical feet, and was equivalent to more than sixty miles of continuous grade of fifty feet to the mile.

The most remarkable and perhaps the most difficult achievement in this reconstruction of the Central Pacific was the building of the so-called Lucin cut-off across the Great Salt Lake. The old line of the road ran around the northern end of the lake, across two mountain ranges, and through a very wild and rugged country where it was practically impossible to get easy grades, or eliminate sharp and frequent curves. This part of the road, as originally built, varied in elevation from 4200 to 4900 feet above the sea-level and contained maximum curvatures of ten degrees and grades as steep as ninety feet to the mile. Very little of the track between Ogden and Lucin was either straight or level, and the topography of the whole region was such that, for a distance of one hundred and forty-seven miles, it was difficult, if not impossible, to find a location that would be much better. When Mr. Harriman acquired control of the Central Pacific, he decided that this part of the line would have to be abandoned altogether, and as there seemed to be no other satisfactory route around the lake, he determined to go directly across it. The idea, however, was not his own. Mr. William Hood, the chief engineer of Collis P. Huntington, had suggested it, some years before, and had even drawn plans for an air line across the lake on embankments and trestles; but the estimated cost of the work was very great, and Mr. Huntington had only begun it. Mr. Harriman, however, soon satisfied himself that the saving which might be made in the running of trains would cover liberal interest on the cost of the improvement, and he therefore directed Mr. Kruttschnitt to complete the construction of the cut-off at once. It proved to be a task of tremendous difficulty. Although the greatest depth of the Great Salt Lake was only thirty-two feet, it had a very insubstantial and treacherous bottom, and many times in the progress of the work the fills and trestles seemed about to be wholly swallowed up in abysses of quicksand and mud. But persistence and unfaltering resolution won out at last, and on the 26th of November, 1903, Mr. Harriman and fifty prominent officials of the Pacific roads assembled at Ogden to celebrate the completion of the great undertaking. By the building of this cut-off, the maximum grades between Ogden and Lucin were reduced from ninety feet per mile to twenty-one feet per mile; four thousand degrees of curvature were eliminated, and the distance between the two points was shortened from one hundred and forty-seven miles to about one hundred and three miles. The cut-off, when completed, was only three tenths of a mile longer than an air line. The cost of the improvement was nearly $9,000,000, a large part of which sum was spent in building twenty-seven miles of fills and trestles across the lake from Lakeside to Promontory.

In discussing the savings made by this cut-off, an official of the Southern Pacific Company said in 1917:

> One hundred and ten million tons of freight have passed over the Lucin cut-off since its completion, and this, in terms of average car-loading, would take about 4,000,000 cars, making a continuous train 37,000 miles long, or enough to reach one and a half times around the earth. Had this freight been hauled over the old line, it would have necessitated the running of 172,000,000 additional car miles and additional work equivalent to lifting a million carloads a mile in the air.[1]

The main line of the Southern Pacific, from New Orleans to San Francisco, ran through a country that was comparatively open and level, so that reconstruction of it involved fewer engineering difficulties than those presented by the Central Pacific

[1] *Railway Age Gazette*, November 2, 1917.

THE LAST SPIKE OF THE LUCIN CUT-OFF ACROSS SALT LAKE

division between Ogden and Reno. It needed, however, almost everywhere, extensive betterments in the shape of heavier rails, new cross-ties, better ballasting, longer sidings, and more substantial culverts and bridges. These improvements Mr. Harriman began at once to make, and in the first two years after he acquired control, he spent on the main line of the Southern Pacific (apart from the Central Pacific division) more than $20,000,000. All the available net earnings of the road were devoted to betterments, and no dividends were paid, even on the preferred stock, until 1905.

Reconstruction work on the Southern Pacific did not differ essentially from that on the Union Pacific, and it is perhaps unnecessary, therefore, to describe it in detail. Suffice it to say that during the period of Mr. Harriman's administration 373 miles of the old main line were abandoned altogether and 322 miles were rebuilt in better locations; new and heavier rails were laid on 4481 miles of track; 27,000,000 new cross-ties were substituted for old; nearly 1000 miles of track were ballasted, or reballasted with better material, and about 30 miles of wooden culverts, trestles, and bridges were replaced with earthen embankments, or permanent structures of concrete or steel. Seven million dollars were spent in building new sidings, or extending those already in existence;

$2,600,000 in providing a second main track where the traffic was densest; $6,300,000 in rebuilding trestles and bridges, and nearly $14,000,000 in purchasing terminal or other real estate and the erection of new terminal buildings.

The most important piece of engineering work done on the main line, and the only one comparable, in cost and magnitude, with the famous Lucin cut-off, was the so-called Bay Shore cut-off, a short and nearly straight line which greatly improved the approach to San Francisco. The old single-track road, which was built in 1863, ran into the city on the western side of the San Bruno Mountain by way of Baden and Ocean View. From San Bruno to the terminal it was only eleven miles long, but in that distance it had 796 degrees of curvature, and rose to a height of 292 feet with a maximum grade of 158 feet to the mile. As an approach to San Francisco it had long been inadequate and unsatisfactory; but the city, in the course of forty years, had grown up around it to such an extent that it was practically impossible to widen the right of way, eliminate curves, or reduce the steep grades. Mr. Harriman decided to abandon it altogether and construct an entirely new double-track line on the eastern side of the San Bruno Mountain along the shore of San Francisco Bay. The building of this cut-off was a very difficult piece of work, inasmuch as it involved extensive grading, the building of a number of new bridges, and the digging of five tunnels whose aggregate length was nearly ten thousand feet; but it saved 2.65 miles in distance, eliminated 592 degrees of curvature, lowered the extreme elevation from 292 feet to 20 feet, and reduced a maximum grade of 158 feet to less than 16 feet per mile. The cost of this improvement, including bridges, tunnels, and right of way for a four-track road, was $9,273,055, or more than $800,000 per mile; but it gave the Southern Pacific easy access to the heart of the city and furnished it with better terminal facilities than it had ever before enjoyed.

The most important and costly piece of new construction in southern California was the sixty-mile cut-off on the main line between Burbank and Montalvo. Like all of Mr. Harriman's improvements it was intended to eliminate curves and heavy grades. The old road, by way of Saugus, was unnecessarily long and roundabout and had a maximum grade of 116 feet to the mile. The new line, by way of the Santa Susana tunnel, saved seven miles in distance and 2276 degrees of curvature; lessened the extreme elevation by 511 feet, and reduced the 116-foot grade to a maximum grade of less than 53 feet.

The total amount spent on the Southern Pacific

System for line changes, grade reductions, and other similar improvements during the period of Mr. Harriman's administration was approximately thirty million dollars, and two thirds of this sum was used in building the three principal cut-offs, namely, Lucin, Bay Shore, and Montalvo. Twenty million dollars seems a great expenditure for track improvement in only three places; but the saving in operating expenses which these betterments made possible was equivalent to from eight to ten per cent interest on the money invested in them.

The most important requirement of the Southern Pacific, next to track improvement, was better and heavier rolling stock. Twenty-five per cent of its locomotives and twenty-four per cent of its freight cars were more than sixteen years old, and very few were of the largest capacity. The average weight of the locomotives on their drivers, for example, was only 40.62 tons, and the average capacity of the freight cars was less than 27 tons. By purchasing 540 new locomotives of greater power and 8869 new freight cars of larger size, Mr. Harriman brought the average engine weight up to 52 tons and the average car capacity up to 37.58 tons. At the beginning of the Harriman administration, the freight cars owned by the road could carry, at a single trip, about 959,000 tons, while at the end of it the company's cars had an aggregate capacity of 1,633,000 tons. In the same period, 510 new coaches of larger size and better design were added to the passenger equipment, and the water service on the Atlantic and Pacific Oceans was improved by the expenditure of nearly $9,000,000 for new steamers. All together, the money invested in new rolling stock and floating equipment, after the Union Pacific Company acquired control of the road, amounted to more than $41,000,000.

One of the most valuable improvements made to the Southern Pacific, upon the personal initiative of Mr. Harriman, was the installation of a very perfect system of automatic block signals. Up to 1901, very little of this work had been done, and on the nine thousand miles of the Southern Pacific system there were less than fifty miles of block-signaled track. Mr. Harriman, at a cost of $2,835,000, provided automatic signals for nearly three thousand miles of track, and thus ensured the safety of moving trains on practically the whole of the main line, including the Central Pacific division from Ogden to Reno. In describing these signals, Mr. Kruttschnitt said:

They notify trains of danger ahead or danger behind. They are maintained at safety by an electric current sent through the rails, and anything that breaks the continuity of that current sets the signal at danger. If a rail breaks, if a switch is left open, or if an iron bar or rail is laid across the track for the purpose of wrecking a train, the automatic signal gives due warning. The signal is set at danger also if there is a train ahead, or if a car has escaped from a siding and run on to the main track. Protection is afforded, therefore, not only against collisions, but against broken rails, open switches, washouts, landslides, and obstructions.

The result of the installation of this system of block signaling on the Harriman lines was a great decrease in the number of train accidents — a decrease that amounted in some cases to more than one half. Employees, and especially engineers, were trained to observe signals attentively, and "surprise" experiments were frequently made to test their vigilance. If, in spite of all precautions, accidents occurred, no attempt was ever made to conceal the facts. On the contrary, boards of inquiry were appointed to fix the responsibility, and representatives of the public, including even local newspaper men, were invited to serve on these boards and to assist the railroad officials in making the investigations. To such a pitch of perfection was this system of safeguards carried that, in 1914, the Harriman gold medal of the American Museum of Safety was awarded to the Southern Pacific as the road that had done most to prevent accidents and protect the lives of passengers. In presenting the medal, President Williams referred to the fact that the percentage of accidents on the Southern Pacific had been reduced by two thirds, and that in the preceding five years not a single passenger had been killed. In receiving the medal, Mr. Kruttschnitt, chairman of the executive committee, said:

During the year ended June 13, 1913, the company's locomotives ran 59,738,000 miles — a figure too large to convey any meaning. At this rate, the miles run in a single week would girdle the earth forty-six times, or nearly seven times in a day, or once in three and one-half hours. With so vast a movement the liability to accident is very great, and yet, 41,783,000 passengers were carried the inconceivably great aggregate distance of 1,756,482,000 miles, equivalent to transporting the entire population of Greater New York, some 5,000,000 people, from New York to Rochester. This was done without a fatality in a train accident, and it had been done in the four years preceding with the same immunity.

Mr. Kruttschnitt attributed these results mainly to the policies of Mr. Harriman and to the coöperation and team-work which he so ardently advocated.

The most important extension of the Southern Pacific made after the Union Pacific acquired control was the branch line into Mexico. "Mr. Harriman," says Alexander Millar, late secretary of the Union Pacific, "visited the City of Mexico in March, 1902, and there met President Diaz and the leading men of the Mexican Republic. As a result of that visit a concession was granted by the Government of the Republic for the construction and operation of lines of railway from Guaymas, on the Gulf of California, up the valley of the Yaqui River, in the State of Sonora, to develop the coal and mineral resources of that region, and also down the west coast of Mexico through the cities of Navajoa, San Blas, Culiacan, Mazatlan, and Tepic to the city of Guadalajara, there connecting with the national lines for the City of Mexico and the South and East, a total distance, with branches, of about fifteen hundred miles. These lines will not only afford the Government of Mexico an easy and natural route for the movement of troops and supplies to the Pacific States of the Republic, but will open up a vast extent of territory rich in mining, agricultural, and shipping interests tributary to our Southwestern States. On the 1st of July, 1909, about eight hundred miles of the Mexican lines had been finished, and in the spring of that year Mr. Harriman went over them to Mazatlan in the first railroad train ever seen by the natives of that place." [1] The cost of the Mexican lines, so far as they had been completed during the period of Mr. Harriman's administration, was about $35,000,000, which, added to the cost of new lines and branches built or acquired by the Southern Pacific in the United States in the same period, make a total expenditure

[1] *E. H. Harriman and the Union Pacific*, by Alexander Millar, secretary of the Union Pacific Railroad Company (New York, 1910), p. 11.

of $114,513,000 for the extension of the system, aside from $127,000,000 spent in the reconstruction and re-equipment of it.

It has sometimes been said that Mr. Harriman was not a railroad-builder, but only an improver of railroads that had been built by others. This, however, is hardly true. He built, or caused to be built, more than fifteen hundred miles of entirely new road, much of it in a very wild, mountainous region, and the money spent under his direction for the improvement of the Union and Southern Pacific Systems would have sufficed, at that time, to build and equip three or four transcontinental lines of wholly new railway from the Missouri River to the Pacific Ocean. Improvement, on such a scale as this, does not differ essentially from new construction. An idea may be gained of the scope and extent of Southern Pacific improvements from the following itemized statement of expenditures:

Extensions:	
New lines and branches built or bought	$114,513,383
	$114,513,383
Track betterments:	
Lucin cut-off	$8,358,833
Bay Shore cut-off	9,273,055
Montalvo cut-off	2,425,911
Other line changes and reconstruction	10,761,484
Second main track	2,699,532
Side tracks	7,293,407
Bridges and trestles	6,298,059
Automatic block signals	2,835,278
Ballast	2,962,206
Total track betterments	$52,907,765

New equipment:

Rolling stock, 9919 locomotives and cars	$32,061,304
Steamers, ferry-boats, etc	8,984,282
Total new equipment	$41,045,586

Buildings and real estate:

Terminals and land	$13,896,985
Station grounds and right of way	3,235,988
Station buildings and fixtures	1,878,217
Pumping stations	1,058,294
Fuel stations	1,827,396
Shops, machines and tools	3,332,711
Miscellaneous structures	1,611,337
Various betterments, docks, engine houses, fencing, etc.	6,636,756
Total buildings and real estate	$33,477,684

Recapitulation:

Extensions	$114,513,383
Track betterments	52,907,765
New equipment	41,045,586
Buildings and real estate	33,477,684
Grand total	$241,944,418

The results of these betterments were summed up by Mr. Kruttschnitt in the following words:

Through a progressive policy and the assistance of an established credit [that of the Union Pacific] enormous sums were expended for betterments and additions; the physical condition of the roads was vastly improved; grades were reduced and curves eliminated; the lines were shortened wherever possible; facilities of all kinds were enlarged; the heaviest and most powerful types of locomotives were freely supplied, and the modern passenger and freight cars furnished were of standards not surpassed on any railroad in the United States. As a result, the general service to the public was much improved; the danger from accidents was reduced; the traffic was handled without increase of rates, even during periods of rising prices for material and labor, and the capacity of the roads was so increased that they carried for the public a volume of business that it would have been impossible to move at all if the improvement in facilities had not been made.

While these changes, made under the administration of Mr. Harriman, improved the return to the stockholders through the development and transportation of a much greater volume of business at lower cost, they were equally beneficial to the public in providing a safer, straighter, and more comfortable road and better equipment for passenger travel, as well as increased capacity for freight with more certainty in movement and promptness in delivery.[1]

Although the Interstate Commerce Commission, which investigated the merger of the Union and Southern Pacific Systems, was strongly prejudiced against Mr. Harriman, it did not venture to deny that his management of the roads had resulted in great material improvement. Commissioner Lane, in his report on "Consolidation and Combination of Carriers," in 1907, said:

> It has been no part of the Harriman policy to permit the properties which were brought under Union Pacific control to degenerate and decline. As railroads, they are better properties to-day — with lower grades, straighter tracks, and more ample equipment — than they were when they came under that control. Large sums have been generously spent in the carrying on of engineering works and betterments which make for the

[1] Unpublished letter of Julius Kruttschnitt, director of maintenance and operation of the Harriman lines.

improvement of the service and the permanent value of the property.[1]

In view of the fact that Mr. Harriman spent in the reconstruction and reëquipment of the two systems more than $400,000,000, or enough, at that time, to build and equip three or four entirely new lines to the Pacific Coast, the Commission could hardly say less than this; but, for reasons of its own, it persisted, nevertheless, in regarding this tremendous scheme of betterment as a menace, in some way, to the welfare of the people whose interests it so effectively promoted. If Mr. Harriman had not lived, there would have been a delay of certainly ten years, and possibly twenty, in the development of the resources of the Great West.

[1] *Report* of the Interstate Commerce Commission on "Consolidation and Combination of Carriers," by Franklin K. Lane (April 5, 1907), p. 281.

CHAPTER X

RAILROAD COMBINATIONS

THE merger of the Union Pacific and Southern Pacific lines in 1901 was the largest and most important combination of railroad properties that had ever been made, and in view of the hostile criticism to which it was afterward subjected and the attacks that were made upon Mr. Harriman as the leading exponent of the consolidation policy, it may be well to consider briefly the reasons for such combinations and the effect that they had upon the public welfare.

The consolidation of railroads into large groups, or systems, had its origin in the demonstrated evils of unrestricted competition. More than forty years ago, railway managers became convinced that unrestricted competition was prejudicial to the interests of both shareholders and shippers. It injured the former by reducing their profits, and the latter by vitiating all commercial contracts that were dependent upon equality and stability of rates. A shipper or manufacturer could not safely make plans for the future unless he felt sure that transportation rates would remain substantially unchanged, nor could he enter into contracts for future delivery unless he had some guarantee that, when the time should come for the shipment of his goods, he could get them carried to their destination as cheaply as could any of his business rivals. Cut-throat competition between railroads, with the frequent changes and wide discriminations that it involved, deprived him of all security and introduced an element of uncertainty into every business transaction.[1]

With a view to avoiding these and other evils of unrestricted competition, the railways, after the disastrous rate wars of 1875 and 1878, entered into what were known as "pooling" agreements, by virtue of which freight was apportioned among the several competing roads, or receipts from traffic were divided among them, in such a way as to secure equality and stability. These agreements were not intended to raise rates, or to keep them at an unduly high level; their object was to steady rates — to avoid the competitive changes, differences, and discriminations which were as upsetting to the calculations of producers and shippers as they were unprofitable to the railroads themselves.

[1] The Interstate Commerce Commission itself said, in 1887, that without stability of rates all business contracts were "lottery ventures." It also admitted that railroad combinations had a tendency "to remove obstacles to the interchange of business and to increase the facilities and conveniences for uninterrupted business intercourse." (*First Report* of the Interstate Commerce Commission, December 1, 1887, pp. 8 and 34.)

For a period of ten or twelve years, the "pooling" system worked fairly well; but the public became obsessed with the idea that rates could be reduced and kept low only by the unrestrained competition of carriers; and every effort of railway managers to secure uniformity and stability was regarded as a conspiracy to extort money from the people. In 1887, Congress, paying more attention to popular clamor and demagogic appeals than to facts or reason, inserted in the Interstate Commerce Bill a section which made it "unlawful for any common carrier to enter into any contract, agreement, or combination with any other common carrier, or carriers, for the 'pooling' of freights of different competing railroads, or to divide between them the aggregate or net proceeds of the earnings of such railroads, or any portion thereof." Although this prohibition, as a well-known economist has said, "was suggested and carried through by one of those spasms of demagogism which have done so much to retard progress," it completely thwarted the attempt of the transportation companies to stabilize rates by means of reciprocal agreements. Railway managers then tried to get the same results by organizing joint-traffic associations, which controlled rates through tariff concessions and coöperative adjustments. This plan also worked well for a time, but just as it was becoming most effective it was prohibited by the Supreme Court, on the ground that it brought about a restraint of trade and consequently violated the provisions of the Sherman Anti-Trust Law.

Urged on by the extreme need of stabilizing rates, as well as by considerations of efficiency and economy, the railroads then began to combine into large systems, each of which dominated traffic conditions over a large area. Some of these combinations were made through purchases or leases, some through stock holdings, and some through that form of unified control known as "a community of interest." Congress, however, was opposed to such combinations, as well as to the "pooling" and traffic agreements that preceded them, for the alleged reason that they had a tendency to raise transportation rates, or to maintain such rates at an unduly high level. But, as a matter of fact, did they have such a tendency? During the period of "pooling" and joint-traffic associations — that is, between 1870 and 1890 — there was a decrease in freight rates of about fifty per cent. In 1870, the average rate per ton-mile was 1.889 cents. In 1880, it was 1.232 cents, and in 1890, 0.941 cent. The decrease on Eastern roads was from 1.61 to 0.55; on Western roads from 2.61 to 0.94, and on transcontinental lines from 4.50 to 0.99. If railroad pools and agreements had a tendency to increase rates, or even to maintain them, why did not such tendency become apparent?

If we take the era of railroad mergers and combinations — the period during which the grouping of railroads into large systems proceeded most rapidly — the decline in rates is equally noticeable. In the quarter of a century that ended with 1903, when nearly all the great railroad combinations were formed, including that of the Union Pacific with the Southern Pacific, freight rates per ton-mile decreased from an average of 1.22 cents to an average of 0.77 cent, or nearly forty per cent. The saving to shippers by this reduction of rates was approximately one billion dollars in eighteen years on only one of the large Western systems — the Great Northern.

In the half-century that followed the Civil War, there was never a time when railroad pools, agreements, or combinations increased rates, or even maintained them at a fixed level. On the contrary, there was, throughout that period, a steady and continuous decline, which brought down ton-mile rates, on such a railroad combination as the Pennsylvania System for example, from two and a half cents to six mills. The conclusion seems to be irresistible that the high-rate evil, against which so much prohibitory legislation was directed, did not exist — it was wholly imaginary.

The only other evil alleged as a reason for prohibiting combinations was that the size of the systems that might be formed would tend to produce monopolistic conditions over a wide area and thus give the railroads undue power. But they could exercise that power to the prejudice of the public interest only in one way, namely, by making an excessive charge for the service that they rendered. Theoretically, of course, railroad managers, if they had a complete monopoly of transportation in a given area, or between two given points, might fix almost any rates; but practically they would still be subjected to a very effective economic restraint. If they made charges too high, they would lessen, cripple, or destroy the traffic upon which their profits depended. Mr. Harriman, long ago, pointed out the fact that no railroad, or combination of railroads, can charge exorbitant rates without throttling or paralyzing the industries along its lines. "It is impossible," he said, "for a railroad to sever its interests from those of its patrons. Its life-blood is drawn from their prosperity, and it must furnish them with adequate and ever-increasing facilities at reasonable rates. The widespread popular impression that a railroad company can extort money from the public at will, and in defiance of the laws of trade, is not justified by the facts."

As a matter of history, the great railroad combinations formed between 1887 and 1905 — combinations that were said to be monopolistic in nature or tendency — did not fix unnecessarily high rates. Proof of this is furnished by the records of the Interstate Commerce Commission. In response to a Senate resolution of inquiry, adopted January 13, 1905, the Commission reported that in the eighteen years of its existence it had heard 9099 complaints, relating to all sorts of railroad methods and practices. Thousands of them charged unjust discrimination between persons or places, but not one alleged exorbitant rates. More than eight thousand of the cases of supposed discrimination were informally and amicably settled, and of the forty-five complaints that were carried into the courts only eight were sustained.[1] If the great railroad combinations accused of monopoly had charged exorbitant rates, it is inconceivable that in the course of eighteen years complaint of it should not have been made by some one of the nine thousand shippers who came before the Commission.

The records of the great railroad combinations that were in existence during the period covered by

[1] *Railroad Regulation in Its Political Aspects*, by Joseph Nimmo, Jr. (Washington, May 4, 1909), p. 5; *Highways of Progress*, by James J. Hill (New York, 1912), p. 271.

the Commission's report furnish additional proof that, although the grouping of railroads into large systems enormously increased the service rendered, it did not increase the rates charged. Between 1898 and 1909, for example, the Union Pacific Company increased its capacity for handling freight by about one hundred and forty per cent, while at the same time it lowered rates by an average of sixteen per cent. Abundant facilities are often as important to shippers as low rates; the Union Pacific furnished both. On the Great Northern system, during approximately the same period, there was also a great increase of facilities, accompanied by a reduction of rates which saved shippers one hundred million dollars in a single year (1909).[1]

The low rates on the Western combined lines were undoubtedly due, in part, to the reduction of grades, the straightening of curves, the use of heavier equipment, and the many other improvements in the art of railroading which Mr. Harriman, in particular advocated or introduced; but they were also due, in very large part, to the increased efficiency and economy which the grouping of railroads into big systems made possible. This, as will presently be shown, was particularly true of the Union Pacific–Southern Pacific merger.

[1] *Highways of Progress*, by James J. Hill (New York, 1912), pp. 260–61.

Not one of the Western combinations had anything like a complete monopoly of the territory that it served; but the results of a nearly complete monopoly may be found in the history of one of the great Eastern systems, namely, the Pennsylvania.

For many years [says Professor Mead] the Pennsylvania has been dominant in the State of Pennsylvania, and has enjoyed the largest advantage from the traffic of the middle Atlantic seaboard. Its rivals have cut into long-distance traffic, but in the most valuable portions of this eastern territory the Pennsylvania Railroad Company has supplied the majority of shippers with their transportation facilities. If there were any truth in the assertion that railroad monopoly is injurious to the interests of the shipper, it would appear in the territory which the Pennsylvania controls. As a matter of fact, the unprecedented growth of this section in wealth and prosperity offers a striking refutation of the claim that competition is the life of trade. It is not to the interest of the Pennsylvania Company, although its power in most of this eastern territory is unquestioned, to exact unfair rates from the shipper. Not by such methods can a large traffic be built up. A railroad which abuses its power and follows a policy of extortion is working directly against its own interests. The policy of the Pennsylvania has been to leave a liberal margin of profit to the shipper, in order to encourage him to expand his business and furnish more freight to the railroad. The success of this policy is written in the prosperity of the corporation, and even more legibly in the prosperity of the territory which it serves.[1]

[1] "The Great American Railway Systems: The Pennsylvania," by Edward Sherwood Mead, Professor of Finance and Economy in the University of Pennsylvania. (*Railway World*, February 20, 1904.)

There have undoubtedly been a few monopolies which, under the direction of greedy and short-sighted managers, have tried to make large and immediate profits by charging unreasonable rates; but such monopolies must always be self-destructive for the reasons that Mr. Harriman and Professor Mead have given. They cannot possibly last long, even though there be no anti-trust law to suppress them.

If the evidence above set forth shows, as it seems to show, that combinations do not raise rates, and that transportation monopolies injurious to the shipper or the public are self-destructive and short-lived, what remains of the case against railroad consolidations? Nothing, apparently, except the vague and unsupported charge that big combinations of carriers are "a menace to the public welfare." But this assertion, for which no proof is offered, was discredited nearly four centuries ago. In 1522, the Diet of Nuremberg appointed a committee to investigate the evils said to be caused by the combination of merchants into great companies. In explaining its reasons for doubting the expediency of a restrictive policy, the committee said:

It is impossible to limit the size of the companies, for that would limit business and hurt the common welfare. The bigger and more numerous they are, the better for everybody. If a merchant cannot do business above a certain amount, what is he to do with his surplus money? Some people talk of limiting the earning capacity of investments. This would be unbearable and would work great injustice and harm by taking away the livelihood of widows, orphans, and other sufferers who derive their income from investments in these companies. . . . Hence any one can see that the idea that the companies undermine the public welfare ought not to be seriously considered.

This ancient record of one of the earliest investigations of trusts might well be thoughtfully considered by Congressmen who sought to restrain railroad combinations because they were "a menace to the public welfare," and by Interstate Commerce Commissioners who limited the earning capacity of transportation companies and thus "took away the livelihood of widows, orphans, and other sufferers" who were dependent upon investments for support. We are supposed to have learned something in the course of four hundred years — but have we? The Diet of Nuremberg, in 1522, seems to have had a clearer comprehension of economic law than had the Congress that passed the Anti-Trust Bill and the courts that afterward interpreted it.

Let us see now to what extent the combination of the Union Pacific with the Southern Pacific benefited the latter, and what the effect of the merger was upon the public welfare. When Mr. Harriman bought the Southern Pacific and began the reconstruction of it, his ultimate object was to transport over it more freight and more passengers at a relatively reduced cost. He saw, as his famous rival James J. Hill saw, that the greatest possible economy in railway operation was to be effected by carrying a greater volume of traffic with fewer trains, or, to speak more accurately with a decrease in the aggregate mileage of trains run. If he could increase the tonnage carried by, say, twenty per cent, while, at the same time, he reduced the number of miles run by, say, ten per cent, he would make an immense saving in fuel, wages, and the cost of operation generally. The only way in which this could be accomplished was by using larger cars and more powerful locomotives. But in order to run economically this heavier equipment, he would have to have a better track — a track with stronger rails and bridges, fewer curves, and more moderate grades. It was for this reason that he rebuilt nearly four hundred miles of the Southern Pacific line; spent $20,000,000 for track improvement in only three places, and substituted permanent structures of earth, concrete, or metal for about thirty miles of wooden bridges and trestles. He wanted a track on which he could use safely and economically powerful locomotives and cars of large capacity. He therefore put nearly $53,000,000 into track betterments alone. As soon as he had made the track fit for heavy equipment, he spent more than $30,000,000 for new rolling stock, including 540 locomotives and 8869 freight cars. The increase in traffic, from year to year, which accompanied this increase of facilities is shown in the following table:

Years	Average miles operated	Tons carried all frt.	Tons carried 1 mile all frt.	Tons carried 1 mile per mile of road all frt.	Frt. train mileage including ¾ mixed	Tons of freight per train including ¾ mixed
1901	8,774.37	17,725,632	5,694,770,640	653,802	18,650,784	305.34
1902	8,809.21	20,260,573	6,059,873,410	691,965	18,997,981	318.97
1903	8,933.43	22,230,367	6,308,502,359	711,099	19,344,658	326.11
1904	9,135.49	23,684,348	6,562,648,418	727,196	19,823,619	331.05
1905	9,142.01	24,464,827	6,561,349,589	718,041	18,886,016	347.42
1906	9,216.83	27,589,004	7,236,786,873	784,590	18,468,406	391.85
1907	9,451.27	30,810,518	8,011,974,964	849,420	20,677,172	387.48
1908	9,591.82	28,998,913	7,845,002,515	824,251	18,988,586	413.14
1909	9,734.03	28,122,443	7,213,993,420	749,394	15,261,631	472.69

From the above table it appears that the Southern Pacific carried, in 1909, 10,000,000 more tons of freight than it carried in 1901, but with a reduction of 3,400,000 in the number of freight-train miles run. This was made possible by increasing the capacity of the average freight car from 26 tons to 37 tons, and the average train-load from 305 tons to 472 tons.

In the passenger traffic there was a similar increase without a proportionate increase in the passenger-train mileage. Between 1901 and 1909 the number of passengers carried one mile increased 65 per cent. while the increase in passenger-train miles run was only 43 per cent. The relative economy in the operation of passenger trains was not so great as in that of freight trains, for the reason that in the former it was not possible to increase the car and train capacity so much. Nevertheless, 606,000,000 more passengers were carried one mile in 1909 than in 1901, with an addition of only 5,800,000 to the passenger-train mileage.

Great economy was also effected by pooling the whole equipment of the Union and Southern Pacific systems. The Southern Pacific, prior to its consolidation with the Union Pacific, was composed of a number of organizations and subsidiary companies, many of which had their own managing officers, and were operated, in some respects, independently of one another. This prevented the effective and economical distribution of rolling stock over a large area, and resulted in the returning of many cars empty to the places where they had been loaded. The traffic demand for freight cars varies greatly in different places and at different seasons of the year, and the utmost possible economy in operation can be secured only by redistributing rolling stock, from time to time, in such a way as to place cars where, at the moment, they happen to be most needed, thus keeping them constantly employed. It costs almost as much to haul an empty car as one that is loaded, and the great advantage that a combination has over a number of unrelated or loosely connected roads is that it can distribute cars more widely, in accordance with varying needs, and thus avoid the unnecessary hauling of empties on return trips.

One of the first things that Mr. Harriman did, after he acquired control of the Southern Pacific, was to appoint J. C. Stubbs as director of traffic for both Pacific Systems.[1] Then, when the work of reconstruction in charge of Mr. Kruttschnitt had been largely completed, he appointed him director of maintenance and operation for all the Harriman lines, and authorized him to work out as perfect a system as possible of pooling equipment and unifying traffic on both of the great Pacific Systems. The results more than justified his anticipations.

> On June 1, 1904 [says Mr. Kruttschnitt], we commenced pooling freight equipment on all the lines of the Union Pacific System and the Southern Pacific Company. The object of this was to increase efficiency and reduce unnecessary haul by permitting the cars of all the roads to be used as though they were of one ownership. It had previously been the practice, and is still the practice for roads of different ownership, to return cars to their owners empty when they cannot be promptly reloaded, in order to escape rental payments on them. In the next two years after we inaugurated the system of pooling equipment, we so reduced our empty-car haul that, in the two years, we saved the running of

[1] Mr. Stubbs had been in the freight-department service of the Southern Pacific Company for nearly thirty years, and was generally regarded as one of the ablest traffic experts in the United States. At the time of the consolidation he was third vice-president and traffic manager.

53,213,791 car-miles unnecessarily, which would be equivalent to operating one average freight train a distance of 1,400,900 miles.[1]

It can readily be seen that this saving in the number of car-miles run greatly reduced operating expenses, while, at the same time, the pooling of equipment accommodated shippers by devoting to their use on one road, or system, the cars which, at that particular time, were not needed on another. It was like giving to a military commander on a wide front the resources and motor-trucks of two or three army corps instead of one.

The consolidation of the Union and Southern Pacific systems enabled Mr. Harriman to make another improvement, which, from the point of view of economy, was almost as important as the pooling of rolling-stock, and that was the standardization of equipment generally. Under his administration, all material things used in the operation of a railroad, from locomotives and cars to rails, frogs, switches, wrenches, nuts, bolts, oil-boxes, and journal-bearings were, as far as possible, standardized and made uniform. On the lines of the separate companies that made up the two systems there were originally nearly fifty patterns of frogs; they were reduced to four. There were nearly a hundred different kinds of jour-

[1] Unpublished letter of Julius Kruttschnitt, director of maintenance and operation of the Harriman lines.

nal-bearings; they also were reduced to four. This policy of standardization, which would not have been possible without unified control, not only reduced cost by enabling the allied companies to purchase such supplies in immense quantities, but effected a great saving in time in the making of repairs. If, before the merger, a Union Pacific car lost the use of an oil-box at San Francisco, it might be necessary to send to Ogden, or Omaha, for a new one. If a Southern Pacific car broke down at Butte, Montana, the part needed for repair might have to be brought from Sacramento, or from some Southern Pacific center a thousand miles away. Combination and standardization made it possible to get almost any needed part of equipment at almost any place from Ogden to San Francisco and from New Orleans to Portland.

Sometimes Mr. Harriman was disposed to carry this policy of standardization too far, as in one case where he proposed that classes of locomotives on the two systems be made uniform. When, however, his director of operation showed him that this was impracticable, and that it would result in a decrease of efficiency on certain parts of the lines where engines of an exceptional type were needed, he yielded to Mr. Kruttschnitt's better judgment.

On the other hand, he often suggested improvements or economies that the most experienced of his assistants had never thought of.

One day [says Mr. Kruttschnitt] I was walking with Mr. Harriman on the road. He noticed a track bolt and asked me why so much of the bolt should protrude beyond the nut. I replied, "It is the size which is generally used." He said, "Why should we use a bolt of such a length that a part of it is useless?" I replied, "Well, when you come right down to it, there is no reason." We walked along and he asked me how many track bolts there were to a mile of track, and I told him. Thereupon he remarked, "Well, in the Union Pacific and Southern Pacific we have about eighteen thousand miles of track and there must be some fifty million track bolts in our system. If you can cut an ounce off from every bolt, you will save fifty million ounces of iron, and that is something worth while. Change your bolt standard."

A similar change was made, at Mr. Harriman's suggestion, in the width of what is technically known as the "shoulder of ballast"; that is, the width of ballast between the ends of the ties and the beginning of the downward slope to the level of the terrain. The elimination of a few inches of superfluous "shoulder" would not lessen much the cost of ballasting a mile or two of track; but even this small saving, multiplied by thousands of miles, would amount, as Mr. Harriman said in the case of the track bolt, to "something worth while."

The increase in carrying capacity made possible by Mr. Harriman's betterments, and the economies that resulted directly from the consolidation of the two systems, were reflected, of course, in the earnings of the Southern Pacific Company. In 1901, when the combination was made, the gross operating revenue of the road was about $78,000,000. In the next six years it increased to $126,000,000. During the same period the net surplus, after paying all operating expenses and putting vast sums into reconstruction and improvements, grew from $10,000,000 to $24,000,000. Up to 1901, the company had never paid a dividend. In 1907, it paid $2,769,000 in dividends on its preferred stock and had nearly $25,000,000 left for the common, after having put $30,000,000 of the year's earnings into maintenance of way and equipment.

These results, the captious critic may say, were due to the natural growth and development of the territory that the Southern Pacific served. This, of course, is partly true; but if the transportation facilities afforded by the road had not been immensely increased, the growth and development of the country would have been greatly retarded. It would be almost as true to say that the reconstructed railroad caused the growth of the country as to say that the growth of the country caused the prosperity of the road. They reacted on each other, but the transportation facilities, under the far-sighted management of Harriman, Kruttschnitt, and Stubbs, were always ahead of the territorial development. In his testimony before the Interstate Commerce Commission in 1907, Mr. Harriman himself said, "If we had not had the power to buy the Southern Pacific with the credit of the Union Pacific, the territory tributary to the Southern Pacific would have been ten years behind what it is now." [1]

One of the most important advantages of railroad combination is, undoubtedly, the physical improvement of weak or financially embarrassed roads as the result of incorporation in richer or more powerful systems. When a strong railroad, with large earning power and high credit, combines with a weaker or poorer competitor, it enables the latter to serve the public far better than it ever could alone. A weak road generally has difficulty in getting money for improvements, and it always has to pay high rates for its borrowed capital. At the minimum price fixed by a State commission it may not be able to sell a single share of its stock, in which case it must borrow on bond and mortgage, or on short-term notes, and thus increase fixed charges which may already be dangerously great. All railroad managers are reluctant to do this, because it lessens financial strength; so they avoid it as long as possible by cutting down

[1] Testimony in the investigation by the Interstate Commerce Commission of "Consolidation and Combination of Carriers," p. 163.

expenditures for maintenance and betterments, thus impairing the road's efficiency and usefulness. Scores of railroads have deteriorated physically because they have been forced to economize in this way, and many more have been thrown into the hands of receivers as the result of trying to carry a large floating debt, or of increasing their bonds out of all proportion to their stock. Combination with a rich and powerful road immediately changes this state of affairs. The stronger company lends its money or its credit to the weaker and thus enables the latter to improve its track and increase its equipment without running the risk of financial insolvency.

This was what Mr. Harriman did for the Southern Pacific. That road never would have been able to spend $242,000,000 for additions and betterments in eight years, if, by its merger with the Union Pacific, it had not secured the benefit of the latter's credit and Mr. Harriman's incomparable management. Its improved service and increased public usefulness, therefore, were the direct result of what the United States Supreme Court afterward called an illegal "combination in restraint of trade." Such results have almost always followed the combination of a strong road with a weaker rival, and its beneficial effect, so far as the public welfare is concerned, hardly needs to be pointed out.

Mr. Harriman would have acquired and greatly improved other railroad properties in the West and Southwest if he had not been prevented from doing so by prohibitory State or Federal legislation. In his testimony before the Congressional Joint Committee on Interstate Commerce in March, 1917, R. S. Lovett, formerly counsel for the Union and Southern Pacific Companies, said:

During the life of Mr. Harriman, he planned to build a low-grade line connecting with the Union Pacific at Kansas City, thence to the boundary of Texas at Denison, there connecting with the Houston & Texas Central Line, controlled by the Southern Pacific, and practically to rebuild that line from Denison to Houston and Galveston, in order to establish a low-grade line from Kansas City to the Gulf. As counsel, I was obliged to advise him that, under the Texas law and the ruling of its railroad commission, not a dollar in bonds could be issued for the money required in the reconstruction of the Houston & Texas Central; and even if stock could be issued at one hundred cents on the dollar for the money thus expended, as a practical matter it could not be sold, since stock ownership was the only way by which the Houston & Texas Central could continue as part of the Southern Pacific System, a lease or sale of the railroad itself to the Southern Pacific Company, or any foreign corporation, being forbidden by the laws of Texas. The result was that a great project for improving the facilities for interstate and international commerce had to be abandoned, and the choppy grades of the Houston & Texas Central continue as they always have been, and probably always will be as long as the Texas law remains unchanged.[1]

[1] *Railway Age Gazette*, March 23, 1917.

A new line from Kansas City to the Gulf would not have been injurious to the public welfare; on the contrary, it would have been highly beneficial to all concerned; and yet, construction of it was prevented by the votes of short-sighted legislators who feared that railroad combinations would promote the interests of stockholders rather than the interests of the people. In the railroad field, as in other fields of industrial enterprise, combinations made for the purpose of rendering better service, or furnishing more commodities at lower cost, are as useful as they are practically inevitable. Mr. Harriman, who perhaps more than any other single man personified the idea of combination and centralized control in the railroad field, said, in his address at the opening of the Louisiana Purchase Exposition:

Within the present generation vast improvements have been made in railway transportation. It was impossible to supply the needs of commerce by the railways originally constructed and operated. It became necessary not only to reconstruct and reëquip these lines, but to bring them under uniform methods and management, which was possible only by the combination and unification of the original short lines of railway into systems, each under one management or control. The combination of different railroads should be regulated by law. So far as may be necessary, the public interest should be protected by law; but in so far as the law obstructs such combinations, without public benefit, it is unwise and prejudicial to the public interest.

Another great master in the art of railroading, Mr. James J. Hill, has approved railroad combinations in language equally clear and emphatic. In his "Highways of Progress" he said:

> The tendency toward combination is simply a part of that coöperation in the production, the distribution, and the exchange of wealth with which everybody has been familiar for centuries. When the pioneers in this country united to help build one another's houses, when they had a barn-raising, it was combination. When the owners of land, or implements, or capital in any other form, entered into partnership with labor to produce more wealth, it was combination. When the corporation came into existence, through which many small amounts of capital could be massed, it marked an era, just as much as when two men first lifted by their united strength some stone or tree-trunk too heavy for them singly. Exactly as society and the work of the community have become more complex, so have the means by which material ends are achieved grown larger and more powerful. The union of numerous weak and disconnected railroads in one orderly and efficient system is part of the natural and inevitable evolution of united action among men. Every legitimate railroad combination is intended to produce, and does produce, better service and lower rates on the side of the public, and either larger or more certain profits, or both, on the side of the stockholder.[1]

These economically sound statements of Harriman and Hill were supported and confirmed by the whole history of the Union Pacific–Southern Pacific lines.

[1] *Highways of Progress*, by James J. Hill (New York, 1912), pp. 114–15.

The combination policy, it is true, was ultimately condemned by the Interstate Commerce Commission of 1907; but long before Mr. Harriman adopted it with such brilliant success, it had been distinctly approved by the Interstate Commerce Commission of 1887. Fourteen years prior to the amalgamation of the Union Pacific and Southern Pacific systems, Thomas M. Cooley, who was perhaps the ablest and most far-sighted chairman that the Commission ever had, said, in the Omaha Board of Trade case:

> The more completely the whole railway system of the country can be created as a unit, as if it were all under one management, the greater will be the benefit of its service to the public, and the less the liability to unfair exactions.

Although Judge Cooley may have seen the advantages of combination as clearly as Mr. Harriman or Mr. Hill did, he could hardly have foreseen that, thirty years later, the Government itself would do what it had forbidden Mr. Harriman to do, and for precisely the reason that Mr. Harriman assigned, namely, to secure greater efficiency.

CHAPTER XI

CONTROL OF THE BURLINGTON

THE struggle for control of the Chicago, Burlington & Quincy Railroad, which began soon after the acquirement of the Southern Pacific by the Union Pacific in 1901, was one of the most striking and spectacular incidents in Mr. Harriman's career. Possession, or control of the Burlington was desired by two powerful and far-sighted managers, each of whom was striving to strengthen his position, or increase his business, in the great transportation field lying west of the Missouri River. This field was partly occupied at that time by four important railroad systems, namely, the Great Northern, the Northern Pacific, the Union Pacific, and the Chicago, Burlington & Quincy. The first two of these systems, which were dominated by James J. Hill and J. P. Morgan, extended from Lake Superior and the Mississippi River to the Pacific Coast; but neither of them had an outlet of its own in Chicago. The Burlington had its eastern terminus in Chicago, but it did not extend westward beyond Denver. Between that city and the Missouri River, however, it closely paralleled the Union Pacific, and its great network of branches and feeders in Kansas, Nebraska, and Colorado gathered up or distributed large quantities of freight originating in, or destined for, Union Pacific territory.

Such being the situation, it was almost inevitable that Hill and Harriman should both seek to get possession of the Burlington system. Hill and Morgan wanted it because it would give their roads an entrance into Chicago, while Harriman wanted it, partly because it was a competitor for business in Union Pacific territory, and partly because it might at any time extend its main line from Denver to the Pacific Coast and thus become a rival of the Union Pacific in transcontinental as well as local traffic.

The Burlington, at that time, was

> one of the best constructed, best managed, and most profitably operated systems in the West. . . . It had its own line from Chicago to St. Paul, well built, well handled, and with good terminal facilities and connections. It had a network of lines in northern Illinois; reached Peoria and Quincy, and ran thence to St. Louis. It covered southern Iowa and northern Missouri from Burlington to Omaha, and from Omaha to St. Joseph, St. Louis, and Kansas City. Its lines stretched across southern Nebraska, with termini at Denver and Cheyenne. Northwest, it had a line straight up to and through the Black Hills to Billings in Montana. . . . The total length of lines operated by it in 1901, exclusive of systems leased or otherwise controlled, was 7911 miles.

It had been organized under another name as early as 1849. It absorbed one line after another and built steadily, growing rich and powerful because it ran through one of the best traffic countries in the West. Tributary to it were the fertile lands of Illinois, Iowa, and Nebraska, the coal mines of Illinois and Iowa, the river valleys of the Mississippi and its tributaries, and the mining industries of Colorado and the Black Hills. During its existence it had paid out, up to 1901, cash dividends of more than $127,000,000, besides $6,700,000 in stock distributed[1]

Its capital stock was approximately $110,500,000, and it had a funded debt of a little more than $145,000,000.

To purchase such a road as this, or even to acquire stock control of it, would obviously require a large amount of capital — a greater amount than Mr. Hill at that time could secure. He discussed the matter with friendly financiers in London as early as 1897, but they thought it too big an enterprise for the Great Northern alone to undertake. The Northern Pacific, of course, was equally interested, because it too needed an outlet in Chicago; but the Northern Pacific was not then financially strong enough to participate. It had gone into the hands of a receiver in the panic of 1893 and was not reorganized until 1896. J. Pierpont Morgan and the Deutsche Bank then took

[1] *Life of James J. Hill*, by J. G. Pyle (New York, 1917), vol. II, pp. 114–15.

its affairs in hand, set the company on its feet, and allowed Mr. Hill, in behalf of the Great Northern, to buy about $16,000,000 of its reorganization stock. Subsequently the Great Northern added largely to its holdings, and before 1900 the two roads were practically being operated as a single system, under Mr. Hill's management, and were known as the "Hill Lines." Both roads were then prospering, and when, in 1901, Mr. Hill renewed his effort to get control of the Burlington, he had the support of both companies and the powerful backing of J. P. Morgan and his associates.

Meanwhile, however, Mr. Harriman was not blind to the consequences that might follow a consolidation of the Great Northern, Northern Pacific, and Burlington systems under the skillful and far-sighted management of his rival in St. Paul. Such a combination was sure to be injurious to the interests of the Union Pacific, and might even affect them disastrously.

Late in 1899, therefore, Mr. Harriman and Mr. Schiff had conferences with the president and some of the leading directors of the Burlington Company for the purpose of ascertaining whether the purchase of the road would be possible. The negotiations, however, came to nothing, either because the managers of the Burlington were disinclined to sell, or because Harriman and Schiff did not offer enough.[1]

In the spring of 1900, after the failure of these negotiations, Mr. Harriman called a conference of some of the most powerful friends of the Union Pacific, for the purpose of considering the situation and discussing the best means of preventing the Morgan and Hill interests from buying or controlling the Burlington system. There were present at that conference E. H. Harriman, Jacob H. Schiff (senior partner in the firm of Kuhn, Loeb & Co.), James Stillman (president of the National City Bank), and George J. Gould. Mr. Harriman pointed out the danger involved in the possible acquirement of the Burlington system by Morgan and Hill, and suggested that it be averted, or at least minimized, by the formation of a stock pool to purchase a large enough block of Burlington shares to prevent any hostile interest from acquiring control. As the stock of the Burlington was very widely scattered, and held in small lots of sixty or seventy shares each by fifteen thousand permanent investors, it was not at all certain that enough of it could be obtained in

[1] Mr. Hill's biographer says that Mr. Harriman "made an offer, but it was too low to be taken into serious consideration. Then, believing he could make terms satisfactory to himself later, he went back to New York." (Pyle's *Life of James J. Hill*, vol. II, p. 121.) Mr. Schiff, however, could not remember that any definite offer was made.

the open market to give the Union Pacific a substantial hold on the company; but the experiment seemed to be worth trying. It was decided, therefore, to form the pool and secure as much Burlington stock as could be had up to 200,000 shares.

Kuhn, Loeb & Co. began purchasing for the syndicate in May, and by the 6th of June had accumulated 69,800 shares. The market supply at current prices then seemed to run short and in the next six weeks the syndicate was able to add only 10,000 shares to its holdings. By that time it had become apparent that to get enough of the stock to establish even partial control of the company would be difficult, if not wholly impracticable; and on the 25th of July the syndicate suspended operations, after having acquired 80,300 Burlington shares at a cost of approximately $10,000,000. In speaking of this episode, a year or two later, Mr. Hill said that when the Union Pacific interests tried to get control of the Burlington by stock purchases, they "found themselves up against a stone wall consisting of the great body of small shareholders" (fifteen thousand, or more, who did not wish to sell their holdings).[1]

Throughout August and September Burlington stock remained inactive; but in October the demand for it began to increase, as the result, apparently, of

[1] Pyle's *Life of James J. Hill*, vol. II, p. 139.

bids made by speculators, or friends of the Hill Lines, who based their calculations on reports that the Great Northern and Northern Pacific intended to buy the Burlington road. From that time the price of Burlington shares steadily increased until, in December, it reached 140.[1]

The scanty market supply of the stock and the increasing demand for it apparently convinced the members of the Harriman syndicate that they could not get enough of it to answer their purpose; so about the 1st of November they decided to sell their shares, take the profit they had made, and liquidate the pool. Kuhn, Loeb & Co. began selling on the 7th of November, and between that time and the 21st of December sold 60,300 shares at prices ranging from 130 to 140⅝. The 20,000 shares that remained were then divided among the members of the syndicate, each taking 5000 shares.

The next steps in the contest for possession of the Burlington were taken by Morgan and Hill. In testifying as a witness in the Northern Securities case, two or three years later, Mr. Morgan said:

[1] Mr Hill always contended that he never tried to buy stock control of the Burlington and that the purchases which raised the price of the shares from 130 to 140⅝ in the fall and winter of 1900 were neither made nor inspired by him. This is doubtless true, because if he contemplated buying the road outright from its directors and stockholders he would not run up the value of its shares by bidding for them in the open market. That would only encourage the owners of the property to demand a higher price for it.

I made up my mind that it was essential that the Northern Pacific Railway should have its terminus practically in Chicago. I talked it over with a great many people interested in the Northern Pacific, and I found that all agreed with me, and the question came up as to how it could best be done. I came to the conclusion that there were but three lines available, the St. Paul, the Chicago, Burlington & Quincy, and the Wisconsin Central. I made up my mind that I would rather have the St. Paul. Soon after that I met Mr. Hill and I said: "Mr. Hill, I think the best thing we could do — I think your line perhaps is in the same condition — I think we had better go to work and secure the St. Paul road, or a road to Chicago, and if you will share with us we will do it together." He said: "All right; who would take it up?" I said: "I will. I think we had better take the St. Paul." He said he thought we had better take the Burlington. I said I would rather have the St. Paul, because the financial responsibility would be less. He did not agree with me, but he acquiesced in my decision, and I took it up with the directors of the road. They refused to sell the road on any terms — they would not even name terms — so I went to Mr. Hill and told him; "You can go ahead and see what you can do with the Burlington."[1]

Inasmuch as Mr. Morgan's main object was to get an entrance into Chicago for the Northern Pacific — the road in which he was most interested — he would have been quite satisfied with the acquisition of the Chicago, Milwaukee & St. Paul. But Mr. Hill had other aims. He, too, needed a Chicago terminus, but he needed still more some means of independent

[1] J. Pierpont Morgan's testimony in the Northern Securities case.

access to the prairie States of Kansas and Nebraska where he could market his lumber, and to the great distributing centers of Omaha, St. Joseph, St. Louis, and Kansas City where he could get cotton and provisions for transportation to the Pacific States, Alaska, and the Orient. The St. Paul line would not give him access to any of these places, while the Burlington would open them all to him. In a letter written a little later to his friend and associate, Lord Mount Stephen, he said:

The best traffic of the Great Northern and Northern Pacific is cotton and provisions west- and lumber and timber east-bound. The San Francisco lines run through the cotton country, from New Orleans through Texas and Arkansas. The great provision centers are Kansas City, St. Joseph, Omaha, Chicago, and St. Louis, none of which are reached directly by the Great Northern or Northern Pacific. Both companies have to divide the through rate with some other line to reach those important points. Now as to lumber from the Coast, we have to divide our rate with lines south to reach Chicago, Illinois, St. Louis, Iowa, Nebraska, Kansas, etc. The Burlington lets us into all these districts and commercial centers, over better lines and with better terminals than any other road.[1]

In the early part of 1901, after having been authorized by Morgan to "go ahead and see what he could do with the Burlington," Hill opened negotiations with the president and directors of that road, with a

[1] Pyle's *Life of James J. Hill*, vol. II, pp. 119–20.

view to buying it outright for the joint use of the Great Northern and Northern Pacific. Of these negotiations Mr. Harriman seems to have been unaware. He was deeply absorbed at that time in the gigantic task of rebuilding the Union Pacific and in plans for the improvement of the Southern Pacific, and it is quite possible that the acquisition of the Burlington had temporarily dropped into the back of his mind, as a matter either of secondary importance, or of no immediate urgency. Certain it is that he did not attempt any active interference with the Hill-Morgan plans, as he probably would have done if they had been known to him.

Mr. Hill afterward maintained that he began and carried on his negotiations with the Burlington people quite openly, so far, at least, as Union Pacific interests were concerned. In a letter to a friend, written on the 16th of May, 1901, Mr. Hill said:

To remove any ground for the charge that we were working secretly to acquire the Chicago, Burlington & Quincy I said to [a representative of the Union Pacific interests] in January that if he at any time heard that we were conferring with the "Q" board of directors looking to the joint acquisition of the property, I wanted to be the first one to tell him that we intended to take the matter up seriously. In April, after Mr. Morgan had gone abroad and the Burlington matter was taking definite shape, I again told him that matters were progressing toward a close. . . . I told him our plan was an open and fair attempt to agree with the "Q" board as the only means of gaining control of the property.[1]

If the unnamed person to whom Mr. Hill made this statement was really a representative of Union Pacific interests, he did not pass on the information to the men who were actively in control of Union Pacific affairs, namely, Harriman and Schiff. Neither of these gentlemen had any knowledge of the Hill-Morgan negotiations until some time in March, 1901. As soon as they became aware of the situation, they asked Mr. Hill to meet them in conference at the house of George F. Baker, a friend and associate of Mr. Hill in New York. The interview, which was brief, failed to establish any basis for agreement or compromise. Harriman, in behalf of the Union Pacific, asked to be given one-third interest in the purchase of the Burlington and offered to furnish one third of the purchase money. Hill declined even to take this proposition into consideration. "Very well," Harriman is reported to have said, "it is a hostile act and you must take the consequences."

In a signed statement published nine months later in the St. Paul "Globe," Mr. Hill explained in the following words his refusal to allow the Union Pacific to participate in the Burlington purchase:

About a year ago, the Union Pacific Company bought

[1] Pyle's *Life of James J. Hill*, vol. II, pp. 138–39.

the Huntington and other interests in the Southern Pacific, and at the same time made an effort to buy the control of the Chicago, Burlington & Quincy. With these lines in the hands of the Union Pacific interests, the Northern Pacific and Great Northern would be largely shut out of the States of Nebraska, Kansas, Missouri, South Dakota, Iowa, Illinois, and Wisconsin, except by using other lines of railway, some of which were in the market for sale and might at any time pass under the control of, or be combined with, Union Pacific interests. We, then, with the Northern Pacific, made proposals to the directors of the Burlington to buy their entire property. When this transaction was about being closed, the people who represented the Union Pacific Company, and who had previously tried to buy the Burlington, asked to be allowed to share with us in the purchase of that Company. This proposal we refused, for the reason that it would defeat our purpose in buying the Burlington, and, further, it was against the law of several of the States in which the largest mileage of the Burlington was located.[1]

If Mr. Hill supposed that, by refusing to allow the Union Pacific to participate in the purchase of the Burlington, he could thwart the purposes of as resolute and resourceful a man as Mr. Harriman, he reckoned without his host. Absorbed in the affairs of the two great Pacific systems which had so recently come under his control, Harriman may have lost sight temporarily of the Burlington danger; but when it became imminent, he acted with characteristic vigor, and met the unlooked-for move of his

[1] St. Paul *Globe*, December 22, 1901.

adversaries with a counter-move which, in the words of Mr. Hill's biographer, was so "daring" in conception and so "swift and unsparing in execution" as to "command admiration from friend and foe." [1]

When Mr. Harriman discovered that the Burlington had been captured and taken into the camp of the enemy, he determined to make a sudden, surprise attack on that camp itself. He had lost the C., B. & Q.; but there was nothing to prevent him from seizing the Northern Pacific by secretly buying a majority of its capital stock. He would then control not only that company, but the half-interest that it had just acquired in the Burlington. By this move Morgan would be ousted and the joint ownership of the disputed property would be vested in the Great Northern and the Union Pacific, with the latter in the stronger if not the dominant position. As Mr. Hill's biographer has justly said:

> The boldness of this plan, so different now in magnitude from the old days when Mr. Villard had realized it — $78,000,000 to put up instead of $8,000,000 — allied it to a work of genius. From those grim old lions [Morgan and Hill] who guarded the way, the quarry was to be snatched before they sensed the presence of an enemy. The implications of the project were tremendous. Suppose the Union Pacific gained control of the Northern Pacific. At once the Great Northern would have to make terms with its new owners, or bear the brunt of in-

[1] Pyle's *Life of James J. Hill*, vol. II, p. 141.

cessant attacks along two thousand miles of battle front. It would be shut into the narrow strip between its line and the Canadian border. As the Union Pacific would succeed also to a half-interest in the Burlington, the situation there would be a permanent deadlock. ... There could be but one issue from a position so intolerable. He [Mr. Hill] would have to make the best terms he could. And the terms dictated by an interest that would then reach from New Orleans and Galveston to Winnipeg, and from San Francisco, Portland, and Tacoma to Chicago, St. Paul, and Duluth, were not likely to be tolerable. The victor could make them almost what he pleased.[1]

Although an agreement between Mr. Hill and the directors of the Burlington was virtually concluded in March, 1901, the purchase and sale were not formally authorized until about a month later. On the 20th of April, the directors of the Great Northern empowered its president, with the coöperation and participation of the Northern Pacific Company, to buy the whole, or not less than two thirds, of the Burlington capital stock. The two companies thereupon bought 1,075,772 shares, or 96.79 per cent of the whole, and in payment therefor issued their joint collateral trust bonds and scrip to the amount of $215,154,000. The price that they had to pay was high. The market value of the shares was less than 180, but the Burlington directors and stockholders would not sell for less than 200, and that was the price paid. Mr.

[1] Pyle's *Life of James J. Hill*, vol. II, pp. 141–42.

Hill, however, believed that he had made a good bargain.

> It is true [he said], we pay a great price for the property. This could not be avoided. . . . The Burlington road had a very heavy sinking fund. For many years the miles of main track — something more than 8000 miles — had a bonded debt, less the sinking fund, of $15,800 a mile, and its stock was about $13,000 a mile. Take the Burlington stock at 200, and add to it the bonded debt per mile of the road, and it would give the average cost of the Burlington about $42,000 a mile, which is about what it cost us; that is, $10,000 or $12,000 less a mile than any of these granger roads are selling at on the market. In other words, the Burlington was the cheapest property altogether and reached the points we desired to reach; and it would cost us less money per mile than it would to have acquired any other.

Satisfied that they had checkmated the Union Pacific and made the Burlington safe, Mr. Morgan sailed for Italy, while Mr. Hill went to the Pacific Coast to look after his interests there. Harriman and Schiff, in the meantime, were swiftly and secretly carrying out their plan to get control of the Northern Pacific by buying more than half its capital stock. The first purchases seem to have been made by Kuhn, Loeb & Co. for firm account; but on the 15th of April they turned over to Mr. Harriman all that they had accumulated — 150,000 shares of the common and 100,000 shares of the preferred — and thenceforward bought steadily and aggressively for account of the Union Pacific. When they began buying, early in April, Northern Pacific shares were selling at 102 for the common and 101 for the preferred; but under the influence of their purchases, together with a large speculative demand from other sources, quotations gradually advanced, on enormous transactions, to 131 for the common and 109 for the preferred.

This speculation in Northern Pacific shares was not regarded, at the time, as anything extraordinary. Nobody suspected that the Union Pacific was accumulating the stock, and the general impression seemed to be that it was being bought by brokers, or by the general public, in anticipation of the enhanced value that it would have as a result of the Burlington purchase. Even the Northern Pacific people took this view, and regarding such anticipations as too sanguine, they sold their holdings, in order to take advantage of what seemed to them absurdly high prices. Mr. Hill himself did not take the possibility of losing control of the Northern Pacific into serious consideration. In speaking of it afterward he said:

As I remember it, one of our directors raised the question that inasmuch as the purchase of the Burlington stock, and the creation of a bond to pay for it, involved the joint and several liability of the entire amount of the purchase, it was a matter of consequence to the Great

Northern to know that the Northern Pacific would not pass into the hands of people who might be interested in other directions — in developing in other directions or other sections of the country; and I remember I answered that, with what my friends held at that time, and what Morgan & Co. held, we would have somewhere in the neighborhood of 35 or 40 millions of the stock out of a total of 155 millions, which is larger than is usually held in any of the larger companies. I did not think, at the time, that it was at all likely that anybody would undertake to buy in the market the control of 155 millions of stock.[1]

Hill's friends were as unaware of Mr. Harriman's operations as Hill himself was, and in many cases they played directly into their adversaries' hands by selling their stock to brokers who were buying for Kuhn, Loeb & Co. One large holder, for example, sold to them 35,000 shares in a single lot. Even the Northern Pacific Company, tempted by the high prices, sold its own stock. As late as the 2d of May, one of its subsidiary corporations, which happened to have in its treasury 13,000 Northern Pacific shares, sold them by direction of the Northern Pacific board itself. So unsuspecting were Morgan & Co. that on the same day they sold 10,000 shares which had happened to come into their hands in the ordinary course of business. All of this stock, or most of it, went directly to Kuhn, Loeb & Co., who were buying for Harriman and the Union Pacific.

[1] Pyle's *Life of James J. Hill*, vol. II, p. 144.

Toward the last of April, Mr. Hill finally took alarm. He happened, just then, to be in Seattle, and noticing in the market reports the enormous transactions in Northern Pacific stock and the rapid advance in the quotations of both common and preferred, he felt a premonition of impending trouble. He did not know what had happened, or what was likely to happen; but inasmuch as his ally, Mr. Morgan, was in Europe, he thought that he himself ought to be in New York, where he could investigate the exhibition of fireworks in Northern Pacific shares, find out what caused it, and follow closely the course of events. He therefore called upon the operating officials of the Great Northern to give him at once the fastest possible special train to St. Paul with unlimited right of way over everything. The superintendent of the western division furnished the "special" immediately and said to the locomotive engineer: "The road is yours to St. Paul; everything else on the line will be held up to let you pass." The train pulled out of Seattle with a clear track ahead of it and made the quickest run to the Mississippi River that had ever been made up to that time.

Mr. Hill arrived in New York on the afternoon of Friday, May 3d, and went at once to the office of Kuhn, Loeb & Co. to see Mr. Schiff.[1] In reply to an

[1] Hill and Schiff were old personal friends and the latter had been a director in the Great Northern Company.

inquiry as to the meaning of the rapid rise in Northern Pacific shares, Schiff informed Hill that Kuhn, Loeb & Co. were buying them on orders from the Union Pacific. "But," said Hill, "you can't get control. The Great Northern, Morgan, and my friends were recently holding $35,000,000 or $40,000,000 of Northern Pacific stock, and so far as I know none of it has been sold." "That may be," replied Schiff, "but we've got a lot of it. You secretly bought the Chicago, Burlington & Quincy and refused to give us a fair share; now we're going to see if we can't get a share by purchasing a controlling interest in the Northern Pacific."

Hill, after a brief talk, left the office, saying that he did not believe it could be done. He evidently feared, however, that it *might* be done, because on the following day, after making further investigations, he went to Robert Bacon, of the firm of Morgan & Co., told him that the situation was critical, and suggested that it might be well to cable J. Pierpont Morgan, who was then in Italy, for authority to buy at least 150,000 shares of Northern Pacific stock, preferably the common, which, for purposes of control, was more valuable than the preferred. The cablegram was sent to Morgan after the close of the Stock Exchange, Saturday, May 4th.

But if Hill was anxious with regard to the outcome of the contest, Harriman was hardly less so. Kuhn, Loeb & Co. had advised him, Friday night, that they had bought, for Union Pacific account, about 370,000 shares of the common stock of the Northern Pacific Company and about 420,000 shares of the preferred, making a total of approximately $79,000,000. This was a clear majority of the two classes of stock taken together, but it lacked 30,000 or 40,000 shares of a majority in the common taken separately. This deficiency in the common gave Mr. Harriman a feeling of uneasiness, which he afterward expressed in the following words:

On the morning of Saturday, May 4th, I was at home, ill. We had somewhat over $42,000,000 of the preferred shares of the Northern Pacific, or a clear majority of that issue, and somewhat over $37,000,000 of the common shares, which lacked being a majority of the common by about 40,000 shares. But we had a majority of the entire capital stock, as represented by both the common and preferred shares, and I had been competently advised, and was convinced, that this holding was sufficient to enable us to control the Company. Nevertheless, the fact that the Northern Pacific could, on the 1st of January following, retire the preferred shares, of which we had a majority, bothered me somewhat, and I felt that we ought not to leave open to them any chance of retiring our preferred stock and leaving us with a minority interest in the common stock, or involving us in litigation about it.

Some of our friends, however, felt that our position was secure enough, and that it would be foolish to go in and buy more Northern Pacific stock at the prices which then prevailed. Nevertheless, I made up my mind that we should have a majority of the common shares, and on that morning I called up Heinsheimer (one of the partners in the firm of Kuhn, Loeb & Co.) and gave him an order to buy, at the market, 40,000 shares of Northern Pacific common for my account. He said: "All right"; and as dealings that day in Northern Pacific common shares continued to be very heavy, I felt that, come what might, I had control of Northern Pacific, common stock and all.

On Monday, the 6th of May, Northern Pacific came strong from London and opened with a burst of activity in the Street; and having had no confirmation from Kuhn, Loeb & Co. of the purchase of the 40,000 shares of Northern Pacific which I had ordered on Saturday morning, I called Heinsheimer up and asked him why I had gotten no report of the execution of my order. He told me that before giving out the order he had to reach Schiff, who was at the synagogue. Schiff instructed him not to execute the order and said that he (Schiff) would be responsible. I then knew that matters were in a serious way and that the whole object of our work might be lost. Meanwhile, the day (Monday) had become so advanced, and prices of Northern Pacific shares had gone so high that I realized the impossibility of buying, in such a market, 40,000 shares of stock. So I determined to go down and see Schiff, find out what it was all about, and fight the question out with what material I had in hand.[1]

Schiff's decision to ignore Harriman's order was based on the belief — which is understood to have been shared by James Stillman — that inasmuch as

[1] As related by Mr. Harriman to G. W. Batson.

the Union Pacific had a clear majority of *all* the shares of the Northern Pacific, taking common and preferred together, it would be unnecessary and wasteful to buy any more. But this proved to be a tactical mistake. If Harriman had been well enough to go downtown and see Schiff personally, his influence and his arguments might have overcome the banker's reluctance to make further purchases; but it must not be forgotten that the time available for deliberation and action, on that critical Saturday morning, was short. There were only a few hours in which business could be transacted before the Stock Exchange closed at noon; Schiff had neither time nor opportunity to consult Harriman, and he was forced to decide quickly on his own best judgment. But the consequences were unfortunate. Before Harriman found out, on Monday, that his order to Kuhn, Loeb & Co. had not been executed, the opportunity to get a majority of the common stock had passed.

Some time in the course of Sunday, May 5th, Robert Bacon received a cablegram from J. P. Morgan authorizing him to go ahead and buy 150,000 shares of Northern Pacific common at the market. Immediately the Hill-Morgan forces took the field. With the reopening of the Stock Exchange, Monday morning, their brokers swarmed over the floor, bidding eagerly for Northern Pacific common, and taking all that could be had at prices that advanced steadily from 110 to 130. Tuesday they continued this aggressive buying, and ran the price of the common up to 149¾ — an advance of nearly forty points in two business days.[1] But they attained their object. Before Tuesday night they were in possession of the 150,000 shares that Morgan had authorized them to buy. With this addition to their holdings, the Morgan-Hill interests had something like 30,000 shares more of the common than they needed; but they had only a minority in the preferred, and lacked also a majority in the common and preferred taken together. Of the whole capital stock of the Northern Pacific Company, Harriman and the Union Pacific owned 781,080 shares, or about 6000 more than one half. As both classes of stock had equal voting rights, this would enable Harriman to choose a majority of the board of directors at the next election; but whether it would give him power enough to prevent the retirement of the preferred shares, in which he had preponderating strength, was an unsettled question. So far as control of the common was concerned, he had lost the fight.

Hill's biographer attributes this partial defeat of the Union Pacific plan to Harriman's "oversight" in not taking into account the right of the Northern

[1] *Commercial & Financial Chronicle*, May 18, 1901.

Pacific Company to retire its preferred stock and thus to leave him with only a minority of the common.[1] But Harriman did not overlook this possibility. On the contrary; it was precisely for this reason that he ordered Kuhn, Loeb & Co. to buy 40,000 more shares of the common on the morning of Saturday, May 4th. He believed, with Schiff, that the holders of a majority of *all* the stock — common and preferred together — could prevent the retirement of the preferred;[2] but he did not wish to take any chances of litigation over this question. He wanted to be *sure*, and his failure to make sure was due not to oversight, but to accident. Illness alone kept him away from the firing line when the contest reached its final and decisive stage. In his absence and without his knowledge his bankers ceased buying, while Morgan & Co. went into the field, practically unopposed, and secured 150,000 shares.

Although the contest for control of the Northern Pacific and the Burlington was carried on with more or less secrecy and was imperfectly understood by the general public, the rapid and sensational advance of forty points in Northern Pacific common created

[1] Pyle's *Life of James J. Hill*, vol. II, pp. 141 and 153.

[2] This belief was based on the unanimous opinion of five eminent authorities on corporation law whom Mr. Harriman had consulted. (*Edward Henry Harriman*, by Otto H. Kahn, New York, 1911, p. 32.)

great excitement in Wall Street, and not only led to an avalanche of "short" selling of the virtually "cornered" stock, but brought on, two days later, the memorable Northern Pacific panic.

CHAPTER XII

NORTHERN PACIFIC PANIC

THE contest for control of the Burlington, which ultimately developed into a struggle for possession of the Northern Pacific, ended, so far as the competing interests were concerned, on the afternoon of Tuesday, May 7th. Each of the contending parties then believed that it had won a victory over the other. Harriman and Schiff were sure that they owned a majority of all the Northern Pacific stock, taking common and preferred shares together, while Morgan and Hill were equally confident that they had a safe majority of the common, which would enable them to retire the preferred and thus leave the Union Pacific with only a minority holding in the capital that would then remain. Both sides, therefore, ceased buying. Their purchases, however, had given a great impetus to speculation in Northern Pacific common. Nobody knew, with certainty, who was accumulating this stock, or why it had risen from 112 to 149¾ in less than a week; but more than half of the public believed that the common shares were selling far above their intrinsic value and that they must soon fall to something like their normal level. Scores of speculators, therefore, sold them "short," with the expectation of being able to buy them for delivery, a few days later, at much lower figures.[1] In this expectation, however, they were grievously disappointed. Northern Pacific common instead of declining, made a further advance of more than fifty points, simply because everybody wanted it while few brokers had any of it for sale. When, therefore, the "shorts" were called upon to deliver, they found it almost impossible to buy or borrow shares enough to meet their urgent needs. Prices continued to advance; money was scarce and hard to get, and, in order to escape involuntary bankruptcy, scores of brokers were forced to sell their other stocks, at ruinous prices, and use the proceeds in buying Northern Pacific. This, of course, depressed the

[1] For the benefit of readers who are not familiar with Wall Street operations, it may perhaps be well to explain that when a dealer sells stock "short," he sells what he does not own, with the expectation of buying it later at a lower price. By the rules of the Stock Exchange he must make delivery to the purchaser on the next day after the sale, or be declared insolvent. If, however, the stock that he has sold does not fall low enough so that he can "cover" at a profit, he borrows it from a dealer who happens to have it, paying the latter a specified sum for the accommodation. With this borrowed stock he makes delivery to the purchaser, and then, until he decides to buy the stock of which he is "short," he continues borrowing it from day to day at whatever rates may be current. It sometimes happens that the whole marketable supply of a particular security has been bought by one or two persons, or groups, who hold it, either for speculative purposes or for control. In the technical language of the Street such a stock is said to be "cornered," and dealers who must buy or borrow it may be compelled to pay for it almost any price that the owners may choose to demand.

general market, unsettled confidence, and eventually brought on one of the worst panics that Wall Street had ever known.

As early as Wednesday noon it became apparent that trouble was impending, and on Thursday, May 9th, when the storm finally broke, Northern Pacific common sold up to $1000 a share, while other standard securities were offered at half their intrinsic value. United States Steel, for example, declined from 46 to 24; Atchison, Topeka & Santa Fé from 76 to 43, and Delaware & Hudson from 163 to 105. Call money, meanwhile, was bid up to 60 per cent, and little could be had even at that exorbitant rate. Before noon on Thursday nearly half the brokerage houses in Wall Street were technically insolvent, simply because they could neither buy nor borrow the Northern Pacific shares that they had sold short.

Such a state of affairs threatened general ruin, and all the conservative, constructive forces in the financial district were set in motion to support the market and reëstablish confidence. At the suggestion of Frederick T. Tappan, fifteen prominent banks formed a "pool," or temporary syndicate, to relieve the money market by loaning about $20,000,000, and at the same time several other banks, including Morgan & Co. and Kuhn, Loeb & Co., agreed not to call for the delivery of short-sold shares of Northern

Pacific stock that day. A little later, Mr. Schiff, with the approval of Mr. Harriman, made a proposition to Robert Bacon, of J. P. Morgan & Co., that the "shorts" be permitted to settle with both firms at $150 a share for all the Northern Pacific common that they had sold to these firms. Mr. Bacon, fearing that if he "let up" on the "shorts" he might lose a considerable part of the stock that was coming to Morgan & Co., seemed, at first, a little reluctant to acquiesce in this proposition; but he finally saw the wisdom of it and agreed to it. As a large part of the short stock had been sold to one firm or the other, and as $150 a share was a very reasonable price for it at that time, the proposal was gladly accepted by the "shorts," and did much to relieve the tension and quiet the excitement.

Morgan & Co., as well as Harriman and Schiff, "had done what they could," and each side believed itself sure of victory. But the fact that the market was bare of Northern Pacific, while buyers were still eager to get it, sent prices rocketing. Many shareholders in the West and South sold their shares, but could not deliver immediately. Speculators who sold short saw the price jump, point after point, but could not furnish the stock to stop their losses. But it was not what was ordinarily called a "corner." Nobody was trying to force prices up that he might sell at a profit. "How could we sell at any price?" said Mr. Hill; "we were investors, not speculators, I never bought or sold a share of stock for gambling purposes in my life, and I don't want to earn money wrung from people by a 'corner.'" [1]

Mr. Hill, however, was unjust to Mr. Harriman — perhaps inadvertently so — in saying that Union Pacific interests "bid Northern Pacific up until there was the largest stock 'corner' ever known." [2] This is an error. Harriman and Kuhn, Loeb & Co. did not "bid Northern Pacific up" until they created a "corner." They made no purchases after Friday, May 3d, and the "corner" was not established until four days later. If anybody created it, Morgan & Co. did so by buying 150,000 shares after Harriman and Schiff had gone out of the market. It was Robert Bacon, not Kuhn, Loeb & Co., who bid the stock up from 112 to 149¾ in the attempt to get control of it.

As a matter of fact the "corner," as the "Commercial & Financial Chronicle" said at the time, was largely if not wholly accidental, and was the result of wild and irrational speculation on the part of the general public.[3] Mr. Hill compared it to an Indian

[1] Pyle's *Life of James J. Hill*, vol. II, p. 151.

[2] Public statement made by Mr. Hill at the time of the formation of the Northern Securities Company.

[3] *Commercial & Financial Chronicle*, May 18, 1901.

"ghost dance." In an interview published in the New York newspapers of Thursday afternoon, May 9th, he was quoted as saying:

All I can do is to liken it to a ghost dance. The Indians begin their dance and don't know why they are doing it. They whirl about until they are almost crazy. It is so when these Wall Street people get the speculative fever. Perhaps they imagine they have a motive in that they see two sets of powerful interests which may be said to be clashing. Then these outsiders, without rhyme or reason, rush in on one side or the other. They could not tell you why they make their choice, but in they go, and the result is such as has been seen here for the past few days.

Mr. Harriman's description of the situation, and particularly his own relation to it, was given in the following words:

Our holdings [of Northern Pacific stock] were all acquired prior to the supposed contest between Morgan & Co. and ourselves. During the days of the panic we did not buy any Northern Pacific stock, nor give orders for any. Many of our shares had been bought in Germany, Holland, or England, for delivery in New York, and the certificates were on their way to their destination. Meanwhile the agents of the foreign sellers were making their deliveries by using stock borrowed from other people. Then, when the supposed contest took place and other parties bought Northern Pacific at very high prices and demanded immediate delivery, the agents of these European sellers had great difficulty in getting stock to fill their contracts. But, in every case, we gave them all the time they needed. We were not in the supposed contest and had no hand in it.[1]

On the day after the panic, brokers in Wall Street were in a state of complete nervous prostration from the strain of anxiety and apprehension; but there were few failures, money soon became comparatively easy again, and the stock market returned to something like its normal state. Millions had been made and lost, and scores of firms had been threatened with ruin; but the panic was local, rather than general, and the country at large was little affected.

So far as possession of the Northern Pacific was concerned, the situation remained substantially unchanged. Hill and Morgan held a majority of the common shares, while Harriman and the Union Pacific owned a majority of the preferred, as well as of both classes of stock taken together. Owing, however, to certain peculiar conditions, neither of the contending parties could regard its hold of the property as absolutely secure. The plan of Morgan and Hill was to retire the preferred shares on the 1st of the next January and thus leave Harriman and the Union Pacific with only a minority holding in the common.[2] There was a question, however, whether

[1] As related by Mr. Harriman to G. W. Batson.

[2] In the reorganization of the Northern Pacific Company in 1896, the right was reserved "to retire this [the preferred] stock, in whole or in part, at par, from time to time, upon any 1st day of January during the next twenty years."

the board of directors then existing (in May, 1901) would have power to do this. If not, Harriman would be able to prevent it, because, at the annual meeting of stockholders on the first Tuesday in October, he, holding a majority of the whole capital stock, could elect directors enough to give him control of the board, and then this newly constituted board would refuse to retire the preferred shares. In order to avoid this contingency, Morgan and Hill proposed to have the annual meeting of stockholders postponed until after January 1, 1902, so as to prevent Harriman from electing any new directors friendly to the Union Pacific, until after the preferred stock had been retired. There was grave doubt, however, whether the board of directors then existing (in May, 1901) would have legal authority either to retire the preferred stock, or to postpone the annual meeting so as to prolong the term of its own existence. Mr. Harriman consulted five eminent legal authorities in different parts of the United States and they all unanimously agreed that the existing board could not lawfully retire the preferred stock, nor, without the consent of a majority of the shareholders, postpone the annual meeting to another year. If this opinion proved to be sound, Harriman, having a majority of the whole capital stock, could elect in October a board of directors friendly to the Union Pacific, and thus prevent Morgan and Hill from getting control through the retirement of the preferred stock.

In order, however, to avoid further controversy, Harriman and Schiff finally decided that if they could bring about a compromise which would safeguard the interests of the Union Pacific by giving that company adequate representation on the Northern Pacific and Burlington boards, it would be better to do this than to keep the affairs of three companies unsettled pending the outcome of long litigation. As Mr. Hill's biographer has said:

> Nothing was to be gained for either side by fighting. Both might have continued to tear up Wall Street and injure large property interests including their own. They could have engaged in endless litigation, which would have cost a lot of money without materially altering anything. They might have maintained their divided ownership and kept up a tug-of-war until the rope broke. The end of that would be two pieces of rope and two parties covered with bruises from severe falls. After all their animosities, and with all that they had done or left undone, it has to be remembered that on both sides there were big men. They were big not only by the measurement of achievement, but also because they were not actuated by a blind, vindictive desire just to crush and kill. They had already accepted, not merely as a theory, but as a conviction, the necessity of community of interest to a certain extent. Recent events had broadened and instructed their view. Things being as they were, they were ready for agreement.[1]

[1] Pyle's *Life of James J. Hill*, vol. II, pp. 153–54. Mr. Harriman

The fact that there never had been any personal animosity between Hill and Harriman made it easier to bring about a compromise than it would have been if they had hated each other. Working, as they did, in practically the same general field, it was almost inevitable that their business interests should clash; but throughout their controversies their personal relations were those of mutual respect and esteem. In a talk with the well-known journalist, Frederick Palmer, soon after the Northern Pacific contest, Mr. Harriman expressed the belief that Hill was not personally hostile to him. "Anyhow," he said, "he calls me 'Ed.'" Eight years later, when Mr. Harriman died, Mr. Hill, in paying a tribute of respect to his character, said:

His properties are in fine shape, but his place at the head of them will be hard to fill. I have done a good deal of business with him, and some of it was pretty strenuous at times, but we were good personal friends throughout. I had a very high regard for Mr. Harriman personally.[1]

never doubted that he had lawful control of the Northern Pacific Company and that if he had fought the case through the courts he would practically have obtained possession of the company. As Mr. Otto H. Kahn has said: "He held, beyond any question of doubt, the winning hand; but instead of boldly playing it, he contented himself with a drawn battle, and with terms of peace which gave to the other side the appearance of victory. The course that he pursued, however, showed his wisdom, foresight, and self-restraint, and his practice of never using any greater force than was necessary for the substantial accompslihment of his object." (*Edward Henry Harriman*, by Otto H. Kahn, in New York, 1911, pp. 32–33.)

[1] *New York Sun*, September 10, 1909.

Throughout the early part of May, 1901, conferences were held, either at Mr. Harriman's office or the office of Morgan & Co., and late in that month Kuhn, Loeb & Co. authorized publication of the following statement.

It is officially announced that an understanding has been reached between Northern Pacific and Union Pacific interests under which the composition of the Northern Pacific board will be left in the hands of J. P. Morgan personally. Certain names have already been suggested, not now to be made public, which will especially be recognized as representatives of the common interests. It is asserted that complete and permanent harmony will result under the plan adopted between all interests involved.

On the 31st of May, at a final conference held in the Metropolitan Club, the "understanding" above referred to was embodied in a written memorandum which was signed by Kuhn, Loeb & Co., Morgan, Harriman, and Hill. By the terms of this memorandum Mr. Morgan was empowered to select directors to fill vacancies on the NorthernPacific board with William K. Vanderbilt as referee in case of further disagreement. Mr. Harriman and a number of gentlemen friendly, or at least not hostile, to him were to become directors of both the Northern Pacific and the Burlington, and the Union Pacific was to have certain trackage rights over the Northern

Pacific between Portland and Seattle. So far as competition between the Union Pacific and the Hill roads was concerned, the Burlington was to remain neutral, and it was not to embark in any new enterprise in the West — such as building through to the Pacific — without the consent and approval of Harriman and the Union Pacific Company.

On the 17th of July, Mr. Morgan, in the following letter to Hill, Harriman, and Schiff, gave the names of the gentlemen whom he had selected to fill vacancies in the Northern Pacific board:

New York, July 17, 1901

GENTLEMEN:

In accordance with a memorandum signed by you under date of May 31, 1901, under which the composition of the Board of Directors of the Northern Pacific Railway Company was to be left in my hands, I beg to advise you of my conclusion as follows:

I nominate the following gentlemen as the new members of the Board to fill the vacancies to be created:

Mr. James J. Hill, President of the Great Northern Railway Company;

Mr. E. H. Harriman, Chairman of the Executive Committee of the Union Pacific Railway Company;

Mr. William Rockefeller, Director of the Chicago, Milwaukee & St. Paul Railway Company;

Mr. H. McK. Twombley, Director of the Chicago & Northwestern Railway Company;

Mr. Samuel Rea, Vice-President of the Pennsylvania Railway Company;

and I would suggest that the attention of the Board be

called to the advisability of arranging for these gentlemen to assume their duties as Directors of the Company as soon as possible, without awaiting the annual election.

It is my opinion that a Board thus constituted will contain within itself the elements best adapted for the formulation of the plan referred to in said memorandum, in connection with Mr. William K. Vanderbilt named therein as Referee. Every important interest will have its representative, who will be brought into close touch with the situation as a whole, and there should be no difficulty in reaching a conclusion that will be fair and just to all concerned and tend to the establishment of permanent harmony among the different lines. To this end I shall be very glad to coöperate in such manner as will seem desirable.

I am, Gentlemen

Very truly yours

J. Pierpont Morgan

Of the gentlemen thus chosen, Rockefeller and Twombley were friendly to the Union Pacific Company, while only Mr. Hill was certainly hostile to it.

In this final settlement of the contest, Mr. Harriman did not gain all that he had hoped for, because the two roads that he wanted remained in the possession of his adversaries. Inasmuch, however, as he himself secured a seat in the directing board of each, he guarded himself against secret, aggressive action on the part of either, and thus made the interests of the Union Pacific reasonably safe.[1]

[1] Mr. Harriman became not only a director on the board of the Northern Pacific, but also a member of its executive committee.

The nearly successful attempt of Mr. Harriman to secure control of the Northern Pacific startled and alarmed not only J. Pierpont Morgan, who was the person most interested in that corporation, but also Mr. Hill and the little group of men who had coöperated with him in the building of the Great Northern. They regarded themselves as responsible for the future of the systems that they had created or reorganized; they had a natural feeling of pride in them, and they wished to have carried out, even after their own retirement or death, the plans they had formed for their future management and operation. They determined, therefore, to bind them together in such a safe and permanent way as to ensure unified control and, at the same time, prevent them from falling into the hands of rival corporations or alien interests. Mr. Hill was the first to think of and suggest the idea of forming a holding company, to be known as the Northern Securities Company, which should acquire the stock of both the Great Northern and Northern Pacific and issue in lieu thereof stock certificates of its own. Such a company would have, including the stock of the recently acquired Burlington, a capitalization of three or four hundred million dollars, and would be so large and strong that, in all probability, no alien or hostile corporation could ever get control of it by purchasing a majority of its shares.

In a letter to a friend written in May, 1901, soon after the Northern Pacific contest, Mr. Hill outlined his plan as follows:

The cost of administering the affairs of a holding company would be practically *nil*, as it would only draw dividends on the shares held by it and divide the money so received by check to its own shareholders. You will see how strong the holding company would be. It would control the Great Northern and Northern Pacific, and those two roads would control by ownership the Chicago, Burlington & Quincy. The holding company could also, if at any time it seemed best, hold the shares of coal or other companies which, while of value in themselves and of value to the railway company for the traffic they would afford, the charters of the railway companies are not broad enough to enable them to hold with safety. I think the completion of the plan of which the above is a fair outline would greatly enhance and insure the value of every share we hold in the railway companies. For myself, I feel that the future would be secure, and we would have a certainty in the situation, and the control of those properties safe. Unless we do something of this kind, we will always be subject to attacks like the recent one to secure control of one or other of our properties.[1]

In a somewhat later statement, Mr. Hill said:

We were particularly anxious to put a majority of that stock [the Northern Pacific] where it could not be raided again as it had been. We wanted to put it in a corporation that was not a railroad company — a company that would hold it as an investment — and the

[1] Pyle's *Life of James J. Hill*, vol. II, p. 166.

larger the company the more difficult it would be to secure a majority of it. . . . We were advised that it would be safer with the shares held by an investment company, the stock of which could only be held by individuals, or by corporations that were not railroad companies, and to that extent we would be more free from such raids by interests that were anxious to destroy or restrict the growth of the country — such raids as had been made by the Union Pacific interests so-called.[1]

In saying that the Union Pacific interests were anxious to "destroy or restrict the growth of the country," Mr. Hill was not quite fair to Mr. Harriman. The latter had no intention of destroying or restricting. He tried to secure control of the Northern Pacific, primarily, as a means of getting the share in the Burlington which Mr. Hill had refused to give him; but he had no thought of injuring the Northern Pacific, or of restricting the growth of the country tributary to it. On the contrary; his aims were, first, to get a share in the Burlington, and, second, to make the Northern Pacific stronger and more useful than it ever had been before. If he had succeeded, he would have done with the Northern Pacific precisely what he was already doing with the Union Pacific and the Southern Pacific; that is, he would have spent tens of millions of dollars in improving it and making it better able to serve the country through which it ran. When he testified as

[1] Pyle's *Life of James J. Hill*, vol. II, pp. 164–65.

a witness before the Interstate Commerce Commission in 1907 he said:

> If we had not had the power to buy the Southern Pacific with the credit of the Union Pacific, the country tributary to the Southern Pacific would have been ten years behind what it is now. If we had acquired the Northern Pacific, the Northern Pacific territory would have been ten years ahead of what it is now.[1]

Mr. Harriman's genius was essentially and fundamentally constructive, and no railroad that he ever acquired suffered injury from his management or control. Eight years after his death, when the securities of all railroads had been depressed by hostile legislation and the restrictions of an incompetent Commission, the shares of the Southern Pacific and the Union Pacific were selling respectively at 115 and 122, while the shares of the Northern Pacific and the Great Northern were offered at 86 and 85. Traffic statistics, moreover, show that the country served by the Hill system certainly did not develop more rapidly than the country served by the Harriman lines. Mr. Harriman planned and built with the future of the country constantly in mind, and the prices of his stocks, as well as the prosperity of his territory, show how sagacious and far-seeing

[1] Hearings before the Interstate Commerce Commission in the matter of "Consolidation and Combination of Carriers," February 25–27, 1907, p. 163.

his plans were and how enduring his influence has been.

The plan of the Northern Securities Company, although suggested and advocated by Mr. Hill, was practically put in shape by John S. Kennedy (representing the Dutch committee of bondholders); George F. Baker (a friend and associate of Mr. Hill); Willis D. James; W. P. Clough; Samuel Thorne and G. W. Perkins (of the firm of J. P. Morgan & Co.).

In a signed statement published in the St. Paul "Globe" in December, Mr. Hill explained the purposes of the company in detail as follows:

Several of the gentlemen who have long been interested in the Great Northern Railway and its predecessor, the St. Paul, Minneapolis & Manitoba Company, and who have always been among its largest shareholders, but not the holders of a majority of its stock, whose ages are from seventy to eighty-six years, have desired to combine their individual holdings in corporate form, and in that way secure permanent protection for their interests and a continuation of the policy and management which had done so much for the development of the Northwest and the enhancement of their own property in the Northwest and elsewhere. Out of this desire has grown the Northern Securities Company.

It became necessary (in order to prevent the Northern Pacific from passing under the control of the Union Pacific interests and with it the joint control of the Burlington) to pay off the seventy-five millions of Northern Pacific preferred. The enormous amount of cash required for this purpose, from a comparatively small number of men, made it necessary for them to act together in a large and permanent manner through the medium of a corporation; and the Northern Securities Company afforded them the means of accomplishing this object without the necessity of creating a separate company to finance the transaction for the Northern Pacific. . . . The Northern Securities Company is organized to deal in high-class securities; to hold the same for the benefit of its shareholders, and to advance the interests of the corporations whose securities it owns. Its powers do not include the operation of railways, banking, or mining, nor the buying and selling of securities or properties of others on commission; it is purely an investment company; and the object of its creation was simply to enable those who hold its stock to continue their respective interests in association together; to prevent such interests from being scattered by death or otherwise, and to provide against such attacks as had been made upon the Northern Pacific by a rival and competing interest.[1]

Although the Northern Securities Company was suggested by Mr. Hill in the spring of 1901, and a plan for its organization drawn up by him and his associates a few months later, it did not actually come into existence until late in the fall. On the 12th of November, 1901, it was duly incorporated under the laws of the State of New Jersey with a capital of $400,000,000.

Its first board of directors consisted of fifteen members, six of whom represented the Northern

[1] St. Paul *Globe*, December 22, 1901.

Pacific, four the Great Northern, three (including Mr. Harriman) the Union Pacific, and two not representative of any specific interest. Mr. Hill was unanimously chosen president of the new corporation, and all holders of Great Northern and Northern Pacific stock (including the Union Pacific) were invited to exchange their shares for the stock of the Securities Company on the basis of $180 for every $100 surrendered (in the case of the Great Northern) and $115 for every $100 (in the case of the Northern Pacific). About 76 per cent of the Great Northern stockholders and 96 per cent of the Northern Pacific stockholders turned in their shares for exchange. Mr. Harriman surrendered all the Northern Pacific stock that he had acquired in his attempt to get control of that road, and received in lieu thereof about $82,500,000 in the shares of the new corporation.

If there had been no interference from outside, the three companies would probably have worked together more or less harmoniously under the terms of the Metropolitan Club agreement and the charter of the Northern Securities Company. Unfortunately however, the latter was almost immediately attacked in the courts, on the ground that it was an attempt to restrain trade in violation of the Sherman Anti-Trust Law. Owing partly to popular ignorance or prejudice and partly to political demagogism, the public mind at that time, particularly in the North-west, was obsessed with the idea that combinations and agreements among railroad companies were made for the sole purpose of advancing or maintaining rates, and that the only remedy for this alleged evil was to enforce unrestricted competition in every case where one railroad ran parallel to another. The formation of the Northern Securities Company was generally regarded as a covert scheme to extort more money from the people by restricting or preventing competition among the Hill and Harriman lines.[1] As we now know, the creation of the holding company was not related in any way either to competition or to rates. It had its origin in a perfectly legitimate attempt, on the part of a number of large shareholders, to keep their associated interests together in the event of their retirement or death, and to prevent seizure or control of their properties by outside corporations, or groups, through the secret purchase of stock. The State authorities of Minnesota, how-

[1] "As a matter of fact, the Great Northern and Northern Pacific did not compete, to an appreciable extent, with each other, and still less with the Union Pacific. Only three per cent of the total interstate traffic was subject to control by them individually in the making of rates. There was competition, of course, for the Oriental trade, but it did not affect at all the people in the Northwest, where only an inappreciable portion of the total interstate traffic was strictly competitive." (*History of the Northern Securities Case*, by B. H. Meyer, University of Wisconsin Bulletin, p. 247.)

ever, as well as the general public, disregarded or disbelieved this explanation of the reasons for combination, and on the 7th of January, 1902, the State of Minnesota began suit against the Securities Company in the United States Circuit Court at St. Paul, on the alleged ground that it was an illegal combination in restraint of trade. A few weeks later, the Attorney-General of the United States advised President Roosevelt that, in his opinion, the so-called "merger" of the Northern Pacific and the Great Northern violated the provisions of the Sherman Act of 1890; and on the 10th of March, 1902, the Federal Government brought suit against the Northern Securities Company, the Northern Pacific, and the Great Northern in the Circuit Court of Appeals, a tribunal consisting of four Circuit Court judges sitting as a trial court under a special Act of Congress.

The decisions in the two lower courts were diametrically opposed to each other. In the State case it was held that the formation of the Northern Securities Company did not involve any act or contract in restraint of trade, while in the Federal case the judges decided that the "Securities Company accomplishes the object which Congress has declared illegal perhaps more effectually than other forms of combination generally known in 1890 when the Anti-

Trust Law was passed." The facts that the combination might have been inspired by "wholly laudable and unselfish motives," and that it was, perhaps, "the initial and necessary step in the accomplishment of great designs," were said to make no difference. If the combination *had power* to "suppress competition between two or more parallel and competing lines of railroad engaged in interstate commerce," no matter whether it had actually exercised that power or not, it was illegal. The Northern Securities Company was, therefore, enjoined from voting stock, acquiring additional stock, paying dividends, or exercising corporate control. The principal difference in the judgments of the two lower courts was this: one held that the mere purchase of a majority of the shares of the Great Northern and Northern Pacific by the Securities Company was illegal, because it gave the holding company *power* to restrict competition and thus restrain trade; the other declared that the mere possession of power does not warrant the assumption that the power will be criminally used.[1]

Both cases were carried by appeal to the United States Supreme Court in Washington, where they were argued by some of the ablest lawyers in the

[1] The records, briefs, and arguments in these cases made about eight thousand pages, or sixteen large octavo volumes.

country. On the 14th of March, 1904, after about two years of litigation, the State case was dismissed for lack of jurisdiction, while the Federal case was decided against the railroad companies by a divided court. Five justices regarded the combination as a violation of the Sherman Anti-Trust Law, while four, including the Chief Justice, could not see in it any contract, or conspiracy — much less any act — that restrained trade, or was intended to restrain trade. Justice Harlan, who read the opinion of the majority, said that Congress, "by the Anti-Trust Act, has prescribed the rule of free competition among those engaged in interstate commerce," and any combination which, by its necessary operation, restrains, or tends to restrain, such free competition is clearly illegal. "The Government charges," Justice Harlan said, "that if the combination is not held to be in violation of the Act of Congress, then all efforts of the National Government to preserve to the people the benefits of free competition among carriers engaged in interstate commerce will be wholly unavailing; and all transcontinental lines, indeed the entire railway systems of the country, may be absorbed, merged, and consolidated, thus placing the public at the absolute mercy of the holding corporation." The majority of the Court coincided in this view and affirmed the judgment of the Circuit Court of Appeals.

The decision of the Supreme Court, it will be observed, is based almost wholly on the assertion that "Congress, by the Anti-Trust Law, has prescribed the rule of *free competition* among those engaged in interstate commerce." It is a noteworthy fact, however, that Congress, in the Sherman Act, did not use the words "free competition," or "restraint of competition," or refer to "competition" in any way whatever. The thing that it forbade was "*restraint of trade or commerce*," which may be, and generally is, a very different thing from "restraint of competition." The word "competition" is not to be found in any section of the Sherman Anti-Trust Act; it was read into that Act by the courts, on the assumption that "restraint of trade" and "restraint of competition" are synonymous expressions.

Justice Holmes, in a dissenting opinion, called attention to this wholly unwarranted assumption, and said that the words "restraint of competition" and "restraint of trade" do not have the same meaning. The latter, which has "a definite and well-established signification in the common law, means, and has always been understood to mean, a combination made by men engaged in a certain business for the purpose of keeping other men out of that business. ... The objection to trusts was not the union of former competitors, but the sinister power exercised, or supposed to be exercised, by the combination, in keeping rivals out of the business. . . . It was the ferocious extreme of competition with others, not the cessation of competition among the partners, which was the evil feared." "Much trouble is caused," Justice Holmes added, "by substituting other phrases, assumed to be equivalent, which are then argued from as if they were in the Act. The court below argued as if maintaining competition were the express purpose of the Act. The Act says nothing about competition."[1]

The minority of the Court, however, did not base its dissent wholly, or even mainly, on this unwarranted substitution of the words "restraint of competition" for the words "restraint of trade." It took the broader ground that the question in the case was "not the power of Congress to regulate *commerce*, but whether that power extends to the regulation of *ownership of stock in railroads*, which is not commerce at all." In the opinion of the minority, "The acquisition and ownership of stock in competing railroads, organized under State law by several persons, or by corporations, is not interstate commerce and therefore not subject to the control of Congress." [2]

In commenting, some years later, on the origin

[1] Senate Documents, vol. 6, 58th Congress, 2d Session.

[2] Dissenting opinion of Justice White, in which the Chief Justice and Justices Peckham and Holmes concurred.

and history of the Northern Securities Company, Dr. B. H. Meyer (afterward a member of the Interstate Commerce Commission) rightly said that its causes were "partly personal and partly economic." The personal cause was the desire of a number of aged stockholders to keep their holdings together after their retirement or death, and to prevent their properties from being seized or controlled by alien or rival interests. The largest economic cause was a desire to secure a permanent basis for the interchange of commodities between great producing sections of the United States and of the Orient.[1] Neither of these causes had anything whatever to do with interstate commerce, or with the rates to be imposed on such commerce. They related to entirely different matters.

Harriman and Hill were both deeply interested in the through traffic to and from the Orient. Harriman already had a trans-Pacific steamship line, while Hill was building on the northwestern coast two of the largest steamers in the world for the Oriental trade. Both wanted the Burlington system, because it would give them access, over a line of their own, to the cotton, provisions, and manufactures of the South and Middle West, which they hoped to exchange for tea, silks, and other products of China

[1] *A History of the Northern Securities Case*, by B. H. Meyer; University of Wisconsin Bulletin, pp. 226–27.

and Japan. The United States, at that time, had only about one-fourteenth part of the total Chinese trade. If, by providing better transportation facilities, the Pacific roads could give American producers cheaper and easier access to this great market, they certainly would not be restraining trade — they would be promoting and extending it. But they could not safely make plans for increasing America's exports to the Orient without forming a combination that would ensure certainty of supply and stability of rates. It was this, and not a desire to suppress local competition, that led Hill and Harriman to struggle for control of the Burlington, and later (by way of compromise) to join in the organization of the Northern Securities Company.

In view of the fact that, for many years, Congress and the people of the United States have made a sort of fetish of railroad competition, it may be well to repeat here that Mr. Harriman, with his synthetic and constructive mind, always favored coöperation and combination, as more advantageous both to the railroads and to the public than unrestricted competition. Indeed, in the last decade of his business career he came to be regarded as the foremost exponent of the policy of combination and consolidation. His motives were then misrepresented and his methods were described as autocratic and monopolistic;

but time has demonstrated the soundness of his ideas. The world is coming at last to see that, in the words of the first chairman of the Interstate Commerce Commission, "the more completely the whole railway system can be created as a unit, as if it were all one management, the greater will be the benefit of its service to the public and the less the liability to unfair exactions."[1]

Dr. Meyer, in his "History of the Northern Securities Case," is perfectly right in saying:

> Competition, as a regulative principle of railways, and as a force which will maintain proper relations between the railways themselves, and between the railways and the public, has failed in every country of the world where it has been given a trial. . . . I regard the application to the railways of the Sherman Anti-Trust Law of 1890 as one of the gravest errors in our legislative history. . . . If railways had been permitted to co-operate with one another, under the supervision of competent public authority, and if the Trans-Missouri and Joint-Traffic cases had never been decided, the railway situation in the United States to-day would be appreciably better than it is. . . . The undiscriminating opposition to all forms of open concerted action on the part of railways is, in my mind, the greatest single blunder in our public policy toward railways. . . . We should have cast away, more than fifty years ago, the impossible doctrine of protection of the public by railway competition.[2]

[1] Opinion of Judge Thomas M. Cooley in the Board of Trade case.

[2] *History of the Northern Securities Case*, by B. H. Meyer; University of Wisconsin Bulletin, pp. 253, 305.

CHAPTER XIII

CONTESTS WITH CLARK AND KEENE

AT no other time in Mr. Harriman's career did he undertake more important enterprises, or carry on a greater number of multifarious activities, than in the three years between 1898 and 1902. During this period he began the reconstruction of the Union Pacific; acquired control of the great Southern Pacific system and began to rebuild that; directed the recapitalization and reconstruction of the Chicago & Alton; undertook the management of the Kansas City Southern; organized and personally conducted an important scientific expedition to Alaska; planned and put up a five-story building for the Boys' Club in New York; carried on a titanic contest with J. P. Morgan and James J. Hill for control of the Northern Pacific, and finally coöperated with these railroad financiers in the organization of the Northern Securities Company, a corporation which had a capitalization of $400,000,000 and which linked together three of the most important railway systems in the West.

One might suppose that activities of such scope and magnitude would overtax the working capacity even of a superman; but Mr. Harriman was able to carry them all on successfully, and at the same time to act as president of the Southern Pacific;[1] president of the Oregon Short Line; chairman of the finance committee of the Illinois Central, and a director of the Baltimore & Ohio. His connection with the last-named road began in 1899 (when F. D. Underwood became its general manager),[2] and lasted till 1901. During this period he was not only a director, but one of the most influential members of the important committee on expenditures.

After the reorganization of the Baltimore & Ohio Company in 1899, the road was found to be urgently in need of capital betterments, and Mr. Harriman aided Vice-President Underwood in raising and expending about $32,000,000 for improvements and new equipment. In an interview many years later Mr. Underwood said: "From the time when I became associated with Mr. Harriman on the Baltimore & Ohio I knew him intimately. I was very much attached to him as well as filled with respect and admiration for his character. He helped me to get about $32,000,000 for improvements on the

[1] Elected September 26, 1901.

[2] Mr. Underwood had previously been general manager of the Minneapolis, St. Paul & Sault Ste. Marie Railway. He became general manager of the Baltimore and Ohio in January, 1899, and second vice-president about five months later. In May, 1901, he was elected president of the Erie.

B. & O. and for that assistance I have always been grateful." [1]

In addition to all the work that he accomplished between 1898 and 1902 (and perhaps by reason of such work), he acquired during this period three very powerful and influential supporters, namely, James Stillman, William Rockefeller, and H. H. Rogers. Mr. Stillman, the president of the National City Bank, had known Harriman slightly before 1898, but it was not until that time that he was brought into close business relations with him. He had, at first, a little prejudice against him, because, as he afterward said:

> A very prominent man had told me to "look out for Ed. Harriman. He is not so smart as some people think, and he is not a safe man to do business with." For that reason I steered clear of him until the matter of the Union Pacific reorganization came up. In my association with him after that time he impressed me as a remarkable man — a man of unalloyed frankness and honesty, and in all respects loyal and trustworthy. He soon showed, moreover, great money-making possibilities. [2]

[1] Speaking afterward of this partial reconstruction of the Baltimore and Ohio, Mr. Harriman said: "I put in eighteen months of hard work at it." He did not mean, of course, that he gave to it his undivided attention, but merely that for eighteen months he made it a subject of study and thought. (See "Harriman: The Colossus of Roads," by Carl Snyder; *Review of Reviews*, January, 1907, p. 48.)

[2] James Stillman, in an unpublished interview with G. W. Batson, February 9, 1911.

The National City Bank, at the time when Mr. Harriman began the reconstruction of the Union Pacific, was the bank of the Standard Oil Company, and James Stillman, its president, was very closely associated with William Rockefeller and H. H. Rogers. It was only natural, therefore, that when he became satisfied that Harriman was "a remarkable man, and a man of unalloyed frankness and honesty," he should introduce him to the Standard Oil managers. This he did about 1901, and Rockefeller and Rogers were soon afterward added to the group of influential and powerful men upon whom Harriman could confidently rely. This group, as John Moody afterward said, "certainly surpassed in financial resources any set of men in the history of the financial world." [1]

Many times in later years its members gave Harriman financial support when he needed tens of millions of dollars, in credit or cash, for the realization of his far-reaching plans.

The first time that the interests of the Harriman lines were menaced, after the purchase of the Burlington by the Northern Pacific, was in 1901, when Senator William A. Clark, of Montana, who had made a great deal of money in the Butte copper

[1] "Masters of Capital in America," by John Moody and George Kibbe Turner; *McClure's Magazine*, December, 1910, p. 347.

mines and who had ambitions in the railway field, projected a road from San Pedro and Los Angeles to Salt Lake City. This road, when completed, would not only open up a new competing route to southern California, but might, by consolidation or agreement with the Gould lines, create a new transcontinental system from the Middle States to the Pacific Coast. Such a combination, if effected, would be more or less prejudicial to the interests of both the Union Pacific and the Southern Pacific, because it would not only compete with those lines for transcontinental business in general, but would very likely take away from them a considerable part of the profitable fruit traffic between southern California and the Eastern markets. Mr. Harriman determined to avert these dangers by building a line of his own from Los Angeles to a junction with the Union Pacific at Ogden.

Upon investigation, he found that ten or twelve years earlier, the Oregon & Utah Northern Railway Company, a subsidiary of the Oregon Short Line and the Union Pacific, had begun and partly completed a road from Salt Lake to Los Angeles over this very route. The section from Salt Lake City to Milford, about two hundred miles in length, had been practically finished, while grading for the track had been carried ninety miles farther into the head of a long, narrow cañon known as the Meadow Valley Wash. In the period of financial depression that followed the panic of 1893, a part of this uncompleted line had been abandoned by the Union Pacific, while in other places the rails had been taken up and carried away for use elsewhere. Harriman was informed by his engineers that any railroad between Ogden and Los Angeles would have to follow the route of this abandoned line and pass through the hundred-mile cañon known as the Meadow Valley Wash. He therefore directed his construction forces to take possession of the old right of way of the Union Pacific through this cañon, while at the same time he gave orders to prosecute the work of construction between the cañon and southern California. Senator Clark's construction parties followed Mr. Harriman's into the Meadow Valley Wash, and after a number of physical clashes between the rival forces, both sides appealed to the courts to sustain the rights which each claimed to have in this narrow gorge. In the course of litigation it was found that, under the laws of the United States with regard to the occupancy of gorges and cañons, neither side could exclude the other, and if both persisted in building through the cañon, their respective tracks would have to cross each other twenty-six times within a comparatively short distance on account of the narrowness of the gorge.

When this state of affairs was realized, a truce was declared and negotiations were begun for a friendly settlement of the controversy. The result was a compromise between Senator Clark and the Union Pacific by virtue of which they agreed to sell to each other a half-interest in their respective properties and rights, and to form a new company for the completion of the road, which was to be called the San Pedro, Los Angeles & Salt Lake Railway. Under this agreement, which was dated July 9, 1902, the road was built and the Union Pacific acquired one half of its capital stock with joint control over its management.[1]

Hardly had this struggle ended when Mr. Harriman became involved in another contest which threatened, at one time, to deprive him of the management, if not the control, of the whole Southern Pacific system. In pursuance of a well-considered and settled policy, he had been putting all the earnings of the Southern Pacific into betterments, instead of into dividends, with the intention of so improving and upbuilding the road as to increase its usefulness as well as its earning capacity. This policy created dissatisfaction among some of the short-sighted holders of the company's shares, and in the

[1] See Hearings before the Interstate Commerce Commission in the matter of "Combination and Consolidation of Carriers," pp. 137–38, and Millar exhibits 52 and 53.

latter part of 1901, the noted speculator and Wall Street operator, James R. Keene, conceived the idea of acquiring a large amount of Southern Pacific stock and then bringing such pressure to bear upon Mr. Harriman as would induce or force him to begin the payment of dividends and thus largely increase the value of his (Keene's) holdings. He seems to have thought, at first, that he could get Mr. Harriman to join him in this speculative scheme, by tempting him to enrich himself at the expense of the road whose best interests he was in honor bound to promote. Failing, however, to make any impression upon him, Keene, in the early part of 1902, with the assistance of the Stock Exchange firm of Talbot J. Taylor & Co.,[1] formed a strong combination, or pool, for the purpose of buying from 200,000 to 400,000 shares of Southern Pacific stock and then forcing the company to begin the payment of dividends. The plan of the managers of the pool was to bring an action in the courts in which they would allege that the Southern Pacific Company was earning more than enough money to pay regular dividends, but that the directors of the Union Pacific, who had control of it, were using it for the benefit of their own road. They (the pool managers) would therefore ask for an injunction to restrain the Union Pacific Com-

[1] Taylor was Keene's son-in-law.

pany from voting its 750,000 shares of Southern Pacific stock. With these shares tied up in litigation, the pool managers hoped to be able, at the next annual meeting of Southern Pacific stockholders, to oust Harriman, elect a board of directors of their own, and begin the payment of dividends. Then, when the market value of Southern Pacific shares had largely increased, the pool members would unload their stock upon the public and pocket their profits.[1]

The history of this scheme, up to the time when litigation began, was briefly given by Mr. Harriman in the following affidavit:

One evening in the autumn of 1901, Mr. Edward Lauterbach[2] called me at my house on the telephone and stated that a friend of his had a matter of importance to communicate to me and he would like me to have an interview with the party at once. To this I assented and during the evening the card of Mr. David Lamar, accompanied by a card of Edward Lauterbach identifying him, was presented to me. I saw Mr. Lamar for about ten or fifteen minutes, during which time he stated that he had friendly relations with Mr. James R. Keene, who had a large holding in Southern Pacific and

[1] The members of the pool succeeded in getting about 240,000 shares of Southern Pacific stock; but there was no evidence that they bought it for permanent investment. They had acquired it for speculative purposes only, and were carrying a large part of it on margins. (See *New York Times*, April 12, 1914, and *Railroads: Finance and Organization*, by William Z. Ripley, p. 217.)

[2] Mr. Lauterbach was Keene's legal counsel and afterward counsel for the pool.

was contemplating some adverse action against its management, and that he (Lamar) was assured that there could be obtained an injunction against the Union Pacific somewhat similar to that obtained against the Georgia Central, in which latter case Mr. Lamar stated he had been an influential and important factor. He stated that he would like to work with me, and that if I would make an alliance which would be of some advantage to him, he had such influence over Mr. Keene that he could induce him not to instigate any adverse action against myself and allied interests. I informed Mr. Lamar that I did not see that I could do anything regarding the matter, but that if I should change my mind I would let him know. I walked to the door with him, and he was very insistent as to when I would again communicate with him. I finally took his telephone number and agreed to telephone him the next day, which I did, and stated to him that I had no desire to pursue the matter further.

About that same time I had several interviews with Mr. James R. Keene, brought about at the requests of others. Mr. Keene stated to me that he had a large holding in Southern Pacific Company stock, that he would like to join with me in purchasing the shares in the market, that he believed there could be a great deal of money made thereby and that he would act for me, either in purchasing for our joint account, or for myself if I wished it; that it would be advantageous for the Union Pacific to take all the Southern Pacific stock and issue its four per cent bonds therefor, and stated that he was an adept in carrying out successful large stock market operations and that he had shown this capacity especially in the manipulation of United States Steel stocks.

I carefully explained to Mr. Keene the requirements of the Southern Pacific properties, such as the replacement of old light rails with new heavy ones; new and heavier equipment — both motive power and cars — to replace old small-capacity ones; that in order to carry this equipment of larger capacity the track would not only require heavier rails, but additional ballasting and renewal of ties, heavier and new steel bridges to replace old light steel and wooden structures, the lengthening of present side-tracks, and additional ones, as well as additional second tracks; the remodeling and enlargement of terminals, as well as the elimination of grades and curvatures; and that all the surplus net earnings for some time would have to be applied for such requirements, improvements, and repairs; that I believed it would be a mistake to create a speculation in the shares of the stock and advance their price to a basis that would justify the buyers in expecting a dividend in the near future; that it was also necessary to make such repairs and improvements from surplus earnings, so far as they would go, in order to establish for the company a basis of credit upon which it could refund the bonded indebtedness of its subsidiary companies, a large part of which would mature in a few years, and that there was nothing between the stock and the bonded indebtedness of those companies which could be pledged to raise the necessary funds for such work, and that I believed that our method of procedure, as outlined to him, would inure to the benefit of the stockholders in the future much more advantageously than in any other way. Mr. Keene assured me that he did not want to act in any way antagonistic to me, and I stated to him that I would let him know if I saw any reason to change my mind, and he said that he would do nothing without informing me.

In the autumn of 1902, through various persons, I was informed that Mr. Edward Lauterbach and Mr. Talbot J. Taylor would make trouble for us unless we settled in some way with them. Mr. Lauterbach tried in various ways, through such third persons, to get an interview with me, and at one time called me on the telephone for such purpose, but I declined to see him, and during the autumn and winter of 1902 and the winter of 1903 I had several calls on the telephone from Mr. Lamar; but my answer through the messenger announcing the call was that I was too much engaged to talk with him. Some time in January, 1903, Mr. Lauterbach approached a mutual friend, a man of high standing and well known, and made to him statements which made him believe that it would be for my interest to take the matter up; and he telephoned and requested an interview with me. At the interview he explained to me that Lauterbach had said to him that Mr. Keene represented a pool holding about 170,000 or 175,000 shares [of Southern Pacific stock] and that Mr. Keene himself held about 70,000 shares; that they contemplated action which would make us a great deal of trouble and might be disastrous to our interests (especially laying stress upon the large expenditures we were making upon the Central Pacific portion of the Southern Pacific properties) unless we purchased such shares from them; that he would sell the pool shares at about 70 and his own shares at about 78. I explained to this friend that there was nothing in the situation which we had to fear from those people, or in the management of the company, which would justify any criticism or objection upon the part of any stockholders, and that I certainly would not be forced by fear of anything they might do into recommending a course which would be adverse to the interests of the general body of stockholders of the Southern Pacific. I had two interviews with this friend on this subject, substantially as above stated, he in the second interview having informed me that he had communicated what I had said to Mr. Lauterbach. Since that time there have been several attempts made by Mr.

Lauterbach and Mr. Lamar to take the matter up with me, but without success.[1]

After trying first to bribe Mr. Harriman by offering him a share in the profits of the speculation, and then to intimidate him by threatening legal proceedings which would cause serious "trouble," if not "disaster," Mr. Keene and his associates, in the spring of 1903, began a suit in the United States Circuit Court at Nashville for the purpose of getting an injunction which would prevent the Union Pacific Company from voting its Southern Pacific shares at the annual meeting of Southern Pacific stockholders to be held at Beechmont, Kentucky, in April of that year. Senator Foraker, of Ohio, who acted as counsel for the Keene pool, was very confident of success, and is said to have declared that if he did not win the suit he would abandon his profession; but the result showed that he was over-sanguine. When the case came to trial, Evarts, of New York, and Maxwell, of Cincinnati, who represented the Pacific roads, argued that the court had no jurisdiction, and as the court itself was of that opinion, the application for an injunction was denied. This practically ended the litigation, because on the very next day after the court rendered its decision the annual meet-

[1] Affidavit of E. H. Harriman in the suit of Talbot J. Taylor & Co. against the Southern Pacific and Union Pacific Companies.

ing of Southern Pacific stockholders was held at Beechmont and the Union Pacific Company was able to vote its shares and retain its control. This, however, would have been the result, even if the Keene pool had obtained the injunction that it sought, because Mr. Harriman, in order to guard against the possibility of an adverse decision in the court, had previously sold 300,000 shares of Southern Pacific stock to his friend and supporter, William Rockefeller, of the Standard Oil Company. These shares would not have been affected by the injunction, and Rockefeller would have voted them against the pool and in support of Mr. Harriman's policy. On the 1st of May, 1903, when the danger had passed, this stock was resold to the Union Pacific Company. Thus Mr. Harriman, through the support of his powerful group of friends, would have been able, in any event, to frustrate the plans of the strongest combination of speculators that had ever been arrayed against him.

The pool, after failing to paralyze the Union Pacific by means of an injunction, was forced to liquidate its holdings on a declining market and eventually sold its stock at a loss, it was said, of about $3,000,000. Talbot J. Taylor & Co., who had cooperated with Keene in the formation of the pool, were so weakened by its collapse that they soon afterward went out of business.[1] Thus ended one of the boldest and best-planned attempts that had ever been made to compel a railroad company to distribute in dividends money that it needed for repairs, betterments, and new equipment. It made for Mr. Harriman a new lot of enemies, but it enhanced his reputation as a conservative railroad manager and as a formidable antagonist in a fight.

A number of successful or unsuccessful attempts were made, in the first decade of the twentieth century, to wrest the control of railroad properties from managers who happened to hold less than a majority of the capital stocks. Harriman and his associates, for example, nearly succeeded in ousting Morgan and Hill from the management of the Northern Pacific by purchasing a majority of that road's outstanding shares, while they themselves, in turn, were deprived of control of the Chicago & Alton by similar means. Many railroads, at that time, were managed by men who owned only thirty or forty per cent of the capital stock. If a single group of associated interests controlled, say, one third of the outstanding shares, its supremacy was regarded as assured, because it could almost always get support enough from the other scattered stockholders to give it a safe majority at every annual meeting. Hill and

[1] *New York Times*, April 12, 1914.

Morgan, prior to 1901, never controlled more than forty per cent of the outstanding stock of the Northern Pacific, and yet they managed the property as if they owned it all. Harriman and his associates, in 1901, held only thirty-seven and a half per cent of the stock of the Southern Pacific, but, so far as the direction of its affairs was concerned, their power was virtually supreme.

There was always a danger, however, that a minority group might be deprived of its control by the secret stock purchases of a similar but perhaps more powerful group. From the correspondence of Schiff with Harriman in 1901 and 1902, it is evident that this danger was always present in their minds, and that they tried to minimize it, as far as possible, by organizing pools or syndicates of friendly capitalists who were willing to buy, and to hold for a term of years, stock or convertible bonds enough to offset any secret purchases that might be made by rival or hostile interests. Such, for example, was the Union Pacific convertible bond pool of 1901 and 1902. In a letter written by Mr. Schiff to Mr. Harriman in September, 1901, the former said:

Concerning the winding up of the Union Pacific convertible bond pool, of which you speak, I think it would be inadvisable to give up the call which you and Kuhn, Loeb & Co. practically now have on these holdings for over two years yet. It cannot be foreseen how this may stand us in good stead hereafter; and until we are absolutely certain that our rear is safe, and that no attempts are likely to be made by others to get control of the Union Pacific, which has become the most important and valuable system in the United States, I should not advise to let go of the convertible bond pool, though we should continue to liquidate it as heretofore. This liquidation must necessarily be slow, assuring us, for a long time, the control of a considerable amount of the bonds in case of need. . . . It is not possible that we permanently hold a sufficient amount of Union Pacific stock to absolutely control the company (nor can any one else), and we shall for this control have to rely, in the first instance, on the good-will of our shareholders.

I have long felt, and feel now more than ever, that we must strengthen our holdings of Southern Pacific stock; for while it is not likely that, with the thirty-seven and a half per cent of stock which the Union Pacific holds, any other combination can get control, it is safer, with so able and unprincipled a manipulator as James R. Keene holding a very large amount of the stock, to have an additional considerable amount in friendly hands.[1]

About a year later (August 31, 1902), Mr. Schiff wrote another letter to Mr. Harriman on the same general subject in which he said:

That we must find ways and means to tighten and make permanent our hold on the Union Pacific becomes more evident every day; but it is also very clear to me

[1] Three hundred thousand shares were afterward placed in the "friendly hands" of William Rockefeller to be used against Keene in case the latter should try to get control. Whether Rockefeller bought for himself, individually, or for a syndicate of which he was the head, does not appear; but the object of the investment was to offset Keene's purchases and thus strengthen Harriman.

that to attempt to lease, until we have a very firm hold, would be extremely dangerous, with all the possibilities that we may have to face. I feel we would have saved ourselves much and frequent uneasiness if we had classified the board.[1]

Mr. Harriman evidently shared Schiff's anxiety, and six weeks later (November 11, 1902), with the coöperation of Kuhn, Loeb & Co., he formed a pool or syndicate of nine members which agreed to buy, as a more or less permanent investment, approximately 500,000 shares of Union Pacific preferred stock. The members and the amounts taken by them respectively were as follows:

E. H. Harriman	$10,000,000
Kuhn, Loeb & Co.	10,000,000
James Stillman	10,000,000
William Rockefeller	5,000,000
H. H. Rogers	5,000,000
W. K. Vanderbilt	5,000,000
James H. Hyde	2,000,000
H. C. Frick	1,250,000
P. A. Valentine	1,250,000 [2]

Harriman, Schiff, and Stillman were made mana-

[1] So as to provide for the election of only two or three directors at a time. This would prevent a clean sweep of the board at any single annual meeting in case hostile interests should succeed in getting temporary control.

[2] Unimportant changes were subsequently made from time to time in the membership of the pool or in the amounts subscribed. Vanderbilt, for example, transferred his stock to the Chicago & Northwestern Railway Company and acted for the latter as trustee. The participants in this pool, taken together, probably represented, potentially, the greatest aggregation of capital then existing in the United States.

gers of the pool, with discretionary power to buy or sell, and it was agreed that, unless previously liquidated by general consent, the pool should continue to hold the stock for a period of five years. This accumulation of 500,000 shares in the hands of a few men who were in sympathy with Mr. Harriman and his plans would have been an almost insurmountable obstacle in the way of any group of speculators who should seek to capture the Union Pacific by means of a sudden and unexpected raid.

Covertly organized pools of this kind were regarded by the public, at one time, with a good deal of suspicion, for the reason that their object was supposed to be the secret manipulation of railway stocks; but for this suspicion there was, in most cases, no valid foundation. Harriman, in reconstructing and reëquipping the Union Pacific and Southern Pacific systems, was engaged in a highly important and beneficent piece of work, and his friends, who had faith in his plans, resorted to defensive combinations as a means of protecting him from alien and often purely speculative interference. Such combinations had to be made secretly, in order to prevent hostile interests from becoming aware of their existence. It would have been little short of a public misfortune if Harriman's plans for the extension and betterment of railroad transportation in the Great

West had been thwarted, and he himself eliminated, as the result of a change in control brought about by alien interests for speculative and purely selfish purposes. It was to guard against such a possibility that the fifty-million-dollar pool was formed; and its managers bought the preferred stock, rather than the common, for the reason that the former had equal voting power, with less liability to extreme fluctuation in market value.

CHAPTER XIV

HARRIMAN AND THE ERIE

ONE of the first of the Eastern trunk-lines to attract Mr. Harriman's attention was the Erie. The fact that his great country estate at Arden was situated on that road naturally gave him a personal interest in it, and in 1894, when it was in the hands of a receiver, he became one of the most energetic opponents of the plan of reorganization that had been devised and proposed by Drexel, Morgan & Co. When that plan failed, as Mr. Harriman predicted that it would fail, he withdrew for a time from active participation in Erie affairs; but, as a security-holder as well as a resident on the line, he continued to take a watchful interest in the management of the property. After Mr. F. D. Underwood was elected president of the company, in 1901, Mr. Harriman expressed a wish to become a director. He and Mr. Underwood had previously been associated in the management of the Baltimore & Ohio, and both were desirous of continuing that friendly association in the Erie. The only obstacle in the way was a possible objection on the part of J. P. Morgan, whose firm had done most of the financing of the company after the receivership, and whose interests were dominant at that time in the board. Morgan had had two or three clashes with Harriman, and it was thought that the latter's election as director without his approval might cause friction. For a time, therefore, the matter was held in abeyance. In September, 1903, the death of Abram S. Hewitt left a vacancy in the board, and Mr. Morgan was informed that it would please the directors if Mr. Harriman could be chosen to fill it. Mr. Morgan expressed neither approval nor disapproval, but merely said that "the matter rested entirely with the board of directors and the president." Thereupon, at a meeting of the board held September 30, 1903, Harriman was elected to fill the vacancy, and a little later (June 28, 1905) he became a member of the executive committee.

As subsequent events proved, the president and directors could not have secured a more valuable adviser and supporter in the great work, which they had already begun, of transforming the Erie into a first-class trunk-line, which could compete, on something like equal terms, with the New York Central and Pennsylvania. The road, at that time, was suffering from a freight-traffic congestion in several parts of the main line where grades were heavy and operating facilities inadequate. This was particularly the case in the New York and Alleghany divisions, where trains had to be moved over grades that ranged from 0.8 per cent to 1.5 per cent. With a view to improving these parts of the system and thus relieving the congestion, the company decided to build two low-grade branches, or extensions; one of them forty-two miles in length in the New York division, and the other thirty-three miles in length in the Alleghany division. These branches subsequently became known as the Erie & Jersey and the Genesee River railroads.

In order to provide funds for this new construction, the directors authorized the issue of Erie convertible bonds; but before the work had been long under way, financial conditions became such that the bonds could not be sold at prices that would warrant their flotation. Meanwhile, contracts had been made for a large part of the construction material and some of it was already on the ground. In 1905, after the company had spent about $1,500,000 on the projected extensions, work was temporarily suspended for lack of funds. Mr. Harriman then proposed that the new lines be organized as independent companies, subsidiary to the Erie, but separate from it. They could then issue their own first mortgage bonds, at an attractive price, and earn the interest on them by leasing the roads to the Erie when completed. This seemed to be a perfectly practicable plan, but, unfortunately, the State Commission fixed a minimum price, at which the bonds could not be sold. Mr. Harriman then proposed, and successfully negotiated, a loan of $5,000,000 upon short-term notes, secured by these bonds and the Erie's guarantee, the two subsidiary companies agreeing not to issue any additional bonds without the consent of the note-holders. In this way the necessary funds were finally obtained and the Erie & Jersey and Genesee River railroads were built.

The completion of these two branch lines greatly benefited the Erie by lowering grades, cutting down operating expenses, and providing capacity for increased traffic. On the New York division, for example, the maximum grade was reduced from 74 feet to 26 feet per mile eastbound, and from 75 feet to 53 feet westbound, while, at the same time, the full train-load was increased from 556 tons to 3193 tons eastbound and from 520 tons to 1812 tons westbound. On the Alleghany division the grade was reduced from 42 feet to 10 feet eastbound, and from 53 feet to 16 feet westbound, while the train-load was increased from 1350 tons to 3812 tons eastward and from 1106 tons to 3071 tons westward.

After these two branches had been completed, Mr. Harriman urged the importance of increasing equipment. "You may fix your grades," he said, "so as to move a large traffic; but you will lose the benefits that should accrue if you don't keep your equipment in balance with your track betterments." Some railroads, prior to that time, had been in the habit of saving money, when hard-pressed financially, by going without equipment that was really needed. In one case, cited by Mr. Harriman, the president of an important railway company in the West made it a practice to go over his line regularly, once every year, and systematically cut down the expense estimates of his subordinates, no matter how reasonable they were. That road never prospered and eventually went into the hands of a receiver. In another case, an equally prominent Eastern road tried to save money by using cheaper lights — and even oil lanterns — in its passenger coaches. Mr. Harriman strongly disapproved of such cheese-paring economy, and when one of the directors of the Erie proposed to stop altogether, for a time, the making of equipment purchases, Harriman interposed an emphatic objection. "The way to save money," he said, "is to spend it." By this he meant not that money should be squandered, but that it should be spent freely where the expenditure would increase earning power and thus bring in more revenue.

At a meeting of the Erie executive committee one

day a requisition was presented for a comparatively small sum of money — ten or twelve thousand dollars — to buy mules for hauling purposes in the company's coal mines. There were differences of opinion with regard to the matter, and after listening to the discussion impatiently for a time, Harriman said: "If the manager in charge cannot be trusted to buy mules without bringing the subject to the executive committee, a new manager should be selected. My time is worth about a mule a minute and I can't stay to hear the rest of this discussion. I vote 'Aye' on the requisition." He then left the room.

On the question of spending money for permanent improvements and better equipment, Mr. Harriman almost always voted "Aye," and his influence, ability, financial experience, and personal prestige were very helpful to the Erie between the years 1903 and 1906, when, with limited resources and impaired credit, the company was taking the first steps toward the realization of a far-sighted and comprehensive plan for the betterment of the property. In speaking of this plan, many years later, the "Railway Age Gazette" said:

The history of the Erie since 1902 is unique, in that it is the only instance in American railroad history where a large system, with a funded debt utterly disproportionate to the value of the property, has been rehabilitated without the intervention of the courts and a receivership, and without reorganization. In the years prior to 1902, not only did the Erie have a top-heavy load of bonds, but its credit was almost exhausted and its physical condition was such as to make its operation uneconomical. The morale of its organization was almost equally bad. The history of the development of the Erie Railroad since then is, in considerable part, an account of the domination of one man's personality, sound common sense and persistence, in the face of an unusually large proportion of "unsurmountable difficulties."

The Erie pulled itself out of its hole by its own bootstraps; or, to put it in another way, its rehabilitation went on "under traffic." The physical condition of the road was such as to make it impossible to effect economies in operation without the additional investment of large sums of money. With the small margin of earnings above fixed charges, the company's credit was such as to preclude the possibility of any large issue of securities to provide funds for a general programme of additions and betterments. Before the service and economy of operation could be much improved, modern facilities would have to be provided, and this was a question of establishing credit, and so the circle of "impossibilities" was complete.

In 1901, Frederick D. Underwood was made president, and among the first things he did was to gain the confidence of his board of directors so securely that he held it even through the trying times of 1907 and 1908. . . . This backing of the directors has been of great importance in the success of the development of the property. There have been numerous instances where a board of directors could be carried, by a more or less temporary burst of confidence, into granting authority to inaugurate a large system of expensive improvements; but the Erie's case demanded a continuing faith in the face of difficulties which arose one after another, year in and year out, for a long period of time. The programme of physical betterments had to be carried out bit by bit as the money could be raised. . . . The keynote to the upbuilding of the Erie has been the orderly carrying out of a plan adopted after careful consideration and thereafter adhered to strictly.

After stating that the road weathered its most difficult time while Harriman was a member of the executive committee, the "Railway Age Gazette" says:

The Erie, unquestionably, owes to Mr. Harriman and his immediate associates much, as regards the breadth and scope of the plan of rehabilitation and the tenacity with which it was adhered to under the most trying circumstances.[1]

Not long after Mr. Harriman became a director of the Erie, there were two serious strikes of workmen in the company's shops. The first one was begun by the boiler-makers, who insisted that no foreman should be appointed without their approval; that the number of apprentices should be limited; that double pay should be given for overtime, and that there should be no piece-work. A little later a strike was begun by the machinists, who made substantially the same demands. The question then came up: Should the company yield, or compromise, or fight? It was Mr. Harriman's judgment that these

[1] "Studies in Operation — The Erie Railroad"; *Railway Age Gazette*, April 28, 1916, pp. 939–42.

two strikes should be fought out to a finish, and it was largely through his courage and his influence in the board that they were so fought out. They cost the company about $1,800,000, but the wisdom of the policy that Harriman advocated and the board adopted was shown by the fact that after the partly new force of workmen had been organized, sixty per cent more work was done than had been done before on the same floor area, and there was industrial peace in the shops for a period of ten years.

One of the most extraordinary episodes in the history of the Erie after Mr. Harriman became a member of the executive committee was the purchase of a controlling interest in the Cincinnati, Hamilton & Dayton Railroad from J. P. Morgan, on the 20th of September, 1905, at a cost of $12,000,000, and the resale of the same interest to the same banker, at the same price, two and a half months later. The circumstances that brought about the purchase were stated by the Interstate Commerce Commission as follows:

The acquisition of the C. H. & D. by the Erie was not a new subject in the minds of Erie officials and directors. It had been seriously considered at different times for several years prior to the actual purchase. The value of the C. H. & D. to the Erie, from a traffic standpoint, had been investigated and favorably reported,[1] the southern

[1] By H. B. Chamberlain, third vice-president and general traffic manager of the Erie Company, in a report dated May 23, 1904.

connections through Cincinnati and western connections through Indianapolis being looked upon as of particular value. . . . According to the testimony of President Underwood, of the Erie, there were no negotiations carried on for this purchase, by him or by any one else in behalf of the Erie, prior to an interview he had with J. P. Morgan, at the latter's request, on August 16, 1905, at which Morgan said:

"When I was more active in the Erie than now, and during Mr. Coster's time, it was always thought that sometime the C. H. & D. would become the property of the Erie. Now I have to say to you that if it is still the intention of the Erie board, and it is desirable on the part of the Erie Company, to acquire the C. H. & D., they will have to move quickly in the matter, for it is to be sold soon and there are other purchasers after it."[1]

He then submitted a statement showing the condition of the C. H. & D., which was taken under advisement by President Underwood and his staff.[2]

Without making an inquiry as to the date, authenticity, or trustworthiness of this statement, and without investigating independently the financial condition of the C. H. & D. Company, the Erie officials decided to make the purchase, and on the very next day (August 17, 1905) President Underwood personally authorized J. P. Morgan to buy for the

[1] The "other purchasers" were the members of a syndicate supposed to represent the so-called "Hawley interests." It was composed of Edwin Hawley, D. G. Reid, Newman Erb, John W. Gates, T. P. Shonts, Paul Morton, and others.

[2] "*In Re* Père Marquette Railroad Company and C. H. & D. Railroad Company," Interstate Commerce Commission *Reports*, No. 6833 (March 13, 1917), p. 159.

Erie a majority of the C. H. & D. stock. In a letter to Mr. Morgan, dated August 18, 1905, President Underwood said that grade reductions and other improvements which were then in progress on the Erie would enable the road to handle more traffic than was then tributary to it; that the properties which it was proposed to acquire would largely increase such traffic, and that they "were worth more to the Erie than to any other interest on the map." He predicted that in five years' time, the increase in revenues from the haul of anthracite coal on the Erie, and the sales thereof in the territory traversed by these lines and their connections across Lake Michigan to the northwest, would, in itself, go a long way toward paying the interest on the proposed investment.[1]

In explaining subsequently the haste with which he acted on Morgan's suggestion, President Underwood said that he was influenced by the rumor that the C. H. & D. was in danger of falling into other hands. "I did not at that time want," he said, "to see the C. H. & D. get into the hands of any interest that would divert its traffic from the Erie Railroad, and that was one of the prime factors that made us move when we did."[2]

On the 9th of September, 1905, J. P. Morgan, as

[1] "*In Re* Père Marquette," etc., p. 160. [2] *Ibid.*, p. 164.

banker for the Erie, entered into a contract for the purchase of about 74,000 shares of C. H. & D. stock at $160 a share. Three weeks later (September 20, 1905,) the board of directors approved the action of the president in orally agreeing to take the stock from Morgan, and on the 10th of October the Erie shareholders ratified the purchase. At the same time, the Erie Company issued its short-term notes for the sum of $11,835,000 in payment to Morgan & Co. for 74,059 shares of C. H. & D. stock, including $392,630 in commissions. It then virtually took possession of the C. H. & D. by electing directors and general officers of that company.

In making this purchase, the Erie relied wholly upon the statement furnished by J. P. Morgan, which seemed to show that the C. H. & D. was earning its fixed charges and was consequently solvent. Such, however, was far from being the case. The real condition of the company, and the causes that had brought about that condition, are briefly summarized by Professor Ripley as follows:

Within three years prior to 1905, the road was passed in succession through no less than four syndicates. The first pool was formed in 1902 to purchase the Père Marquette road, which ran crosswise of the main trunk-lines up into Michigan. The plan was, by threat of extending it east and west to Buffalo and Chicago, to force it upon the Vanderbilt roads at a profit. This project failed, leaving the bankers with a heavy burden of unsalable and non-dividend-paying securities. In the meantime another independent cross-line, the Chicago, Cincinnati & Louisville, had been constructed almost into Chicago by a second syndicate. A third pool already controlled the Dayton road. These three groups all overlapped in membership. All parties finally decided to join forces. The Père Marquette was sold to the Dayton road, by payment in Dayton bonds and notes at the rate of $125 for Marquette stock which had cost $85 per share. This recompensed the first syndicate liberally. The second syndicate, which had built the line toward Chicago, was paid for its services in Marquette notes. The third syndicate, controlling the Dayton road, now made its profit in turn by selling the combined properties to a fourth syndicate.[1]

And it was this fourth syndicate, headed by H. B. Hollins & Co., which offered the C. H. & D. to Morgan, with the intimation that if he did not take it, others would.

As the result of the sales, purchases, stock-watering, and speculative manipulation above outlined, the C. H. & D., when the Erie bought it, was practically bankrupt and was liable for the deficits of three other companies, namely, the Père Marquette, the Chicago, Cincinnati & Louisville, and the Toledo Railway & Terminal. In the words of the Interstate Commerce Commission: "The Erie, in buying the

[1] *Railroads: Finance and Organization*, by Professor William Z. Ripley, pp. 215-16

C. H. & D., was not buying a system which was then paying its fixed charges, but a system which had fallen short of doing so by over a million and three-quarters of dollars," not including interest charges of nearly half a million on the Erie's own securities, issued to raise funds for the purchase.

On June 30, 1905, the C. H. & D. proper had outstanding short-term and demand obligations in the form of loans and bills payable aggregating over $2,300,000. In addition there was $1,009,000 due on audited accounts which were unpaid because of lack of funds, not to mention sundry bills held up and not even vouchered for the same reason. It soon became apparent that the C. H. & D. would be wholly unable to perform its obligations under its lease of the Père Marquette; that neither the Chicago, Cincinnati & Louisville nor the Terminal Company was earning operating expenses, and consequently their interest charges and more would have to be met; that $15,000,000 of C. H. & D. notes would mature in about three years, and that heavy interest charges would fall due in January with no funds to pay them.[1]

President Underwood first began to suspect that all was not right with the C. H. & D. when he made a tour of inspection over that road in November, 1905. In the course of this trip he met the controller of the company, who said "that he was not prepared to give the exact figures of the C. H. & D. finances, because he did not 'have them on the books.'

[1] "*In Re* Père Marquette," etc., p. 170.

Asked to explain, the controller said it was understood that there were contracts and commitments that he knew nothing of. He did, however, disclose some obligations not shown on the books, and it then appeared that the statement Mr. Underwood had looked at, and on which he and Mr. Morgan traded, was inaccurate." [1]

Surprised, if not startled, by these discoveries, Mr. Underwood cut short his trip, left the train at Lima, and hurried back to New York.

It may naturally enough be asked: Where was E. H. Harriman when Morgan and the Erie Company bought a twelve-million-dollar railroad with less inquiry and investigation than a prudent business man would make before purchasing an automobile? As an influential member of the executive committee, could he not have prevented the Erie from making an investment that he must have known would be unfortunate, if not actually disastrous?

Mr. Harriman sailed for Japan on the 16th of August, 1905, and did not return to New York until October 26th. Presumably, therefore, he knew nothing about the transaction at the time, and certainly he was not consulted with regard to it. When, some

[1] *Open Letter to the Stockholders of the Baltimore & Ohio Railroad Company*, by Isaac M. Cate (Baltimore, 1917), pp. 6–7.

months later, he became aware of the facts, he strongly disapproved the purchase, and urged President Underwood to see Morgan and try to have it rescinded. In testifying before the Interstate Commerce Commission some years later Mr. Underwood said:

Several days before the rescindation process was had, I talked with Mr. Harriman in his office in the Equitable Building. Now I cannot give you any idea where he had been in the interim, but I very distinctly remember my conversation with him. I could not forget it, nor could you forget it if you had heard it — about what was necessary to be done. He said: "You made the trade with Mr. Morgan yourself. No one was present. You had better go and see Mr. Morgan, and you had better not depend on any one else but yourself. It is up to you. You had better go and better go now." Then I went down and had an audience with Mr. Morgan and told him that practically the C. H. & D. had a floating debt that was not visible in the statement he showed me. He said: "Well, we will look at the statement," and there was some attempt made to find it, but it was unsuccessful; it was not produced. I said: "Mr. Morgan, the statement that I made to you of the effect of the acquisition of the C. H. & D. on the Erie's finances is null and void, because the statement [the Morgan statement] was inaccurate." He looked at me and said: "Well, if the statement that we made to you was inaccurate, and for any reason you think that the Erie Railroad has made a bad trade, your duty is very simple — you have only to convene your board of directors and rescind it, and I advise you to do it at once." I bade him good afternoon and walked out of his office.[1]

[1] "*In Re* Père Marquette," etc., pp. 172–73.

After buying a twelve-million-dollar railroad from Morgan, unconditionally, in August, it must have required a good deal of courage to go to him in November and ask him to take the road back at the same price that the Erie had paid for it. So far as Mr. Harriman inspired that courage, he is entitled to the credit of saving the Erie Company from a serious, if not a disastrous loss. But perhaps Mr. Underwood would have made the appeal in any event.

On the 28th of November, Mr. Morgan himself appeared before the Erie executive committee, and offered to take back the C. H. & D. stock at the price paid for it, "because," as he said, "he understood that some dissatisfaction was felt, and had been expressed, with reference to the purchase effected by his firm as agents for the Erie." The committee, by a unanimous vote, decided to recommend to the board the acceptance of the offer, and the board did so accept on the following day. At the same time the board authorized the delivery to Mr. Morgan of a copy, "suitably engraved, under the Erie's corporate seal, and signed by every director," of the resolution of thanks adopted at the meeting, "for his extraordinary service and assistance to the company; first in his quick and efficient compliance with the direct personal appeal of the company, through its president, to obtain for it a large majority of the common stock of the Cincinnati, Hamilton & Dayton Railway Company; and, finally, after the development of doubt in this board as to the continuing ability of the Erie Company satisfactorily to maintain and extend that system, in view of the demands of its own railroad, in his magnificent, unparalleled, and absolutely voluntary offer himself to assume the entire purchase, and to relieve the Erie Company from all contracts and cost in connection therewith."

The freeing of the Erie from its purchase was formally accomplished through an agreement with J. P. Morgan dated December 2, 1905, whereby the Erie agreed to sell to him its C. H. & D. stock at the price paid under the purchase contract. While Morgan assumed this obligation personally, the firm paid for the stock and treated it as a firm matter, without formal assignment from him.[1]

Two days after the signing of this agreement, both the C. H. & D. and the Père Marquette went into the hands of a receiver. While the whole transaction above outlined is more or less extraordinary, perhaps the strangest feature of it is the apparent ease with which H. B. Hollins & Co. palmed off upon Morgan and the Erie Company the watered stock of a bankrupt railroad at $160 a share.

[1] "*In Re* Père Marquette," etc., p. 171.

CHAPTER XV

THE CONTEST WITH THE SANTA FÊ

IN the early years of the twentieth century, managers of all the trunk-lines west of the Missouri River were striving to lessen operating expenses and quicken the movement of trains by cutting down heavy grades, eliminating sharp curves, and otherwise improving their tracks. When these transcontinental roads were originally built, comparatively little attention was paid to operating efficiency. The important considerations at that time were economy and rapidity of construction; and in selecting locations, engineers and managers chose routes over which it would be cheapest and easiest to build, rather than routes over which trains could be most economically and rapidly hauled. Experience proved, however, that this was a mistake, and that it would be better to relocate and rebuild parts of the roads where there were sharp curves, or steep grades, than to waste money unnecessarily in heavy operating expenses. Mr. Harriman was one of the first to see this, and between 1899 and 1904 he spent scores of millions of dollars in improving both the Union Pacific and the Central Pacific by relocating and rebuilding their tracks. He turned his attention first to the mountainous region between Ogden and Reno, partly because that section was most important and partly because grades there were heaviest and curves most frequent. He always intended, however, to carry out a plan long contemplated by Mr. Huntington, which was to improve the main line of the Southern Pacific by changing its location between Lordsburg, New Mexico, and Yuma, Arizona, where the road crossed the Rocky Mountains and where maximum grades ran from one and one half to nearly two per cent.

A glance at a contour map of the United States will show that from Canada to Mexico there is no watercourse that cuts entirely through the Rocky Mountains and their outlying foothills except the Gila River in southern Arizona. Everywhere else the range is practically unbroken, and in order to surmount it the builders of the first transcontinental lines had to carry the work of construction up more or less steep grades, where, in many places, there was a rise of one hundred feet or more to the mile. The advantages of the Gila Valley route had been known for many years, and the engineers who made surveys for the Southern Pacific were well aware that by adopting it they could get across the mountains with a maximum grade of only twenty-six feet per mile. They were deterred, however, from taking this course by a very formidable obstacle. Just west of the San Carlos Indian Reservation, the Gila River runs into what is known in Arizona as a "box cañon" — a very narrow defile between high rocky cliffs. This cañon is about eighteen miles in length, and its walls rise perpendicularly, almost from the water's edge, to heights of from eight hundred to a thousand feet. The engineering work involved in building through such a gorge would be very expensive and would take a good deal of time; so it was finally decided that a better plan would be to cross the mountains fifty or sixty miles farther south, where the road could be more quickly and easily built and where the initial cost would be less. Mr. Huntington and Mr. Kruttschnitt, however, always kept the Gila route in mind, and fully intended to build over it as soon as the financial condition of the Southern Pacific should be such as to justify the necessary expenditure.

Meanwhile, the Atchison, Topeka & Santa Fé, the most enterprising and powerful rival of the Southern Pacific, began to show a disposition to get control of the Gila Cañon by building toward it from Phœnix. In the summer of 1902, the Phœnix & Eastern Railroad Company, a corporation backed by Santa Fé interests, obtained an Arizona charter, filed the necessary location maps, and began the construction of a line from Phœnix to Benson, by way of the Gila and San Pedro Valleys. The ostensible object of this enterprise was to secure a connection with the El Paso & Southwestern and thus get an entrance into Texas. To this move the Southern Pacific offered no objection, although the projected road invaded its territory and for a distance of one hundred and eighty-five miles nearly paralleled its main line. In December, 1903, however, the Phœnix & Eastern abandoned the location along the south bank of the Gila River on which it had originally filed, crossed to the north bank, where it had no right of way, and began making location surveys eastward in the general direction of the Gila Cañon. This, and other moves made by the Santa Fé about the same time, seemed to indicate an intention on the part of its managers to preëmpt the only practicable approach to the cañon, and perhaps build through the cañon itself, thus preventing the Southern Pacific from constructing its proposed line from Lordsburg to Yuma by way of the Gila Valley.

When this state of affairs was reported to Mr. Harriman, he took steps at once to protect Southern Pacific interests. By his direction, and under the immediate supervision of Epes Randolph, vice-president and general manager of Southern Pacific lines in Arizona and New Mexico, a new company was incorporated under the name of Arizona Eastern, which was empowered by its charter to build a road from Yuma to Lordsburg by way of Phœnix, Dudleysville, the Gila Cañon, and the San Carlos Reservation. This new company began at once to make location surveys and pushed them with all possible speed to completion. Meanwhile, the Phœnix & Eastern was also making location surveys, with a view to preëmpting a strip of land about eighteen miles long on the northern bank of the river, where, under its original map and location, it had no right of way. As this strip furnished the best and easiest means of access to the Gila Cañon, each of the contending parties strove eagerly to get possession of it by prior location. The Arizona Eastern completed its surveys early in March, 1904, and on the 14th of that month at 9 A.M. filed its route map in the United States Land Office at Tucson, as required by the Act of Congress of March 3, 1875, granting rights of way to railroad companies over the public domain. The Phœnix & Eastern filed its own route map on the same day, but not until 9.20 A.M., so that the Arizona Eastern had a small margin of twenty minutes' priority. Both companies began grading operations on the disputed strip, and as the rival gangs of laborers were working almost side by side, they naturally interfered and clashed frequently with one another.

The contest, thus far, had been for possession only of the eighteen-mile strip on the northern bank of the river below Dudleysville, which may be described as the western approach to the Gila Cañon, but a struggle soon began for possession of the cañon itself. On the 6th of April, 1904, the Santa Fé brought about the organization and incorporation of still another company, called the Gila River Railroad Company, whose charter authorized it to establish a connection with the Phœnix & Eastern at or near Dudleysville, and to build thence through the Gila Cañon and across the Arizona–New Mexico boundary to the terminus of the Santa Fé branch line at Deming. So far as the Gila Cañon was concerned, this route had already been preëmpted by the Arizona Eastern in the map that it filed in the United States Land Office on the 14th of March, 1904; but the Gila River Company, nevertheless, made application to the Interior Department in Washington for right of way.

The various controversies involving preëmption rights on the northern side of the river soon became the subject of litigation, and in the trial court the Arizona Eastern's right of way through the Gila Cañon was sustained. The case was then appealed to the United States Supreme Court, but before a final decision had been rendered, the managers of the Santa Fé, anticipating defeat, approached Mr. Harriman with a proposition to compromise. The negotiations that followed ended in an agreement on the part of the Southern Pacific to purchase the capital stock of the Phœnix & Eastern at cost. This was a clear victory for Mr. Harriman, because it not only gave him undisputed possession of the Gila Cañon and the road leading thereto, but put an end to the encroachments of the Santa Fé upon Southern Pacific territory in that part of Arizona.

Mr. Harriman was always desirous of maintaining peaceful relations with the Santa Fé, and even went so far as to offer its managers seats for two of their representatives in the Southern Pacific directorate, provided they would reciprocate by giving him a similar privilege in their own directorate. "We should work in harmony," he said to them, "and not live in strife. You give me two seats on the board of the Santa Fé and I will give you two seats on the board of the Southern Pacific." But this offer was not accepted. Perhaps President Ripley and his associates were afraid of the influence that might be exerted in their organization by a man of Mr. Harriman's energetic and dominating character. But the privilege that they would not concede voluntarily was eventually extorted from them. In the summer of 1904, while the contest for possession of the Gila Cañon was still going on, Mr. Harriman and his associates bought in the open market 300,000 shares ($30,000,000 par value) of Santa Fé stock. This gave them power to elect two directors, and H. H. Rogers and H. C. Frick were shortly afterward chosen to represent Union Pacific and Southern Pacific interests on the Santa Fé board.

Although Mr. Harriman was a keen rival when competition became necessary, he was always of opinion that competitive railroad-building is not permanently advantageous, either to the public, or to the companies that engage in it; and that where competing lines are already in existence, it is best for them either to work harmoniously together by means of coöperation, or to combine under a single management. This was the central thought in the address that he delivered at the opening of the Louisiana Purchase Exposition in St. Louis on the 30th of April, 1904. "The combination of different railways," he then said, "should be regulated by law. So far as may be necessary, the public interest should be protected by law; but in so far as the law obstructs such combinations, without public benefit, it is unwise and prejudicial to the public interest."

This was not then the view of Congress, or of the

American people. Combination was prohibited by the Sherman Anti-Trust Law, even when it was clearly beneficial to the public. Time and experience, however, showed the soundness of Mr. Harriman's judgment. During and after the World War, the advantages of railroad combination were almost universally recognized, and Congress itself adopted the very policy for which Mr. Harriman had been condemned.[1]

[1] The bill introduced in 1919 by Senator Cummins, chairman of the Senate Committee on Interstate Commerce, authorized railroads to combine voluntarily in geographical groups, and provided that at the end of seven years such combination should be compulsory.

CHAPTER XVI

NORTHERN SECURITIES COMPANY DISSOLVED

WHEN the United States Supreme Court, on the 14th of March, 1904, decided that the Northern Securities Company was "an illegal combination in restraint of trade" and ordered that it be dissolved, the question arose: How should the dissolution be brought about? Should the corporation terminate its existence by cancelling its stock and giving back to every holder the same kind and the same number of shares that the latter had put into it? Or should it dissolve by distributing its total assets, *pro rata*, among its stockholders, without regard to the kinds of stock originally received from them?

Regarded as a question of equity, it would seem to depend upon the nature of the agreement between the parties at the time when the combination was formed. If a Northern Pacific stockholder put in his shares with the understanding that they were to remain his property until the combination should be legally and effectually established, he might rightfully demand the return of those very same shares when the combination was dissolved by judicial decree. If, on the other hand, he *sold* his shares to the combination unconditionally, and without regard to the latter's effectual and permanent establishment, he could equitably claim only his *pro rata* share of the combination's assets. To the average small stockholder it made little difference, perhaps, whether he got back the same shares that he had turned in or not; but to Mr. Harriman it made a very great difference. If, on the dissolution of the combination, he recovered *all* the shares of the Northern Pacific Company that he had originally contributed, he would still retain controlling power in that organization, because he had turned in more than a majority of its capital stock. If, however, he got back only *a part* of his Northern Pacific shares and had to take with them a part of the shares of the Great Northern, he would have only a minority holding in each corporation and comparatively little power in either.

Mr. Hill and his associates, very naturally, preferred to make a *pro rata* distribution of the holding company's assets, including both Northern Pacific and Great Northern shares, so on the 22d of March, 1904, they sent out a circular to the stockholders of the Northern Securities Company, apprising them of the impending dissolution and proposing to return to them, not the same kind and the same number of shares that they had put in, but $39.27 in stock of the Northern Pacific and $30.17 in stock of the Great

Northern for every share of Northern Securities stock that they surrendered. The circular also gave notice of a special meeting of Northern Securities stockholders, to be held on the 21st of April, 1904, for the purpose of voting on the proposition.[1]

On the 2d of April, 1904, only eleven days after the Hill plan of dissolution was announced, counsel for the Oregon Short Line (a subsidiary of the Union Pacific) applied to the courts for permission to intervene, on the ground that it (the Short Line Company) was still the owner of the Northern Pacific shares that had been turned in, and that the proposed distribution of the holding company's assets would be unjust and inequitable. Permission to intervene was denied, whereupon Harriman brought suit in the United States Circuit Court for an injunction to prevent the Northern Securities Com-

[1] Mr. Hill afterward stated, in a letter to a friend, that this plan, when first proposed, had Mr. Harriman's approval (*Life of James J. Hill*, by J. G. Pyle, vol. II, pp. 178–79); but such does not seem to have been the case. The first plan was presented at a conference held in Mr. Hill's office soon after the United States Supreme Court rendered its decision. The gentlemen who attended that conference were Mr. Hill, Messrs. Grover, Stetson, and Johnson, his legal counsel, and R. S. Lovett, general counsel for the Harriman lines. The plan, as presented, was discussed and developed, mainly by Stetson and Johnson, and the conferees separated with the understanding that they should meet again on the following morning. When Mr. Lovett reported to Mr. Harriman what the plan was, the latter dissented at once. Mr. Lovett thereupon telephoned Mr. Grover, counsel for Mr. Hill, that Mr. Harriman was "not prepared to commit himself to the plan suggested," and that he (Lovett) would not return to the conference.

pany from distributing its assets in the manner proposed. The court issued a temporary restraining order, and on April 21, 1904, just before the special meeting of the Northern Securities stockholders, Harriman sent to them the following "Notice":

Notice is hereby given to the special meeting of stockholders of the Northern Securities Company that the undersigned claim that the shares of the capital stock of the Northern Pacific Railway Company delivered by Edward H. Harriman and Winslow S. Pierce to the Northern Securities Company, on or about November 18, 1901, and consisting of $37,023,000, par value, of the common stock of said railway company and $41,085,000, par value, of the preferred stock of said railroad company, and the common stock into which said preferred stock has been converted, belong to the Oregon Short Line Company, as the legal and equitable owner thereof; that the Northern Securities Company is not now, and never became, the owner thereof, but is simply a custodian, and that the undersigned are entitled to the return and delivery to them of certificates for said stock of the Northern Pacific Railway Company, upon the surrender by them of $82,491,871, par value, of the capital stock of the Northern Securities Company and the payment of $8,915,629 in cash received by them on such delivery of Northern Pacific stock to the Northern Securities Company as aforesaid.

Notice is further given that the said Northern Securities Company has no right to distribute the said Northern Pacific stock, *pro rata*, among the stockholders of the Northern Securities Company, or otherwise dispose of the same except to return the same to the undersigned.

Notice is further given that the undersigned have instituted a suit in the Circuit Court of the United States for the district of New Jersey to have it adjudged that they are entitled to the return of the said Northern Pacific stock to them, and that in said suit a restraining order has been granted by the Hon. Andrew Kirkpatrick, U.S. Judge, restraining and enjoining the Northern Securities Company, until the hearing and decision of the application of the undersigned for a preliminary writ of injunction, from parting with, disposing of, assigning, transferring, or distributing said stock of the Northern Pacific Railway Company so received from said Harriman and Pierce, or the certificates which now represent the same, and that a copy of said restraining order and of the bill of complaint, exhibits and affidavits on said motion for a preliminary injunction have been duly served on the officers of the Northern Securities Company.

EDWARD H. HARRIMAN
WINSLOW S. PIERCE
OREGON SHORT LINE RAILROAD
THE EQUITABLE TRUST COMPANY

In arguing this case before the Circuit Court judge, counsel for Mr. Harriman contended that the Hill plan of dissolution, if carried into effect, would put the control of the two roads into the hands of the same men who had combined to organize the Northern Securities Company and who were still endeavoring to secure such control in another way. It would be unfair, counsel argued, to allow the Hill-Morgan interests to take away from the Harriman interests the majority of Northern Pacific stock that they had held prior to the organization of the Securities Company, and to give them in exchange only a minority of Northern Pacific shares and a still smaller minority of Great Northern shares. The latter they had never bought and never desired to buy, and the Hill plan, if carried through, would merely force them to take about $25,000,000 of Great Northern stock in which they had no interest whatever.

Although Mr. Harriman secured an injunction and thus blocked temporarily the proposed distribution of the Securities Company's assets, he was unable to hold his advantage. On the 18th of August, 1904, Hill and his associates carried the case by appeal to the Circuit Court of Appeals, and succeeded, on the 3d of January, 1905, in getting the injunction dissolved. Mr. Harriman thereupon obtained a writ of *certiorari* and took the case to the United States Supreme Court, where it was argued March 2, 1905. Four days later the Supreme Court handed down a decision in which Harriman's plea for the return of his Northern Pacific shares was denied and the Hill plan for the distribution of the holding company's assets was approved and sanctioned. The Northern Securities Company then called in for cancellation ninety-nine per cent of its shares and gave to the holders thereof $39.27 in Northern Pacific stock and $30.17 in Great Northern stock for every share surrendered. This distribution not only deprived Mr.

Harriman of his control of the Northern Pacific Company, but affected his interests injuriously in another way. If he recovered all of the Northern Pacific shares that he turned in when the Securities Company was formed, he would have, at the par value of such shares, $78,108,000, with an annual income (at the current dividend rate) of $5,467,560. If, on the other hand, he got back only his *pro rata* share of the Securities Company's assets (including both Northern Pacific and Great Northern shares), he would have only $56,709,330, at par value, with an annual income of only $3,969,667.[1]

In carrying through his plan for such a distribution of the holding company's assets as would deprive Mr. Harriman of power in Northern Pacific and Burlington affairs, Hill won a decisive victory; but he was not satisfied, nevertheless, with the outcome of the litigation as a whole.

> The dissolution of the Northern Securities Company [says his biographer] was one of Mr. Hill's few great disappointments. It cannot properly be said to mark a failure. The plan, as it was outlined in his mind, away back in 1893 to 1895, was a limited holding company for Great Northern stockholders only. Time and circumstances, rather than individual judgment or desire, had compelled its expansion to the form taken by the North-

[1] *History of the Northern Securities Case*, by B. H. Meyer, University of Wisconsin Bulletin, p. 295.

ern Securities. The forces which struck at this, both State and Federal, were inspired, in part at least, by a political motive. The decision pictures the court in doubt. The vote of five to four was almost equivalent to "not proven." The after event amounted to a vindication. For, just as the reorganization of the Northern Pacific, planned in 1895 and prohibited by the court, was accomplished in another fashion, to the same end but in conformity with the law, so the main business and economic purposes of the Northern Securities have since been realized. The only thing actually accomplished by the court's decision was to prevent eight or ten old men from placing their investments where they would be secure after their death.[1]

If the dissolution of the Northern Securities Company was a disappointment to Mr. Hill, the failure to secure complete control of the Northern Pacific in 1901 and the adverse decision of the United States Supreme Court in 1905 were equally disappointing to Mr. Harriman, because they defeated his plans and left the Union Pacific with only a minority holding of stock in each of the Hill-Morgan companies. Great disappointments, however, are sometimes attended by compensating advantages, and it happened to be so in this case. The Great Northern stock, which Mr. Harriman did not want, but which he was forced to take when the Securities Company dissolved, proved to be a veritable bonanza. In the fall of 1905, the Great Northern Company added

[1] *Life of James J. Hill,* by J. G. Pyle, vol. II, pp. 183–84.

$25,000,000 to its capital stock and gave to its stockholders the privilege of subscribing to the new issue at par. As the stock at that time was selling at a premium, Mr. Harriman, of course, took the amount allotted to the Union Pacific, and thus increased his holdings by 37,444 shares. Then, in the latter part of 1905 and the early part of 1906, there happened to be an extraordinary boom in the stock market which carried railroad securities, and especially the Hill stocks, to almost unprecedented figures. Northern Pacific sold up to $232.50 a share, while Great Northern, notwithstanding the recent expansion of its capital, was bid up to a maximum of $348 a share. During this period of speculative excitement, and upon this steadily rising market, Mr. Harriman disposed of nearly all his Northern Pacific and Great Northern shares at prices that gave the Union Pacific a net profit of about $58,000,000.[1] It is doubtful whether a greater sum was ever made out of a single stock investment, and certainly no investor ever secured $58,000,000 as pecuniary compensation for a series of failures and defeats. Mr. Thomas Woodlock, a

[1] Professor Ripley estimated the profit of the Union Pacific at about $83,000,000 (*Railroads: Finance and Organization*, p. 506); but his figuring, apparently, was based on the assumption that the stocks were sold at the highest prices that they reached. Such, however, was not the case. Mr. Harriman sold the Northern Pacific stock at an average price of $208.75 a share (maximum quotation, $232.50) and the Great Northern stock at an average of $304.51 per share (maximum quotation, $348).

railroad expert of that time, when asked by Carl Snyder what he regarded as Mr. Harriman's greatest achievement, said: "I think it was this; to get licked in a fight and to pull out of it with a colossal fortune as the result." [1] The "colossal fortune," however, was the result of good luck, rather than of clear prevision and deliberate intention. Mr. Harriman took advantage of the stock-market boom and sold the holdings of the Union Pacific at an immense profit; but the causes that brought about the enhancement of value were largely fortuitous.

Mr. Harriman has sometimes been accused of "corporate speculation," and of managing the finances of his railroads "with an eye to the Wall Street situation"; [2] but for this charge (at least in the sense of stock gambling with corporate funds) there never was any justification. He usually spent fifty per cent more for the maintenance and improvement of his properties than was spent by other railway managers in the same territory, and when he invested corporate funds in the securities of other railroad companies, it was not "with an eye to the Wall Street situation," but rather with a view to strengthening the position and increasing the busi-

[1] "Harriman: Colossus of Roads," by Carl Snyder, *Review of Reviews*, January, 1907, p. 48.

[2] *Railroads: Finance and Organization*, by Professor William Z. Ripley, pp. 511, 514, 515.

A NEWSPAPER CARTOON

ness of the Union Pacific and Southern Pacific systems.

His investment in the stock of the Northern Pacific, which is a case in point, was a strategic move rather than a speculative venture. His object was to get a share in the advantages of the Burlington purchase, which Hill had refused to give him. Circumstances and the course of events, however, defeated his original plan and turned what was meant to be a strategic move into an enormously profitable transaction. He failed to get control either of the Northern Pacific or of the Burlington, but, by way of compensation, he was able to put into the treasury of the Union Pacific $58,000,000 in cash by selling Great Northern stock which he had been forced to take and Northern Pacific stock which he had bought without any reference whatever to "the Wall Street situation." He did show, however, an accurate judgment of values when he quickly got rid of these stocks by selling them at prices which he believed to be far above their intrinsic worth.

At the end of the fiscal year 1905-06,[1] the extremely prosperous condition of the Union Pacific

[1] Professor Ripley, commenting upon the company's financial status at that time, says, "its revenues from operation were enormous," "its repayments from advances to subsidiary companies were steadily increasing": and "its treasury was literally bursting with free assets." (*Railroads: Finance and Organization*, p. 507.)

Company and the receipt of $58,000,000 in cash from the sale of Northern Pacific and Great Northern stocks enabled Mr. Harriman to extend the influence of his roads, facilitate traffic, and stabilize rates, by investing largely in the securities of other railway systems with which his own lines indirectly connected or competed. Up to that time he had never bought stocks of other railroad corporations with a view to the establishment of closer and more sympathetic business relations; but in 1906 he began to make purchases for the express purpose of creating what was then known as a "community of interest." Between June 30, 1906, and March 1, 1907, he invested for the Union Pacific more than $130,000,000 in the securities of nine different railway companies, whose lines covered almost the whole country from ocean to ocean and from the Great Lakes to the Gulf. The several amounts of stocks thus bought were as follows:

Atchison, Topeka & Santa Fé, preferred......	$10,395,000
Baltimore & Ohio, preferred	6,665,920
Baltimore & Ohio, common.................	38,801,040
Chicago, Milwaukee & St. Paul	5,997,750
Chicago & Northwestern..................	5,303,673
Fresno City Railway......................	106,410
Illinois Central...........................	41,442,028
New York Central........................	19,634,324
St. Joseph & Grand Island	2,022,540
	$130,368,685 [1]

[1] *Reports* of Interstate Commerce Commission, vol. 12, p. 20.

These amounts of stock were not sufficient, in any case, to secure absolute majority control; but, as Professor Ripley has rightly said, "there can be no doubt that such substantial fractions could exercise a powerful influence upon the traffic policy of the properties concerned." With regard to the wisdom of this policy, or its expediency in view of the state of public opinion at that time, there have been differences of opinion. Mr. Otto H. Kahn, who was a close and sympathetic associate of Mr. Harriman, in commenting afterward upon these large stock purchases, said:

> Whatever be the cause or explanation, he [Mr. Harriman] took action that year which, it has always seemed to me, was the one serious mistake in his management of Union Pacific affairs. I refer to the purchases of very large amounts of stocks of many other companies, which were made for the account and placed in the treasury of the Union Pacific. For some of these acquisitions it must be said, there were valid, legitimate, and, in fact, almost compelling reasons, even at the then prevailing high prices; but for others it was and is difficult to discern sufficient warrant, especially considering the time and the cost at which they were made and the effect which they were likely to have and actually did have upon public opinion. It is but fair to add that the problem of how to deal with the huge cash fund realized by the Union Pacific through the sale of its Northern Pacific stock holdings was an exceedingly difficult and complex one; that the operation of selling Northern Pacific stock and reinvesting the proceeds in the stock of

other lines did largely increase the annual income to the Union Pacific; and that Mr. Harriman . . . never changed his belief that the entire transaction, looked upon primarily as a change of investments, was advantageous to the company, in that it greatly augmented its income, and would ultimately be found to carry with it, as to all the stocks concerned, important and legitimate benefits.[1]

Mr. Kahn's disapproval of Mr. Harriman's policy seems to have been based mainly on the unfavorable effect that it had on public opinion. "It lent color," he said, "to the impression that Mr. Harriman was aiming at a gigantic illegal monopoly of the railroad industry." It may well be doubted, however, whether fear of hostile public opinion ought to deter an experienced and far-sighted railway manager from adopting a policy that he believes will be beneficial to all concerned. Public opinion is seldom well informed, and popular judgments, in many cases, are largely influenced by prejudice, politics, or demagogic misrepresentation. Every business man naturally prefers to have popular approval of his acts, rather than general condemnation of them; but Mr. Harriman never allowed fear of public censure to influence his policies or his decisions. This was shown in many cases. His purchase of a controlling interest in the Southern Pacific "lent color to the

[1] *Edward Henry Harriman*, by Otto H. Kahn (New York, 1911), p. 39.

impression that he was aiming at a gigantic illegal monopoly" of transcontinental traffic; but subsequent events proved that the popular "impression" was an erroneous one, and that the reconstruction of the Southern Pacific with the capital and credit of the Union Pacific was as beneficial to the people of the Great West as it was to the stockholders of the two companies. It is difficult to see why this was not equally true of Mr. Harriman's stock purchases in 1906 and 1907. They affected public opinion unfavorably, for the reason that Mr. Kahn has stated; but it does not appear that they were actually injurious to anybody.

Professor William Z. Ripley, who seldom took a favorable view of Mr. Harriman's financial methods and policies,[1] seems to have seen clearly, in this case, that the investments in question were highly advantageous to the Union Pacific and Southern Pacific systems. After giving a list of the securities bought, he says:

> By this good stroke of business the Union Pacific's income from investments was enhanced by more than fifty per cent. Such income had in fact risen from less than $3,000,000 in 1900 to $6,497,000 in 1905. Now it jumped to $10,333,000 — a sum greater than all the Union Pacific dividend disbursement in the preceding

[1] At least after 1907, when he seems to have been unduly influenced by the Interstate Commerce Commission.

year. . . . The aggregate cost of these securities, purchased within a few months, was, as we have seen, over $130,000,000. As a reinvestment of surplus funds the list speaks for itself. The next question is as to their strategic importance for purposes of transportation. Absolute majority control of none of these properties was secured. Less than one third of Illinois Central; one fifth of Baltimore & Ohio; only about eight per cent of New York Central, with perhaps as much more in friendly individual hands; and even smaller percentages of the granger roads — was all that was held. But there can be no doubt that such substantial fractions could exercise a powerful influence upon the traffic policy of the properties concerned. And considered in their entirety, they made up a network of lines reaching every part of the United States. Most directly valuable, probably, was the Illinois Central, as giving both the Southern Pacific at New Orleans and the Union Pacific at the Missouri River direct access to Chicago. And with the acquisition of the Central of Georgia in 1907,[1] a through line from the South Atlantic ports to the West was afforded. The important coal and iron and cotton manufacturing districts of the South were given their first through routing to important inland and Oriental markets over a single system. And of course, contrariwise, the Illinois Central gave opportunity for participation in the large grain export business through the Gulf ports, as well as ready access to the new trade routes to be opened up by the Panama Canal. Incidentally, it may be noted that the distance to Chicago from the Atlantic seaboard was, by comparison with the

[1] This road was bought by Oakley Thorne and Marsden J. Perry from the Richmond Terminal Reorganization Committee in June, 1907. It was shortly afterward sold by them to E. H. Harriman who turned it over to the Illinois Central. (*The Earning Power of Railroads*, by Floyd W. Mundy, New York, 1913, pp. 329 and 365.)

northern trunk-lines, shortened by about one sixth by this new southeastern trade route.

The Union Pacific now also enjoyed part control of two great Atlantic trunk-lines. The New York Central, with its trans-Mississippi extension, the Chicago & Northwestern, had long made up, with the Union Pacific, the shortest and probably the best ocean-to-ocean line. And the Baltimore & Ohio shares, being one half of the Pennsylvania's former holdings, gave access to the remaining North Atlantic seaports, as well as amounting, in connection with powerful joint directors in the Union Pacific and Pennsylvania boards, to a sort of partnership with this most powerful company. As for the St. Paul road, was that not an important rival in a rich western territory? And even more important, was it not, at that very time, announcing a Pacific Coast extension which should give entry to the North Pacific ports, served by the rival Morgan-Hill properties? [1]

From the above statement of the advantages secured by Mr. Harriman's stock purchases, it seems to appear, not only that they were highly profitable to the two Pacific systems, but that they conferred a benefit also upon the general public by opening more

[1] *Railroads: Finance and Organization*, by William Z. Ripley, pp. 508–10.

Authorities on railway economics generally agree that when purchases of stocks are made — as Harriman made them — for the purpose of "opening communications, or modifying competition, they have a sound foundation." (See *Railroad Reorganization* by Stuart Daggett, Cambridge. Mass., 1908, p. 260.) With regard to purchase made to establish a "community of interest" see also *American Railway Transportation*, by Emory R. Johnson, Professor of Transportation and Commerce in the University of Pennsylvania (New York, 1911), pp. 253–55.

direct through routes, by stabilizing rates, and by greatly improving traffic facilities. Incidentally, of course, they increased Mr. Harriman's power; but if he did not use that power to promote corporate interests at the expense of the public welfare, his policy in making such investments can hardly be regarded as unwise, or mistaken.

In the light of all that we now know of transportation affairs in the first two decades of the present century, Mr. Harriman's activities between 1899 and 1909 were, to say the least, far more beneficial to shippers, producers, and consumers than were interstate regulation and Government control between 1909 and 1920. He left every railroad that he managed better than he found it; he stimulated production throughout the Great West by furnishing adequate transportation to markets, and he moved many million tons of freight that never would have been moved if he had not lived.

CHAPTER XVII

EQUITABLE LIFE INVESTIGATION

ALMOST every man, at some time in the course of his life, becomes involved in a contest, or controversy, which he did not originate and for which he is not in any way responsible. Such was the case when Mr. Harriman, in 1905, was drawn into a fight for control of the Equitable Life Assurance Society. He did not begin this fight, nor was he at all interested in the outcome of it; but circumstances happened to make him a participant, and, as Mr. Kahn has said, he soon "became the principal and probably the most attacked figure of the conflict, both the warring factions pausing in their fight with each other to pour their fire of abuse and innuendo upon him." [1]

The history of the Equitable, so far as it seems necessary to give it here, may be briefly summarized as follows:

About the year 1859, Henry B. Hyde, a well-to-do employee of the Mutual Life Insurance Company of New York, conceived the idea of organizing an in-

[1] *Edward Henry Harriman*, by Otto H. Kahn (New York, 1911), p. 19.

surance company of his own — or at least one that he himself could control. As he did not have money enough for such an undertaking, he applied for assistance to his friend and pastor, Rev. Dr. J. W. Alexander, of the Nineteenth Street Presbyterian Church. Through the latter's influence, he succeeded in raising nearly fifty thousand dollars, in addition to what he already had of his own, and with a capital of $100,000 he organized and incorporated the "Equitable Life Assurance Society of the United States," a joint-stock company, a majority of whose shares he held. In recognition of the aid given him by Dr. Alexander, he made the latter's brother, William C. Alexander, president of the society; but he himself, as vice-president, was the real manager, partly because he had had experience in the business and partly because he owned more than half of the capital stock. When, some years later, William C. Alexander died, Hyde took the presidency, and caused the election of J. W. Alexander, a son of Dr. Alexander, as vice-president.

The society was prosperous and successful almost from the first, and under Hyde's skillful management its business steadily and rapidly increased, year by year, until, toward the close of the century, its available assets amounted to more than $400,000,000. When Henry B. Hyde died, in 1899, he left most of his property, including his Equitable stock, to his son, James Hazen Hyde; but as the latter was then only twenty-three years of age, the will contained a stipulation that he should not become president of the company until he reached the age of thirty. J. W. Alexander was, therefore, elected president and acted as a sort of regent until young Hyde should become old enough to take his place. Meanwhile, the latter filled the position of vice-president.

Under the terms of its charter, the Equitable had a board of fifty-two directors, who were supposed to control its policies and manage its affairs; but, as is often the case in large corporations, they discharged their duties in a merely perfunctory way and left the real management of the company to its president and vice-president.

Control of any great insurance company carries with it control of a vast amount of money; and there are many ways in which such a corporation can be "milked" — to use a colloquial expression — without actual criminality or flagrant dishonesty. Its officers, for example, may establish a trust company, get possession of a large amount of its capital stock, and then favor it by depositing with it one, five, or even ten million dollars of the insurance company's money at a very low rate of interest. If the trust company pays only two per cent for the use of such deposits, and then loans them out at five per cent, it obviously makes a large profit, and in this the officers of the insurance company share as stockholders of the trust company. Then, too, the president or vice-president of an insurance company can buy stocks or bonds as an individual (although perhaps with the money of the policy-holders) and then resell them to the insurance company at an advanced price. Finally, by carrying in their own names stock in other corporations that belongs to the insurance company, officers of the latter can get themselves elected as vice-presidents of such other corporations and draw large salaries from them in addition to those that they receive from their own company. All these and various other methods of "milking" an insurance company were practiced by one or another of the Equitable's high officers, but they did not become known to the public, or even to a majority of the directors, until a quarrel between the president and vice-president brought them to light.

Under the terms of his father's will, James Hazen Hyde, owner of a majority of the Equitable Company's stock, would become eligible to the presidency when he reached the age of thirty — that is, in June, 1906. Early in February, 1905, just before the annual meeting of directors, President Alexander and thirty-five other officers, who composed what may be called the Alexander faction, sent to the directors severally a so-called "petition," in which they set forth their views with regard to the existing state of the company's affairs, and recommended that the society be changed from a joint-stock to a mutual corporation. Such a change was permissible under its charter, and the petitioners expressed the belief that it would be better for all concerned if the controlling power were vested in the policy-holders, rather than in the stockholders. James Hazen Hyde, who regarded this as a covert attempt to keep him out of the presidency when he should reach the age of thirty, gathered together the supporters who composed his own faction and offered strenuous opposition to the proposed change. This led to a bitter personal controversy which lasted for weeks and filled the newspapers with charges, counter-charges, and accusations. Hyde declared that Alexander was actuated by selfish motives and desired only to retain power, while Alexander rejoined that Hyde was "an unsafe official" who had been guilty of various irregularities and improprieties which affected injuriously the company's reputation and standing.

It was at this stage of the proceedings that Mr. Harriman became involved in the controversy. He had had relations with the Equitable as early as the spring of 1901, when, in the ordinary course of business, he borrowed from the society $2,700,000, putting up, as collateral security, stocks and bonds which had a market value of about $3,200,000. This loan was renewed several times, at intervals of six months or a year, but was finally liquidated, in 1904, when the society demanded a higher rate of interest than Mr. Harriman was willing to pay.

In November, 1902, for reasons given in a previous chapter, Mr. Harriman, with the assistance of Kuhn, Loeb & Co., organized a syndicate for the purpose of buying 500,000 shares of Union Pacific preferred stock. Regarding this purchase as likely to be a profitable one, he offered Mr. Hyde a small share in it. Hyde was more than willing to associate himself with such men as Stillman, Schiff, Rockefeller, Rogers, and Vanderbilt, and he therefore became a member of the syndicate and took 20,000 shares of the stock.

With the exception of these two transactions — the $2,700,000 loan and the syndicate proposal — Mr. Harriman never had any business relations with the Equitable or any of its officers; but he became involved in the company's affairs in another way. In the spring of 1901, about the time when the Equitable loaned him $2,700,000, Mr. Hyde proposed to him that he become one of the society's directors. "I told him," Mr. Harriman afterward said, "that

I had very little time to give to such things, and that I did not think the method of management of the Equitable was the right one." Hyde replied that "he intended, as time went on, to change it, and that his desire was to surround himself with independent men, who would have no other interest than that of the Equitable, to help him in his management"; because, as he said, "Mr. Alexander was growing old, and his (Hyde's) succession (to the presidency) was probably not far off. I told him that if that was so and that was his intention, I would become a director."[1]

Mr. Harriman then went on the Equitable board and served as a director from 1901 to 1905; but his connection with the management was purely nominal, as was that of Frick, Bliss, Schiff, Depew, and many other members of the board. He attended meetings and listened to reports; but he was never appointed on any committee, and in all the four years of his term his advice was solicited only once. On that occasion Vice-President Hyde consulted him with regard to a vacancy to be filled in the board of directors, and Mr. Harriman recommended James J. Hill, president of the Great Northern Railway Company, as a suitable man for the place.

[1] Testimony of E. H. Harriman before the Armstrong legislative committee appointed in 1905 to investigate the business of life insurance companies.

When the fight for supremacy began between the Hyde and Alexander factions, Mr. Harriman suggested that a committee of the board be appointed to investigate the charges and counter-charges made by the contending parties. Several of the directors, including Chauncey M. Depew, thought that such action would be premature, and at their request Harriman refrained from putting his suggestion into the form of a motion. Some time later, however, the committee was appointed, and he himself was made a member of it. The other members were H. C. Frick (chairman), Brayton Ives, Cornelius N. Bliss, and M. E. Ingalls. This committee, after a thorough and impartial investigation, reported that the organization and management of the Equitable were generally bad, and that neither Hyde nor Alexander was fit for the place that he occupied. The committee therefore recommended that the company be reorganized; that the president, first vice-president, and second vice-president be requested to resign, and that a special committee of seven be appointed to nominate candidates for election in their places.

In view of the possible loss of their positions and power, both factions then combined, temporarily, for self-protection; and at the next meeting of the directors succeeded in having the report rejected by a majority vote. Frick, Bliss, and Harriman thereupon resigned as directors of the society. Mr. Harriman, however, continued to take an interest in its affairs and spent a good deal of time in trying to reconcile conflicting views, get an amended charter, and put the corporation on a sound basis.

Although Alexander and Hyde had been able to prevent the adoption of the Frick report, they were not strong enough to withstand the tide of public opinion which turned against them when that report was given to the press. Both therefore tendered their resignations, and Hyde sold his Equitable stock to Thomas F. Ryan, a noted speculator and promoter of that time. Mr. Harriman did not think that Ryan was a suitable man to have control of the Equitable, with its $400,000,000 of assets, and he therefore tried to buy from him a part of the Hyde stock. Ryan declined to sell, but proposed to put the stock into the hands of trustees. Harriman had no objection to this, provided Ryan would sell him half the stock and allow him to name two of the five trustees; but Ryan would not consent. Harriman thereupon notified him that he should use his influence against him.[1] In July, 1905, the Equitable Society was re-

[1] Testimony of E. H. Harriman before the Armstrong legislative investigating committee in November, 1905. Mr. Harriman was put on the stand a second time, at his own request, in order that he might reply to certain statements made by Ryan in testifying before the same committee.

organized, with Paul Morton, ex-Secretary of the Navy, as president; but it was not mutualized, and Ryan, as owner of a majority of the stock, had virtual control of it, whether he exercised such control or not.

Mr. Harriman's intervention in the affairs of the Equitable and his negotiations with Ryan brought upon him a storm of criticism and censure. By signing the Frick report he had incurred the hostility of both factions. Hyde, whom he had advised to vote for the adoption of the report, denounced him as a traitor; the Alexander party, whose methods he had condemned, also attacked him, while his enemies outside of the insurance company availed themselves of the opportunity to prejudice public opinion against him by accusing him of "borrowing huge sums of money from a company of which he was a director; of foisting off upon it millions of securities of railroads with which his name was identified; of treachery to young Hyde while pretending friendship; of attempting to manipulate the funds of the policy-holders, and of a conspiracy to oust the warring factions and gain control of the society himself." [1]

To these unwarranted and often malicious attacks Mr. Harriman made no reply. In commenting

[1] "Had Harriman Lived," *Metropolitan Magazine*, May, 1910, pp. 147–48.

upon them, after his death, Mr. Otto H. Kahn said:

> Amongst the many campaigns of vituperation of which Mr. Harriman was the object in the course of his career, none succeeded so well in poisoning and embittering the public mind against him. Under this avalanche of unfair, baseless accusations he went the even tenor of his way, declining to dignify them by defending himself in public. On this and similar occasions I urged him to speak out — to make use of the means at his command for hitting back at his detractors and those who willingly and eagerly gave circulation to their slanders. I was never able to move him. "Let them kick," he used to say. "It's all in the day's work. After a while they will tire of it. Nothing tires a man more than to kick against air. Moreover, it disconcerts him, and not finding any point of resistance he is apt to kick himself off his feet. Besides, for immediate effect they have the advantage, because they will tell lies about me, and I won't about them. As for the effect in the long run, why, the people always find out what's what, in the end, and I can wait. Let those fellows shout and kick against air. I need my time and energy to *do* things." [1]

Harriman's attitude toward persons who attacked him was almost exactly that of President Lincoln. William Roscoe Thayer says, in his "Life of John Hay":

> When Fox, Assistant Secretary of the Navy, said that retribution had overtaken Hale and Winter Davis, "two fellows who have been especially malignant to us," Lincoln replied: "You have more of the feeling of

[1] *Edward Henry Harriman*, by Otto H. Kahn (New York, 1911), pp. 19-20.

personal resentment than I. Perhaps I may have too little of it, but I never thought it paid. A man has not time enough to spend half his life in quarrels. If any man ceases to attack me, I never remember the past against him."[1]

It may well be doubted, however, whether the policy of non-resistance, in Mr. Harriman's case, was justified by its results. When a man's character and motives are assailed and he does not defend himself, the public is apt to assume that he is unable to do so, and that the charges made against him are probably true. But Mr. Harriman almost invariably remained silent, even when he had a perfect defense in an absolutely impregnable case. "I have n't time to bother with newspaper attacks," he once said to a friend. "It'll all come right in the end." "But," his friend rejoined, "if you continue to ignore the newspapers, they'll eventually get your scalp."

That Mr. Harriman's reputation often suffered as the result of his refusal to defend himself publicly, there can be no doubt. In several notable cases, he drew up in manuscript a reply to charges, which, if it had been published, would have been absolutely convincing; but in none of these cases was the reply given to the press. Just before he sailed for Japan, in the summer of 1905, he dictated to his stenog-

[1] *Life of John Hay*, by William Roscoe Thayer; vol. I, pp. 215–16.

rapher the following statement of his relations with the Equitable Society; but it was never published.

There has been nothing in the relations of myself, or the interests I represent, to the Equitable Life Assurance Society and its allied companies [1] that will not bear the closest scrutiny. We have never requested or received a favor from them. The financial transactions between our interests have been insignificant, and never on terms that could not have been readily obtained elsewhere. On the other hand, we have given the Mercantile and Equitable Trust Companies many valuable trusteeships, and all the transactions between us have resulted in material advantage and profit to the Equitable and its allied companies.

I, personally, had one loan with the Equitable Life which could have been obtained without difficulty at any other like responsible institution on as good or better terms. It was paid because the rate of interest was higher than I was willing to pay, and without my even attempting to have it reduced.

There is nothing in the Union Pacific preferred stock syndicate that can be criticized. Mr. Hyde availed himself of an opportunity to join myself and associates in the acquisition of Union Pacific preferred stock on a favorable basis. There was no profit or advantage to any one member of the syndicate over another, and neither the Equitable nor any of its allied companies, or any one else, was ever requested to aid in any way in financing the syndicate.

Like many other of the fifty-two directors I attended

[1] The Equitable owned 64 per cent of the capital stock of the Mercantile Trust Company, 44 per cent of the stock of the Equitable Trust Company, and 35 per cent of the stock of the Commercial Trust Company of Philadelphia.

the regular meetings, which were held quarterly, but I was not a member of any committee, nor active in the management.

The Equitable controversy was started by an attempt on the part of the Alexander faction to oust the Hyde faction, and it was during that contest that the main body of directors became informed, for the first time, of the prevailing methods of conducting the company's business by both of these factions. This led to the appointment of the Frick committee, of which I was a member, and to the Frick report, which I signed and which fully expressed my views. I believe the new management will correct the extravagant methods of conducting the company's business pointed out in that report. In my opinion these methods involved a vastly greater loss to the policy-holders than the particular transactions dwelt upon so extensively by the public press.

There has been too much mystery surrounding the Equitable affairs. I have always been ready and willing to answer any questions asked by any one entitled to make inquiry, and have not tried in any way to avoid it. I will return [from Japan] in ample time to give any testimony that may be desired.

The presumption is that Mr. Harriman made this statement, not for immediate publication, but for future use in case he should be accused, during his absence, of leaving the country to avoid investigation. As such a charge was never made, the statement was not given to the press, although it would manifestly have been better to publish it in any event.

In the fall of 1905, the New York legislature appointed a special committee "to investigate the affairs and conduct of business of life insurance companies," and Charles E. Hughes, afterward governor of the State, was employed as its counsel. This committee called a large number of witnesses, including Mr. Harriman, and made an exhaustive investigation of Equitable affairs. The result was to confirm and sustain the facts and conclusions set forth in the Frick report of the previous summer; but nothing was elicited that threw discredit upon Mr. Harriman except the fact that he had acted as a director of the Equitable for a number of years without participating in its management or knowing anything about it. In this, however, he was not alone. Half the members of the board were as ignorant of its affairs as he was. Mr. Schiff, for example, when he was examined by the committee with regard to his acts and duties as director, said:

I directed as much as, under the prevailing usages in corporations, I was permitted to direct. In other words, I went to the meetings of the society when they were called; I listened to the reports as submitted by the executive officers; I voted upon the same, and gave such advice as was asked of me. The system of directorship in great corporations of the city of New York is such that a director has practically no power. He is considered in many instances, and I may say in most instances, as a negligible quantity by the executive officers of the society. He is asked for advice when it suits the executive officers, and if, under the prevailing system, an executive officer wishes to do wrong, or wishes to conceal anything from his directors, or to commit irregularities, such as have been disclosed here, the director is entirely powerless, and can only judge of such things as are submitted to him.[1]

Mr. Harriman never regarded his connection with the Equitable as particularly useful, to himself or to anybody else. When he went into the society, in 1901, at the request of James H. Hyde, he thought perhaps that he might be of service to a young and inexperienced man; but Hyde never became president, and Harriman, between 1901 and 1905, was so absorbed in the gigantic enterprises in which he was engaged that he gave little attention or thought to an insurance company in which he had no financial interest. In November, 1905, shortly after he gave his testimony as a witness before the Armstrong legislative committee, he wrote to his friend David Willcox, vice-president and general counsel of the Delaware & Hudson Company, the following letter:

New York, November 24, 1910.

DEAR DAVID:

Thank you very much for your kind expressions in letter of 16th. My wonder is when I think over the Life Insurance matters how I allowed myself to be in any

[1] Testimony of Jacob H. Schiff before the Armstrong legislative investigating committee, September 29, 1905.

way mixed up in them. Nearly twenty years ago I foretold the probability of just what is happening. When Hyde came to me, he seemed to want to correct the existing methods, and I believe he was sincere; but he fell to temptation.

Yours sincerely
E. H. HARRIMAN

At some time before Mr. Harriman died, probably two or three years before, he succeeded, after persistent and long-continued negotiation, in buying from Thomas F. Ryan one half the latter's holding of Equitable stock; but he never disposed of it, nor made any use of it. What he would have done with it, if he had lived, is a matter of conjecture; but so long as he held it, Ryan could not control the Equitable Society, or exercise any preponderating influence in its affairs. All the Ryan and Harriman holdings of Equitable stock eventually went into the hands of J. P. Morgan.

END OF VOLUME I

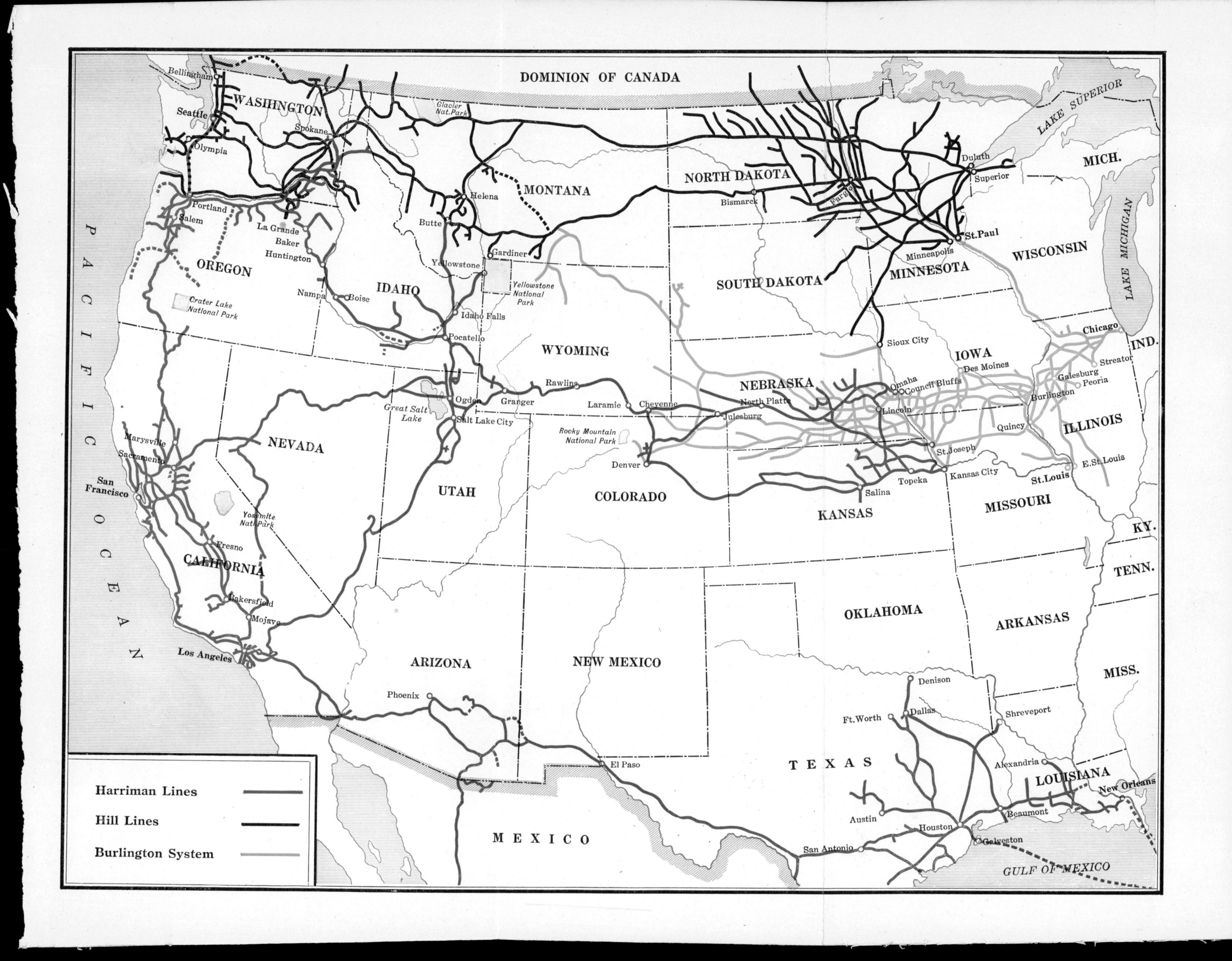
DOMINION OF CANADA
LAKE SUPERIOR
LAKE MICHIGAN
PACIFIC OCEAN
GULF OF MEXICO
MEXICO
WASHINGTON
OREGON
CALIFORNIA
NEVADA
IDAHO
MONTANA
WYOMING
UTAH
ARIZONA
NEW MEXICO
COLORADO
NORTH DAKOTA
SOUTH DAKOTA
NEBRASKA
KANSAS
OKLAHOMA
TEXAS
MINNESOTA
IOWA
MISSOURI
ARKANSAS
LOUISIANA
WISCONSIN
ILLINOIS
MICH.
IND.
KY.
TENN.
MISS.
Bellingham
Seattle
Spokane
Olympia
Glacier Nat. Park
Portland
Salem
La Grande
Baker
Huntington
Crater Lake National Park
Nampa
Boise
Helena
Butte
Gardiner
Yellowstone
Yellowstone National Park
Idaho Falls
Pocatello
Ogden
Granger
Rawlins
Laramie
Cheyenne
Great Salt Lake
Salt Lake City
Rocky Mountain National Park
Denver
Julesburg
North Platte
Marysville
Sacramento
San Francisco
Yosemite Nat. Park
Fresno
Bakersfield
Mojave
Los Angeles
Phoenix
El Paso
Bismarck
Fargo
Duluth
Superior
St. Paul
Minneapolis
Sioux City
Chicago
Streator
Des Moines
Omaha
Council Bluffs
Galesburg
Peoria
Burlington
Lincoln
Quincy
St. Joseph
E. St. Louis
St. Louis
Kansas City
Topeka
Salina
Denison
Ft. Worth
Dallas
Shreveport
Alexandria
New Orleans
Beaumont
Austin
Houston
Galveston
San Antonio
Harriman Lines
Hill Lines
Burlington System